Faith First

Grade Six

Faith First Development Team

RESOURCES FOR CHRISTIAN LIVING®

"The Ad Hoc Committee to Oversee
the Use of the Catechism,
National Conference of Catholic Bishops,
has found this catechetical series, copyright 2000,
to be in conformity with
the *Catechism of the Catholic Church.*"

NIHIL OBSTAT
Rev. Msgr. Glenn D. Gardner, J.C.D.
Censor Librorum

IMPRIMATUR
† Most Rev. Charles V. Grahmann
Bishop of Dallas

March 10, 1999

The Nihil Obstat and Imprimatur are official declarations that
the material reviewed is free of doctrinal or moral error. No
implication is contained therein that those granting the Nihil
Obstat and Imprimatur agree with the contents, opinions, or
statements expressed.

Send all inquiries to:
RCL • Resources for Christian Living
200 East Bethany Drive
Allen, Texas 75002-3804

Toll Free   877-275-4725
Fax   800-688-8356

Visit us at www.RCLweb.com
              www.FaithFirst.com

Printed in the United States of America

20306   ISBN 0-7829-0928-0 (Student Book)

20316   ISBN 0-7829-0929-9 (Teacher Guide)

20326   ISBN 0-7829-0930-2 (Catechist Guide)

4 5 6 7 8 9 10
01 02 03 04 05

ACKNOWLEDGMENTS

Scripture excerpts are taken or adapted from the *New
American Bible with Revised New Testament and Psalms*
Copyright © 1991, 1986, 1970 Confraternity of Christian
Doctrine, Washington, DC. Used with permission. All rights
reserved. No part of the *New American Bible* may be
reproduced by any means without the permission of the
copyright owner.

Excerpts are taken or adapted from the English translation
of *The Roman Missal* © 1973, International Committee on
English in the Liturgy, Inc. (ICEL); excerpts from the English
translation of *Rite of Confirmation*, second edition © 1975,
excerpts from the *Book of Blessings* © 1987; excerpts from *The
Liturgy of the Hours* © 1974, ICEL. All rights reserved.

Photograph and Art Credits appear on page 336.

Faith First Development Team

Developing a religion program requires the gifts
and talents of many different individuals
working together as a team. RCL is proud
to acknowledge these dedicated people.

Advisory Board

Rev. Louis J. Cameli
Judith Deckers
Rev. Robert D. Duggan
Rev. Virgil Elizondo
Jacquie Jambor
Maureen A. Kelly
Elaine McCarron, SCN
Rev. Frank McNulty
Rev. Ronald J. Nuzzi
Kate Sweeney Ristow

Grade 6 Writers

Student Book	Catechist/Teacher Guides
Rev. Louis J. Cameli	Mary Beth Jambor
Yvette Nelson	Yvette Nelson
	Anna Dolores Ready

Editorial

Blake Bergen
Patricia A. Classick
Ed DeStefano
Nancy M. DeStefano
Jack Gargiulo
Karen Griffith
Keith Ksobiech
Ronald C. Lamping
Joan Lathen
Ed Leach
Myrtle E. Teffeau

Art and Design

Pat Bracken
Andrea Friedman
Kristy Howard
Sheila Lehnert
Karen Malzeke-McDonald
Margaret Matus
Carol-Anne Wilson

Production

Mark Burgdorff
Laura Fremder
Becky Ivey
Jenna Nelson

Executive Board

Maryann Nead   Kim Duty

Richard C. Leach

Contents

Welcome to Faith First

My name is _Liboria Marsala_

I like to be called _Libs but nobody does_

The name of my parish is _Notre-Dame des Écores (St-Bruno)_

The name of my diocese is _Father Giuseppe_

The sacraments I've already received are _my baptism, my first_
confession and my first communion

One of the best things about me is _that I'm caring_

As a Christian I believe _in God our lord and Jesus Christ_

One thing I would like to know more about my religion is
God, Jesus, saints, what is the Confirmation and why
do we have to do it

People I Admire and Respect

my parents, my brothers,
my aunts and uncles, my
cousins and my grand-
parents

Favorite Things

Animal _the rabbits_

Bible Story _Noa's Ark_

Book _Harry Potter and the chamber_ _of secrets_

Food _cotolette_

Game _the game of Life_

Movie _Miss Conginiality_

Music _of the backstreet boys_

Sport _basketball_

TV Show _Friends_

A Prayer for the Beginning of Sixth Grade

Dear God,

I pray to you for some help to do good during my
sixth grade and pass with good marks. I ask you
to help me when I'm going to be ching my exams
to get in the private schools. To help me during
the rest of my school years. Please & Thank you
Amen.

The Gift of Faith

We Pray

We thank you, Father
for the life
and knowledge
you have revealed
to us through
your Son
Jesus.
Glory be yours
through all ages.
DIDACHE

God has made himself
known to us in many ways.
How do you come to
know God?

*Praise the LORD from the earth,
You mountains and all hills.*
Psalm 148:7, 9

God's Own Word to Us

Faith Focus

How do we access God's light that shines within all of us?

Have you ever worked at a computer? You know it contains a lot of information and other helpful data. Sometimes, though, it is a challenge to access this data. Knowing God is something like that for some people too.

God's Word Within Us

God writes his word on our hearts, plants his love deep in our souls. Jeremiah the Prophet shared this truth about God and ourselves when he wrote:

> [God said:] "I will give them a heart with which to understand that I am the LORD. They shall be my people and I will be their God, for they shall return to me with their whole heart."
>
> JEREMIAH 24:7–8

Whether we are happy or sad, successful or in trouble, God's word is always there. God's word placed within us is at work in everyone. It acts like the sun to light up our days and like the moon to help us see at night.

Now our challenge is to access and understand the light of God's word. Here are some ways that will help us.

1. We need to pray to the Holy Spirit. The Spirit is our helper and teacher. He is the One who helps us truly understand all that God makes known to us and has revealed to us in Jesus Christ. It is the Spirit who lives in our hearts and gives us the power to call God Abba, our Father, whom we trust with all our heart.

2. We need to get to know Jesus Christ personally. In giving us Jesus, God gave us himself. Everything God wants to say to us can be found in Jesus Christ.

3. We need to grow in our understanding of God's revelation of himself through the prayerful reading and study of Sacred Scripture. Sacred Scripture and Sacred Tradition make up a single deposit, or source, of the Word of God. Together they are like one mirror the Church on earth looks at and contemplates God, who is the source of all our riches. When we read the Scriptures, we open ourselves to listen to what God is saying to us.

4. We need to grow in our understanding of God's Word and revelation of himself through our study of Sacred Tradition and the teachings of the Church. When we share and discuss our faith with other believers, reflecting on Sacred Tradition and Sacred Scripture, we have a better sense of what God is trying to say to us.

5. Finally, we access God's word within us through the preaching and teaching of the pope and the bishops. They teach us in the name of Christ and help us to understand God's revelation more clearly and to live it in practical ways.

To Help You Remember

1. What did God place within our heart?

2. Why did God place his word within our heart?

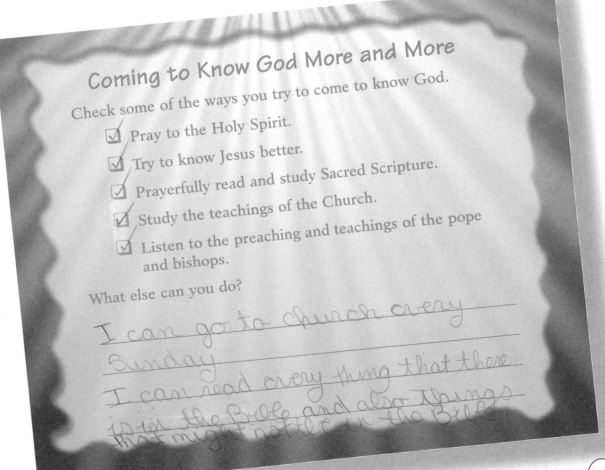

Coming to Know God More and More

Check some of the ways you try to come to know God.

- ☑ Pray to the Holy Spirit.
- ☑ Try to know Jesus better.
- ☑ Prayerfully read and study Sacred Scripture.
- ☑ Study the teachings of the Church.
- ☑ Listen to the preaching and teachings of the pope and bishops.

What else can you do?

I can go to church every Sunday

I can read every thing that there is in the Bible and also things that might not be in the Bible

must pray for the grace to truly know and respond to that love.

This kind of trust is not so easy to give. This kind of faith is not easy or automatic. That is why the Letter to the Hebrews describes faith this way: Faith is the realization of what is hoped for and evidence of things not seen.

HEBREWS 11:1

Faith Focus

How do we respond to God's word written on our hearts?

Faith Vocabulary

trust. To have confidence in someone because of the person's character, strength, ability, or truth; to depend with confidence on someone.

faith. The gift of God's invitation to us to believe and trust in him; it is also the power God gives us to respond to his invitation.

With My Family

Talk about the things your family "gives its heart to." How are these a sign to others that you are followers of Christ?

Who are the teachers or relatives you **trust** and admire completely? You know that they really like you and that they will guide you well. You know that they will not do anything to harm you. What response do you give to such people? You trust them. You depend on them and reach out to them to give you guidance.

Trusting God

God places his Word within us. So what do we do about it? We are free to say, "So what?" and reject God. We might also say, "Okay, God, there is a lot I don't understand; so help me believe in you." In other words, we can try to grow in confidence and understanding of God. This is called **faith.**

Faith is like a good friendship. It is a gift. It is not something we can earn or deserve like a good grade or a scout badge. We cannot claim that we have achieved a deep faith through our own efforts. Growing in faith does not work that way. We should work hard to appreciate God's love, but we also

Jesus, the Word of God

Jesus showed us that God is the One we can and should trust the most. God knows everything about us and everything we need before we ask him. He wants nothing but the best for us.

The Gospel tells us that is why Jesus, the Son of God, became one of us and lived among us on earth. Jesus' whole life on earth showed us that God wants our happiness now on earth and with him forever in heaven. He will never leave us. He is always at our side as our helper and guide.

When we come to know this about God, we grow in our love and trust of him. We love and trust him with our whole mind, our whole strength, and our whole soul. We come to depend on him more than anyone and anything else. This is what faith in God is all about.

Such faith is truly a gift. We could never place our faith in God without his first reaching out to us. It is God's gift to us.

A Story of Faith

Moses and Miriam both were willing to submit their lives in faith to God. Recall what you have learned about the story of Moses and the Israelites.

The Israelites were powerless slaves in Egypt, where Pharaoh's army was the strongest in the world. Nonetheless, Moses and Miriam were willing to believe that God somehow would deliver them to a new homeland that he had promised to them.

Moses and Miriam were willing to trust in God when all the odds were against them. They trusted God would keep his word to them. God did. Successfully, the Israelites journeyed from slavery to freedom.

God invites us to trust him as Moses and Miriam did. Like Moses and Miriam we are free to say yes or no. We are also free to ask God questions, as Moses did, so we can grow in our faith and trust in God.

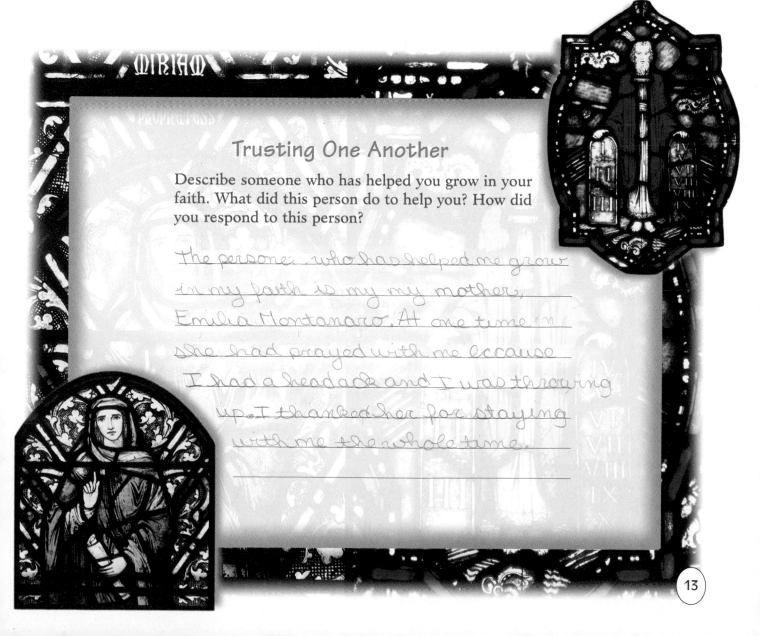

To Help You Remember

1. How would you define faith?

2. How did Moses and Miriam demonstrate their faith in God?

3. What are some of the ways that you can demonstrate your faith in God?

Trusting One Another

Describe someone who has helped you grow in your faith. What did this person do to help you? How did you respond to this person?

The person who has helped me grow in my faith is my my mother, Emilia Montanaro. At one time in she had prayed with me because I had a headache and I was throwing up. I thanked her for staying with me the whole time.

13

Faith Vocabulary

creed. A summary of the principal beliefs of the Church that are often proclaimed as a profession of faith. Creeds are also called symbols of our faith.

redemption. The saving activity of God through Christ delivering humanity from sin. We call Jesus Our Redeemer.

We Express Our Faith

If we really believe in someone or something, we usually want to tell others about that person or share that truth with others. That is especially true about our faith in God. Our faith in God is such a valuable gift that we proclaim or profess that faith in as many ways as we can.

From the beginning, the Church has proudly proclaimed our faith in God in the **creeds** of the Church. Creeds are a way of expressing the heart of the Church's faith. When we proclaim the creed at Sunday Mass, we rejoice in what God is doing for us. We express our trust in God the Father, the Son, and the Holy Spirit.

Throughout the Church's history, those about to be baptized have always professed their faith in creeds before they are baptized.

When we were baptized as infants, our parents and godparents professed the creed in our name.

Now we profess our faith when we pray the Nicene Creed at Sunday Mass. We unite ourselves with believing Christians throughout the world. By doing so, we unite ourselves with Christians past, present, and future.

The Apostles' Creed

The Apostles' Creed is one of the earliest creeds of the Church. It is divided into three parts.

- The first part speaks of our faith in God the Father and the creation of the world.
- The second part speaks of Jesus Christ, the Son of God, and our **redemption**.
- The third part speaks of God the Holy Spirit and our sanctification.

The Apostles' Creed

I believe in God, the Father almighty,
    creator of heaven and earth.

I believe in Jesus Christ, his only
    son, our Lord.
He was conceived by the power of
    the Holy Spirit
and born of the Virgin Mary.
He suffered under Pontius Pilate,
was crucified, died, and was
    buried.
He descended into hell.
On the third day he rose again.

He ascended into heaven and is
    seated at the right hand of the
    Father.
He will come again to judge the
    living and the dead.

I believe in the Holy Spirit,
    the holy catholic Church,
    the communion of saints,
    the forgiveness of sins,
    the resurrection of the body,
    and the life everlasting.

              Amen.

Symbols of Our Faith

In the circles create symbols that represent each part of the Apostles' Creed. Describe each symbol with a statement of belief.

To Help You Remember

1. Why do believers feel a need to express their faith?

2. Describe the main beliefs contained in the Apostles' Creed.

3. Name some of the ways you can share your faith with others.

I eclaire that the God our lord did indeed create the world

Jesus Christ

I eclaire that the Jesus Christ is our redeemer because and our redemptiom which mean

I eclaire in the Holy Spirit and the the Holy Spirit gave the message to Virgin Mary the she would give birth to God son.

15

Faith is like a good friendship. It is the gift of God inviting us to share in his life and love. It is also the gift of the power to respond to that invitation. Our lives are lives of faith.

World Youth Day

Catholic youth from all over the world gather together every two years to profess and share their faith. They gather with the pope, with bishops and priests, with youth ministers and parents, and with teachers and religious sisters and brothers. These gatherings are called World Youth Day.

In 1997 Catholic youth from over 140 countries gathered in Paris, France. This was the sixth time World Youth Day was celebrated.

The five other World Youth Days were held in 1987 in Buenos Aires, Argentina; in 1989 in Compostela, Spain; in 1991 in Czestochowa, Poland; in 1993 in Denver, United States of America; and in 1995 in Manila, Philippines.

During World Youth Day celebrations, Catholic youth celebrate their faith. They discuss ways to live their faith. They deepen their understanding of the teachings and practices of the Catholic Church. Above all they celebrate their unity with one another and with Jesus and with the Church.

How does your parish bring youth together to celebrate and grow in their faith?

World Youth Day, Paris, France, August 1997.

Each day you show that you love and trust God by your words and actions. By trusting in God's love, you grow in your friendship with him.

Professing Our Faith

Think about what you believe. Write three statements that express your faith in God, Jesus, and the Holy Spirit.

My Faith Decision

I profess my faith each day both by my words and by my actions. This week I will profess my faith by

_____

_____ .

And now we pray.
We believe in the Holy Spirit . . . who proceeds from the Father and the Son.
FROM THE NICENE CREED

CHAPTER REVIEW

Match each term in Column A with its meaning in Column B.

Column A

_a_ 1. faith

_d_ 2. trust

_c_ 3. creed

_b_ 4. redemption

Column B

a. Our acceptance of God and our willingness to receive his revelation

b. The saving activity of God through Christ delivering humanity from sin

c. A summary of the principal beliefs of the Church

d. Confidence in someone because of the person's character

Answer the following questions.

1. Name some of the ways we can grow in our understanding of God's revelation of himself to us.

   We can try to know Jesus better, Pray to the Holy Spirit and read the Sacret Sciptures.

2. Describe the three main parts of the Apostles' Creed.

   1st part: speaks of God and creation of the world
   2nd part: speaks of Jesus Christ and our redemtion
   3rd part: speaks of the Holy Spirit and our sanctification

3. Why does the Church express our faith in creeds?

   Because creeds are ways of expressing the heart of the church's faith.

Discuss with your family.

What can we do as a family to grow in our faith?

Visit our web site at www.FaithFirst.com

God's Own Word to Us

We Pray

Your word is a lamp
for my feet,
a light for my path.

PSALM 119:105

The Scriptures are God's own word to us. They are the story of God's love for us and how God's people responded to that love. What is your favorite Bible story? Share how it tells about God's love for us.

*"With all my heart I seek you; . . .
In my heart I treasure your
promise, . . .
Blessed are you, O LORD.*
Psalm 119:10, 11, 12

19

Going to the Source

Faith Vocabulary

Bible. God's own word to us; the collection of forty-six books in the Old Testament and twenty-seven books in the New Testament.

When we want to study history, we turn to a history book. When we wish to do a science project, we use a science book. Of course, we can use the Internet to learn many things too. However, when we want to learn about God, we can go to God's own word to us. We can read the **Bible**, or Sacred Scripture. Through the Scriptures God continues to talk to us about himself and his love for us.

God's Inspired Word

The Bible is the inspired word of God. What does that mean? Did God dictate his words to the various human authors? Did God write it down and then have writers make copies of it? No, God used human writers to communicate what he wanted to tell us. These human writers wrote in their own language and used expressions their readers and listeners were familiar with. This helped their people better understand what God was communicating to them. However, the human writers only wrote what the Holy Spirit helped them to understand about God and his saving love for us.

Why would God give us the Sacred Scriptures? The reason is very simple and moving: God wants to share himself with us. He wants us to know him, to love him, and to become one with him. The Bible is a gift from a generous God. The best way to appreciate that gift is by reading and studying it. To start this process, let us first identify the books that are contained in the Canon of

Section of Dead Sea Scroll found at Qumran.

Sacred Scripture, or the Church's official list of books in the Bible.

Old Testament

In the Old Testament there are forty-six books. This first main part of the Bible tells the story of God's covenant with the Israelites and the promise of a new covenant. The books of the Old Testament are often grouped in the following way:

- The Pentateuch, or the first five books of the Bible, tells the story of God's covenant with his people and the laws they were to follow to live and celebrate that covenant.
- The sixteen historical books tell the story of how God's people sometimes lived the covenant well and at other times did not.

- The seven wisdom books share with us advice on how to live our covenant with God.
- The eighteen prophetic books remind God's people to be faithful to their covenant and that God is always faithful to them.

New Testament

In the New Testament, the second main part of the Bible, there are twenty-seven books. They are grouped in the following way:

- The four written accounts of the Gospel pass on the Church's faith in Jesus Christ.
- The Acts of the Apostles tells the story of the early Church.
- The thirteen epistles, or letters, of Saint Paul help us understand our faith in Jesus and how to live that faith.
- Eight other letters in the New Testament also help us understand and live our faith.
- The Book of Revelation.

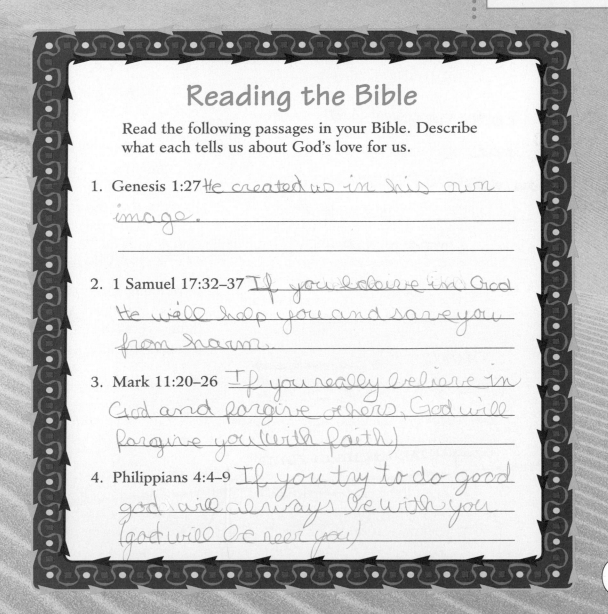

Reading the Bible

Read the following passages in your Bible. Describe what each tells us about God's love for us.

1. Genesis 1:27 He created us in his own image.

2. 1 Samuel 17:32–37 If you believe in God He will help you and save you from harm.

3. Mark 11:20–26 If you really believe in God and forgive others, God will forgive you (with faith)

4. Philippians 4:4–9 If you try to do good god will always be with you (god will be near you)

Contemporary art of Moses and the burning bush.

Faith Focus

What does the name that God gives to himself tell us about God?

Faith Vocabulary

Yahweh. A name meaning "I am who am;" the name God used for himself.

When we tell our name to another person, we give them a part of our true selves. We volunteer a piece of our identity. God freely chose to share his name with Moses and the Israelites. By doing so, he astonished humanity with his openness and compassion. This is how it happened.

God Reveals His Name

Before leading his people out of Egypt, Moses was visited by God. One day while he was tending his sheep, Moses saw a burning bush. He was surprised that the bush was in flames but was not being consumed by the fire.

As Moses approached this strange sight, he heard a voice speaking from the bush. It was God speaking to Moses. "Moses! Moses! . . . I am the God of your father, . . . the God of Abraham, the God of Isaac, the God of Jacob. . . . Come, now! I will send you to Pharaoh to lead my people, the Israelites, out of Egypt." EXODUS 3:4, 6, 10

You can just imagine how confused Moses must have been. So he asked:
"[W]hen I go to the Israelites and say to them, 'the God of your fathers has sent me to you,' if they ask me, 'What is his name?' what am I to tell them?" EXODUS 3:13

God replied:
"I am who am. . . . Tell the Israelites I AM sent me to you." EXODUS 3:14

Through this Old Testament story God shares his name with Moses, with the Israelites, and with us. He says, "I am who am." In Hebrew that name is **Yahweh.**

יְהֹוָה

Hebrew writing of Yahweh.

In calling himself Yahweh, God shared something very important about himself. In naming himself Yahweh, God tells us that he is always with us. Wherever we are, God is always there for us.

In thinking about the name Yahweh, these are some of the things we have come to believe about God:
- God is a mystery who will never be fully grasped.
- God says, "I will be with you."
- God is faithful to his people.
- God enters history in a loving way.
- God is close to his people.
- God knows his people and their needs.
- God is ready to stand by his people in their times of trouble.

God's Love and Fidelity

The Old Testament offers us many examples of individuals who had great faith in God who they knew as Yahweh. One of the most striking stories is about Ruth and Naomi. Ruth was not an Israelite. She was from Moab. Moab was a nation east of Israel. It was the ancient kingdom of Syria. Ruth had married an Israelite man who was the son of Elimelech and Naomi. Both husbands had died, leaving Ruth and Naomi widows. Ruth decided to remain with her mother-in-law, even though by Jewish law she had the right to return to her own family in Moab.

Naomi loved Ruth but knew Ruth would be better off with her own people, the Moabites. She felt Ruth deserved a fresh start and another opportunity to raise her

own family. Ruth, however, would not abandon Naomi.

Ruth's devotion to Naomi is a reflection of God's devotion to his people. He reveals himself as "I am who am." In naming himself this way, God is telling us that he is the One who will always stand by his people in love and faithfulness.

To Help You Remember

1. What did God reveal about himself at the burning bush?

2. Describe what the story of Ruth and Naomi tells us.

3. What are some of the ways you can be faithful to others?

Signs of Loyalty

Name someone you know or have learned about who is or was loyal. Write the person's name and describe some of the things the person did that are examples of loyalty.

Elijah

Esther

Daniel

Rebecca

Faith Focus

Why did God send prophets to his people in the Old Testament?

Faith Vocabulary

prophet. A man or woman who speaks for God, who utters divinely inspired words.

hope. Trust in God and in his promises above everyone and everything else.

The Prophets

The history of the Jewish people, right up to the time of John the Baptist, was filled with holy men and holy women. Rebecca, Esther, Elijah, and Daniel are four holy people who spoke in God's name. Through these holy men and women God reminded his people of his loyalty, or faithfulness, to them.

Many of these people were called **prophets.** Even when the people did not want to listen to them, the prophets kept at it. They never gave up reminding God's people who God is, the One who always loves them and will never abandon them even when they abandon him.

The Scriptures tell us, over and over again, the story of God's love for and fidelity to his people.

Even when they were breaking the covenant agreement that they entered into with him by serving other gods, by violating the Ten Commandments, and by placing God's people and the nation in grave peril, God's love and fidelity never failed them.

God gave the prophets the gift of his Spirit and placed his word on their tongues. God's Spirit filled the prophets with courage to challenge his people and their leaders to wake up and return to God.

You can just imagine how unpopular the prophets were. Their honesty often got them into trouble, especially when people were guilty of abandoning God. If you have ever had to stand up for an unpopular truth, then you have walked in the shoes of the prophets.

The heart of the prophets' message, however, was not doom, but **hope**. They brought God's word of hope and promise to the people. They kept alive a sense of expectation that God would fulfill his promise to them and deliver his people by sending them a new leader, who would come to be known as the Messiah or Savior. They encouraged the people and proclaimed that the poor would find protection and fulfillment in God.

The prophets always kept this hope alive and drew the people back to their covenant with God. Their messages pointed to a new and everlasting covenant intended for all people. A new law would be engraved on their hearts. As we soon will see, all of these promises are fulfilled in Jesus Christ.

To Help You Remember

1. Who were the prophets?

2. Describe the message the prophets brought to God's people.

3. How do the words and promises of the prophets help us?

The Work of Prophets

Name some people you know or have learned about who remind us of God's love for us and how we are to live as his people. Choose one person and describe what he or she has done or is doing.

The pope even though he is very sick continues to travel all over the world and talk about the Word of God

With My Family

Talk about people you have come to trust. What are the qualities of a trustworthy person?

God shares his life with us through the Sacred Scriptures. He inspired the human writers of the Scriptures. This means that when we read the Scriptures we are reading God's own word to us. In the Bible we will find God's word, wisdom, and inspiration.

Bible Services

Bible reading is a very important part of our faith life. We can gain a great deal of inspiration and understanding of our faith by reading the Bible quietly to ourselves. The Church also provides a way to read the Bible prayerfully as a group.

To provide more involvement in reading the Bible, the Church encourages Bible services. Bible services consist of the reading of and meditating on Sacred Scripture, as well as opportunities for prayer and song. When priests are not available, deacons or laypersons may preside at the celebration of a Bible service.

Bible services connect the word of God with our daily lives. Vatican Council II encourages us to take part in Bible services on the vigils of solemn feasts such as Pentecost, on Sundays, and on holidays. Taking part in Bible services on the weekdays of Lent and Advent helps us prepare for Easter and Christmas.

Prepare a Bible service as a class. Celebrate it together.

God always wants to communicate with you. When you read the Bible and listen to it read at Mass, God himself speaks to you and to all the People of God, the Church.

Reading and Studying the Bible

Describe some ways that reading and studying the Bible is a source of inspiration and knowledge about God for you.

Because he sent the Holy Spirit into the the people to write the Scriptures and I know he's talking to me

My Faith Decision

This week I will read the Bible. I will listen to God and share my thoughts and feelings with him.

And now we pray.
Praise the LORD, who is so good;
God's love endures forever.

PSALM 136:1

Write a sentence to explain the meaning of each term.

1. Bible

the Bible is Where you can find the old and new testaments and read them.

2. Yahweh

It means "I am who I am" in Hebrew.

3. prophet

A person who is inspired by the Holy Spirit to spread the word of God

4. hope

To trust in God without any doubt

Answer the following questions.

1. What does it mean to say the Scriptures are God's own word to us?

The scriptures were inspired to be written by God's spirit that talk about is love.

2. What does God tell us through the story of Moses and the burning bush?

That he is who he is and that

3. What was the role of the prophets in the Old Testament?

To remind people of God's loyalty/Hope and faithfulness to them and the promise of the coming of a Messiah(savior)

Discuss with your family.

Why is it important for us to read the Bible regularly? When might we read the Bible together as a family?

Visit our
web site at
www.FaithFirst.com

Living the Covenant

A Scripture Story

We Pray

Teach us to count our days aright, that we may gain wisdom of heart.

PSALM 90:12

The prophets in the Bible spoke to the people in God's name. Name some of the prophets in the Bible you have learned about. Share one message that a prophet shared with the people.

Byzantine art of six unnamed Old Testament prophets.

Bible Background

Isaiah

Ezekiel

Jeremiah

Faith Focus

What were the names of the prophets? What were some of their primary concerns?

Faith Vocabulary

covenant. The faithful, loving commitment God made with the People of God and was renewed in Christ, the New Covenant.

The Prophets

The Catholic Bible contains the teachings of eighteen prophets. The prophetic books include the writings of the major prophets (Isaiah, Jeremiah, Ezekiel), the twelve minor prophets, and the books of Baruch, Lamentations, and Daniel. The major prophets have the longest prophetic books. The minor prophets have shorter works represented in the Bible.

The Prophets' Message

All the prophets shared a common calling. God spoke through them to his people. Their message centered on the two themes of fidelity, or loyalty, to the **covenant** with God, and hope in the future.

Often a prophet simply preached this message. At other times, the message was delivered in a more dramatic way, like wearing a yoke that was used to control oxen. This really got the attention of their listeners.

Fidelity

When the prophets spoke about fidelity to the Israelites' covenant with God, they addressed three specific issues:

- true worship,
- the relationship with other nations, and
- doing works of justice for the people, especially the poor and the weak.

The very first chapter of the Book of Isaiah helps us understand what these three issues were all about.

1. **True worship.** The prophet Isaiah told the people that they had forgotten to worship God from their hearts (Isaiah 1:11).

2. **Relationship with other nations.** Isaiah warned the people that they had become like pagan nations (Isaiah 1:9).

3. **Doing justice.** Isaiah also told the people to act justly and, in a special way, to help the poorest and weakest people (Isaiah 1:16–17).

Baruch

them his faithful servant whose work Isaiah described:

> Through his suffering, my servant shall justify many, and their guilt he shall bear.
> ISAIAH 53:11

Above all, the poor and humble will be signs of this hope. Such holy women as Sarah, Rebecca, Rachel, Miriam, Deborah, Hannah, Judith, and Esther kept this hope of Israel's salvation alive. Mary, the mother of the Savior, is the greatest woman of hope among them.

We should always have hope for the future. We believe the promises God made through the prophets pointed to Jesus, the Messiah, the Suffering Servant. In him God established a new and everlasting covenant. In him we place our hope.

Hope

God also spoke through the prophets to give them hope for the promised future. While God's people were not always faithful to him, he would always be faithful to them. He would be true to his name, YAHWEH. He would send

To Help You Remember

1. Into what two groups are the prophets divided?

2. Explain the three issues often addressed by the prophets.

3. What things can you do to live a life of hope?

A Prophet's Message for Today

What can we do today about these three issues from the prophet Isaiah?

1. True worship _we can keep talking about God and Jesus_.

2. Relationship with other nations _we can help the poor_.

3. Doing justice _we can go to an old folks home._

31

Reading the Word of God

Faith Focus

How did God challenge and bring hope to his people during the Exile?

Faith Vocabulary

Exile. The time in the history of God's people when they were forced to leave their homeland and live in the country of their conquerors.

A People in Exile

There was a time in the history of God's people when they seemed to have very little hope. It was the time in their history known as the **Exile**. It was a time of great infidelity to God.

The Assyrians and Babylonians were conquering the countries surrounding Israel and Judah, the countries in which God's people lived. During this time of suffering, God sent the prophet Baruch to speak to his people who were living in exile in Babylonia.

The Book of Baruch is only six chapters long. It contains different kinds of writing. This passage that we are about to study is in the form of a poem. It is called "Praise of Wisdom in the Law of Moses."

Hear, O Israel, the
  commandments of life:
listen, and know prudence!
How is it, Israel,
  that you are in the land of
    your foes,
  grown old in a foreign land,
Defiled with the dead,
  accounted with those destined
    for the nether world?
You have forsaken the fountain
  of wisdom!
  Had you walked in the way
    of God,
  you would have dwelt in
    enduring peace.
Learn where prudence is,
  where strength, where
    understanding;
That you may know also
  where are length of days,
    and life,
  where light of the eyes, and
    peace.

Who has found the place of
  wisdom,
  who has entered into her
    treasuries? . . .

Yet he who knows all things
knows her;
he has probed her by his
knowledge—
He who established the earth
for all time,
and filled it with four-footed
beasts;
He who dismisses the light,
and it departs,
calls it, and it obeys him
trembling;
Before whom the stars at
their posts
shine and rejoice;
When he calls them, they answer,
"Here we are!"
shining with joy for their Maker.
Such is our God;
no other is to be compared
to him:
He has traced out all the way
of understanding,
and has given her to Jacob,
his servant,
to Israel, his beloved son.

Since then she has appeared
on earth,
and moved among men.

She is the book of the precepts
of God,
the law that endures forever;
All who cling to her will live,
but those will die who
forsake her.
Turn, O Jacob, and receive her:
walk by her light toward
splendor.
Give not your glory to another,
your privileges to an alien race.
Blessed are we, O Israel;
for what pleases God is
known to us!

BARUCH 3:9–15, 32–38; 4:1–4

In this poem, Baruch was
speaking to the people who were
suffering terribly. Taken from
their homes in Jerusalem, they
were forced to walk many miles
away to the foreign country of
Babylon. Baruch tried to help
them understand how this had
happened and how they could
find true happiness. They were
unfaithful, but God would remain
faithful to them. They should
have hope.

To Help You Remember

1. What national tragedy had befallen the people when Baruch wrote this passage?

2. What does Baruch say about wisdom?

3. What advice from this passage can help you live as a follower of Jesus?

With My Family

Talk about a time when your family had hope because of your belief in God's love and faithfulness. How did that hope help you at that time?

Acting Wisely

Think about choices we make that result in our unhappiness. Describe one of those choices. What can you do to make better choices?

Once I called a person bad names and that made me unhappy because it was a mean thing to do. We can always think about how our choices can affect others.

33

Understanding the Word of God

Faith Focus

What is the meaning of Baruch's message to his exiled people?

Faith Vocabulary

prudence. A virtue that helps us know what is truly good for us and how to choose the right way of achieving that good. It is one of the four moral virtues; the others are justice, fortitude, and temperance.

wisdom. One of the seven Gifts of the Holy Spirit; it helps us keep God and our relationship with God at the center of our lives.

End of the Exile, or Captivity, of God's people in Babylon. Illustrated manuscript of Flavius Josephus, Jewish historian born in AD 37.

Baruch's Challenge

Baruch was very honest with God's people. He laid out before them their responsibility for the terrible situation in which they found themselves.

Baruch told the Israelites that they had brought this tragedy upon themselves. It was the consequence of their own choices. If only they had followed the way of God more closely, they would have lived securely in their own homes. In so many words, Baruch told them that their own bad choices had sent them into exile. They did not act wisely.

You have forsaken the fountain of wisdom!

Had you walked in the way of God, you would have dwelt in enduring peace.

BARUCH 3:12–13

Baruch's message did not end there. The prophet gave the Israelites hope for the future. He told them how to make wise decisions. Such decisions would return them to their homeland and they would live in peace. They needed to learn and act with **prudence**.

Prudence is a blend of good judgment and self-control. It is the ability to realize that bad judgment can lead to bad consequences.

God's people did not act prudently when they turned their backs on God and broke God's law. They thought not keeping God's law would benefit them. They thought worshiping the false gods of their neighbors would bring them power and wealth. They were wrong. The real consequence of their decision was this: They lost their homeland.

God's Wisdom

When Baruch speaks of God's **wisdom**, he refers to it as a person. He writes:

All who cling to her will live, but those will die who forsake her.

BARUCH 4:1

The wisdom contained in God's commands keeps us alive. The prophet urges people to realize that if they are looking for life, they can find it only in God's word.

The people need to turn away from whatever would carry them away from God's wisdom and commands. They need to turn to God's wisdom and keep their eyes fixed on it. When they do, they will leave their sadness behind and come into God's wonderful light.

To Help You Remember

1. What are prudence and wisdom?

2. According to Baruch, what will happen when his people learn prudence and focus on God's wisdom?

3. How might people today be acting in a way similar to the people in Baruch's time?

Baruch's Message

What was Baruch's message to the people?

What They Must Do	What Will Happen
Believe in God	(Messiah) Savior will come
Have prudence on God's Wisdom	Be happy, Be free

Stained-glass window of Saint Mother Cabrini.

Prophets spoke in God's name. They reminded God's people to remain faithful to their covenant with God. "Doing justice," especially for the poor and weak, was an important sign of that faithfulness.

Doing Justice

Martin de Porres and Frances Xavier Cabrini are two examples of the many Christians who have listened to and followed the message of the prophets. They devoted their lives to working with the poor, the sick, and others with special needs.

Mosaic of Saint Martin de Porres.

Martin de Porres (1579–1639) was born and worked in Lima, Peru. In 1603 he became a Dominican brother, a follower of Saint Dominic (ca. 1170–1221), and worked among the sick, the poor, and enslaved Africans. He was named a saint in 1962 and is the patron saint of people working for interracial justice.

Frances Xavier Cabrini (1850–1917) came to the United States from Italy in 1889. Mother Cabrini, as she was called, and the sisters who worked with her helped other immigrants. They set up schools, hospitals, and orphanages in the United States. Mother Cabrini was canonized in 1946. She is the first U.S. citizen to be named a saint and is the patron saint of immigrants.

Who reminds you to live as a faithful follower of Christ? Who helps you grow as a person who makes wise and prudent choices?

When people see you doing what is good, you remind them of how God wants us to live. You are making wise and prudent choices. Your choices benefit not only you but other people too.

Actions Speak Louder Than Words

Describe a time when you have needed to make an important choice about living your Catholic faith. Tell who helped you. What wisdom did that person share with you?

Don't have any times. At least I can't
remember any times.

My Faith Decision

This week I will have many opportunities to make good choices. I will try to think about what my choices are saying to others. I will remember that my actions speak louder than my words.

And now we pray.
Blessed are we,
O Israel;
for what pleases God
is known to us!
BARUCH 4:4

Circle the term in the parentheses that best completes each statement.

1. The prophets centered their messages on the theme of (**fidelity, relationships**) to God's covenant and hope in a future God promised to his people.

2. The major prophets are Isaiah, Jeremiah, and (**Ezekiel, Hosea**).

3. When Baruch wrote to the people, they were living in (**exile, freedom**) in Babylon.

4. The gift by which we gain understanding of ourselves and of God through prayer is called (**prophecy, wisdom**).

Answer the following questions.

1. What work did the prophets do among God's people?

   They spoke God's message in God's name.

2. What does Baruch say about God's wisdom?

   That wisdom is in God's words.

3. Where does Baruch say the people can find life?

   In god's word.

Discuss with your family.

How does God make known to us what pleases him?

Visit our
web site at
www.FaithFirst.com

The Mystery of God

We Pray

God and Father of all
    gifts,
we praise you, the source
    of all we have
    and are.
Teach us to acknowledge
    always
the many good things
    your infinite love has
    given us.
Help us to love you with
    all our heart and all
    our strength.
Amen.

*OPENING PRAYER
MASS OF THANKSGIVING*

Think about all the things
you have come to know
about God. If you could
share one thing you have
learned about God, what
would it be?

*"As the heavens tower over
    the earth,
    so God's love towers over
    the faithful."*
Psalm 103:11

The Mystery of God

Faith Focus

Why do we say that God is a mystery?

Faith Vocabulary

mystery. Unknown or unknowable. God is, and his loving plan for us is, a mystery. We only know who God is and what his plan for us is because he revealed it, or made it known to us.

revelation. God making himself known to us.

Holy Trinity. The one God, who is three Persons—God the Father, God the Son, God the Holy Spirit.

With My Family

Brainstorm words or phrases that describe images that help you express your faith in who God is. Choose one and talk about how that word or phrase might describe your family.

Usually, when we talk about a mystery, we think of something like a puzzle. A mystery is something that we do not quite understand but hope eventually to figure out. Usually, if we have enough time, we can figure out how the pieces of a puzzle fit together. When we put our heads together and look at the clues, we can figure out "who done it."

Stained-glass window depicting our faith in the mystery of the Holy Trinity.

The Revelation of God

When we speak of the **mystery** of God, we mean much more than a puzzle. The mystery of God is different, very different. We can never fully grasp who God is. We can never fully know God, never completely have God "figured out." Saint Augustine put it this way: "If you understood him, it would not be God."

God has revealed, or unveiled, the mystery of himself in many ways. We can get a glimpse of the mystery of God by looking at the wonders of creation: the unique design of fingerprints, the beauty of a sunset, the delicate tracings of a flower petal, or the rhythms of the seasons. All the wonders of creation tell us how wonderful and powerful God is.

We can get another glimpse of the mystery of God when we see evil people succeed while saintly ones appear to fail.

But the truth is that if we are going to get a clue about the mystery of who God is, then God himself must share that with us. Our own minds cannot understand the holy mystery of God. God is like and, at the same time, unlike anyone or anything we know. While we can come to know God exists on our own, we really cannot come to know much about the mystery of who God is without his revealing himself to us.

We believe God has done just that. That **revelation** has been passed on to us in Sacred Scripture and the Tradition of the Church. God has shared many things about himself with us. God has revealed to us that he is:

- Faithful—the One who is always faithful to his people (Exodus 34:6);
- Truth—all his promises come true (Deuteronomy 7:9);
- Love—God is love (1 John 4:8, 16).

All these qualities, and many others God has revealed about himself, help us come to know something about God. But who has God revealed himself to be?

The Mystery of the Holy Trinity

God has revealed himself as the mystery of one God in three Persons: Father, Son, and Holy Spirit. This is who God is. We only know this about God because he has revealed it to us. We could never have come to know this about God unless he chose to share it with us.

We call this revelation of God the mystery of the **Holy Trinity.** The mystery of the Holy Trinity is at the very center of our faith. Many other mysteries of our faith have their beginning in this mystery of mysteries.

For example, the story of the human family begins with God creating us in love. Then, when we had sinned, the Father sent the Son, who became human so that we could become like him. The Word became flesh so that we could become sharers in his divinity. To save us from sin, he died and was raised from the dead. The Father and the Son have sent the Holy Spirit to make us holy, or sanctify us, and to reconcile us with God who created us.

To Help You Remember

1. When we say that God is a mystery, what do we mean?

2. How would you explain our belief in the Trinity?

3. How can you come to know more about God, the Holy Trinity?

The Mystery of the Trinity in Our Lives

Write in each section what that person in the Trinity does in our lives.

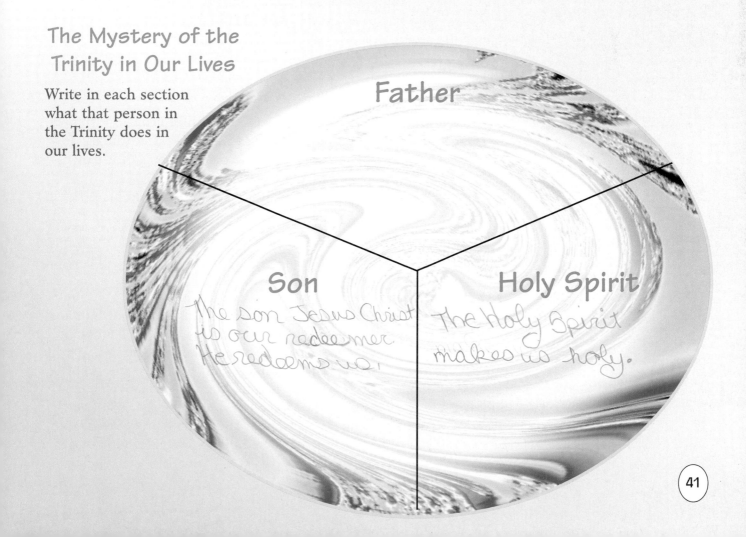

Father

Son

The son Jesus Christ is our redeemer He redeems us.

Holy Spirit

The Holy Spirit makes us holy.

Faith Vocabulary

creation. God bringing the world and humanity into existence from nothing.

soul. Our innermost being; that which bears the imprint of God's image.

eternal. Having no end; timeless; everlasting.

God the Father

The very first words of the Bible begin with the story of God's love for us. The world did not "just happen." It was not made out of "something" that was already there. The first words of the Bible say:

> In the beginning . . .
> God created the heavens
> and the earth.
> GENESIS 1:1

If we listen carefully to these words of Scripture, which are God's word to us, we can begin not only to come to know something about God but also to understand more about the world and ourselves.

- God created the universe and keeps it in existence by his Word, the Son, "who sustains all things by his mighty word"(see Hebrews 1:3), and by his Creator Spirit, the giver of life.

- "In the beginning" means that there was a beginning. The world was not always in existence.

- The words "God created" mean that God is the one who, out of love, made everything that we see and know. Only God creates; that is, only he makes things out of nothing.

- The "heavens and the earth" is simply another way of saying, "everything." There is nothing that our eyes can see, our hands can touch, our ears can hear, that is not created by God. Everyone and everything exists because, and only because, of God's love.

- In the Nicene Creed, we profess that God the Father is the maker of all that is "seen and unseen." We believe that angels are part of God's "unseen" creation. Angels are spiritual creatures who never stop giving glory to God and who serve God's saving plan for all creatures.

Images of God

In God's plan of **creation**, human beings have an extraordinary and unique place. This is God's own word to us:

> God created man in his image;
>   in the divine image he
>   created him;
>   male and female he
>   created them.
> GENESIS 1:27

What does this say about human beings? Every human is an image of God. It does not matter whether the person is an infant, a feared enemy, a prisoner on death row, or a homeless person living in an alley—each and every person is an image of God and is loved by God. The greatness of every person rests on that truth.

When we reflect on this, it helps us understand who we are and who other people are. God shares his love and life with everyone. Thus, we proclaim with the psalmist:

> You formed my inmost being;
>   you knit me in my mother's womb.
> I praise you, so wonderfully you made me;
>   wonderful are your works!
>
> PSALM 139:13–14

To help us understand this great mystery of who we are, the Church teaches that God created us, body and **soul.** At the very first moment of our existence, or conception, God immediately or directly creates each person with a human soul. Our soul is the innermost part of us; our souls are **eternal.** This gives us the ability to share in God's life and love forever.

In all of creation, our special human task is to carry with honor the image and likeness of God. Our responsibility is to share God's love and compassion with all of creation. This means we are to respect the unique dignity of every other human being. It means acting as good stewards of all that God has created. What does this mean? People and all creation are destined for the glory of God.

When you think about it, being created in the image and likeness of God is a mystery too. It is the mystery of the eternal God sharing the gift of his own life and love with us.

To Help You Remember

1. What does it mean to say God created the world?

2. Describe why God created us.

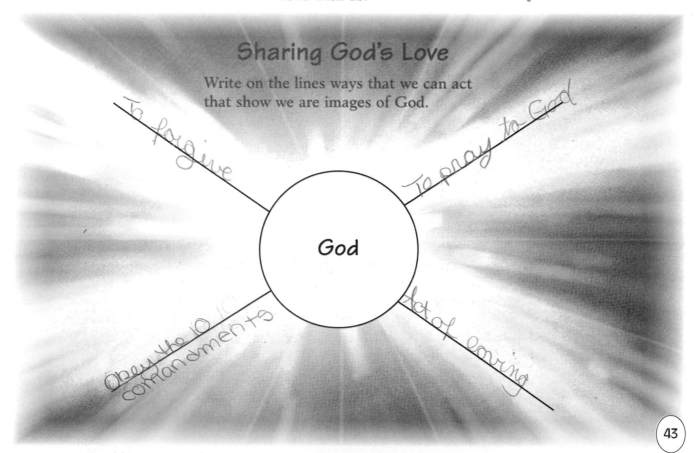

Sharing God's Love

Write on the lines ways that we can act that show we are images of God.

God

To forgive

To pray to God

Obey the 10 commandments

Act of caring

Faith Focus

What was the sin of our first parents at the dawn of creation?

Faith Vocabulary

sin. An offense or violation of God's law; freely choosing to do what we know is against God's will.

original sin. The sin Adam and Eve committed by turning away from God and freely choosing to do what they knew God did not want them to do.

temptation. A strong feeling to do or say something that is wrong or not to do something good we know and can do.

God's Good Creation Is Marked by Sin

The first chapter of the Book of Genesis describes both the creation of the world and of human beings. At the end of the chapter, we read,

> God looked at everything he had made, and he found it very good.
> GENESIS 1:31

It is important for us to remember that all of God's creation is good. God's revelation makes known to us that God created us in a state of original holiness and justice. This was at the center of our friendship with God. This friendship with God was the source of Adam and Eve's happiness. This conviction that humans were first created in a state of friendship with God shapes the way we view our world and ourselves.

Sin, the Bible tells us, made its way into the good world of God's creation. This happened through the sin of our first parents, whom the Bible calls Adam and Eve. Their sin is called **original sin**. Since the moment our first parents committed this sin, which took place at the beginning of the

history of the human race, original sin has become part of our human nature. By this sin, the original holiness and justice human beings received from God was lost. Every human person shares in this sin from the very first moment of our existence, or conception.

The story of the Fall, which this story has been named, begins with a snake, or serpent, tempting Eve. What was at the heart of that **temptation?** The Bible describes it by putting these words in the mouth of the serpent,

> ". . . you will be like gods . . ."
> GENESIS 3:5

The first humans were not happy just being number two; they wanted to be number one. Their sin, therefore, was a combination of pride, ambition, and selfishness. This combination still is in great evidence among people today.

After the sin of our first parents, God's creation remained good, and humanity remained good. Now, however, there was a sad difference. The world and all of us in the human family are marked by sin. All of us are broken people who need God's healing. All of us need to be saved from sin and death, which were introduced to the world by the first humans, the parents of humanity.

We believe that the Son of God became human, lived on earth, and was raised from the dead. In Jesus Christ we have been saved from sin and death and have been healed, or reconciled, with God, with one another, and with all creation. Saint Paul writes:

> [T]hrough one person sin entered the world, and through sin, death. . . . But the gift is not like the transgression. For if by that one person's transgression the many died, how much more did the grace of God and the gracious gift of the one person Jesus Christ overflow for the many."
>
> ROMANS 5:12, 15

Paul was sharing with us our faith in who Jesus is and the meaning of his work on earth. Adam and Eve, by their disobedience, brought sin and death into the world. By his obedience, Christ, the new Adam, brings life to the world. He is the son of Mary, the new Eve.

To Help You Remember

1. What is original sin?

2. Describe what Paul says about the work of Jesus.

3. What can you do that shows you believe Jesus Christ is our Savior?

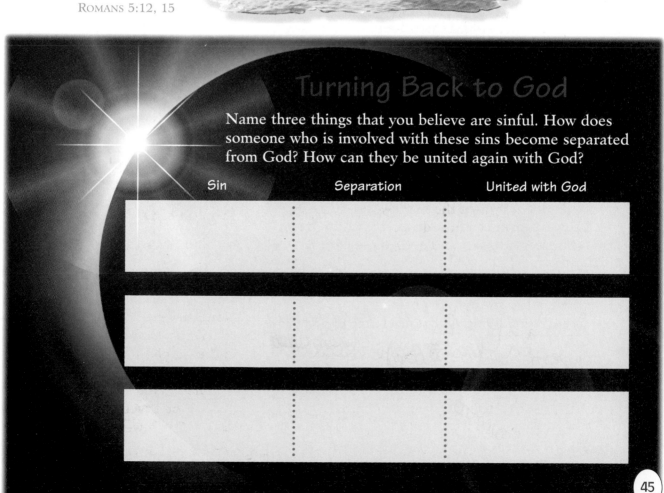

Turning Back to God

Name three things that you believe are sinful. How does someone who is involved with these sins become separated from God? How can they be united again with God?

Sin	Separation	United with God

Belief in the Holy Trinity is the central belief of Christians about God. We believe there is one God in three Persons—God the Father, God the Son, and God the Holy Spirit. Out of love God created us, saved us from sin, and shares his life and love with us.

Mosaics

Long before we had Bibles for everyone to read, Christians used art so people could "hear" the word of God by looking at it. One of the earliest forms of art used by Christians were mosaics. This is an art form consisting of colored pieces of glass called tesserae. These glass pieces are pressed into soft plaster to form pictures.

Mosaic over the altar in the Church of Saint Apollinarius, Ravenna, Italy.

Mosaics give drama and life to scenes from the Bible. They convey a sense of mystery in their portrayal of Jesus and representations of God the Father and the Holy Spirit. Often decorating the ceilings and walls of churches, they instruct the faithful concerning the lives of the saints and the majesty of God.

Some of the most beautiful mosaics were created in Italian churches from A.D. 535 to 1027. The art form is still used in churches today.

What other art forms are being used today to inspire and teach us? What have artists created in your local church?

Mosaic of the Risen Jesus with disciples casting net into sea (John 21:1–8).

If you look closely, there are many clues that give you a glimpse into the mystery of God. God's love for you is so great he never stops giving you signs of that love.

Sharing Life

Make a collage of words and pictures that show what you have come to know about God. Use words from this chapter as part of your collage.

My Faith Decision

This week I will try harder to show that I am made in the image and likeness of God. I will

_____

_____ .

And now we pray.
Come and see the works of God, awesome in the deeds done for us.

PSALM 66:5

Use each word in a sentence that explains its meaning.

1. mystery

   God is a mystery. He remains unknown unless he reavels himself to us

2. Holy Trinity

   The Holy Trinty is one god in 3 persons

3. creation

   A creation is to existance from nothing

4. soul

   Our soul is an imprint of god image

5. original sin

   It is the first sin of the first parents

Answer the following questions.

1. What does it mean to say that God is a mystery?

   We know who god is ecause he reveiled himself to us

2. Why are humans God's greatest creation?

   Because he loves us and created us in his own image

3. How did Jesus save us from sin and death?

   Being freely crucified for us and was raised from the dead.

Discuss with your family.

Where can we go to appreciate the beauty and mystery of God's creation?

Visit our web site at www.FaithFirst.com

Jesus Christ, the Son of God

We Pray

Come, Lord Jesus;
give new courage to your
   people who trust in
   your love.
By your coming, raise us
   to the joy of your
   kingdom,
where you live and reign
   with the Father and
   the Holy Spirit,
one God, for ever and
   ever. Amen.

*DECEMBER 24
MASS IN THE MORNING*

Each Sunday at Mass
we profess our faith in
Jesus Christ. In the creed,
what do we say we believe
about Jesus?

*Lord, by your cross and
   resurrection
you have set us free.
You are the Savior of the
   world.*

Memorial Acclamation

49

God Fulfills His Promises

Faith Vocabulary

salvation. Humanity's deliverance from the power of sin and death through Jesus Christ who "died for our sins in accordance with the Scriptures."

How many promises have you made? How many promises have others made to you? Think about what a big role promises play in our lives. When we join in a game, we promise to play by the rules. The leaders of our towns, cities, states, and country make a solemn promise, or take an oath, to uphold the laws and lead us justly and fairly. We can also describe the Bible as "The Story of the Promise."

The Story of God's Promise

The Bible is the story of God's covenant, or promise, made between God and his people. That story begins in Genesis, the very first book of the Bible. It is told over and over again with more and more details added in each book of the Bible. You might say that all of God's promises in the Bible are part of one big promise.

Let us review some of the promises we read about in the Old Testament.

- In the creation story, God promises that from Eve's descendants will come one who will conquer the tempter, the devil.

- When sin so divided people, God entered a covenant with Noah and all living things. It will remain in force as long as the world lasts.

- Later, God made a covenant with Abraham, promising that Abraham would be the father of a great nation.

- God also made a covenant with Moses. Through Moses, God led the Israelites out of bondage and revealed his law to them. He would be their God and they would be his people.

- God's people became a great nation respected by all their neighbors. However, they soon forgot their promises to God. God sent the prophets who announced a new covenant.

Jesus Is the New Covenant

We believe that all these events and promises point to Jesus Christ. Jesus did not abolish the Law and Covenant of Sinai. He fulfilled it and perfected it. Jesus said, "Do not think that I have come to abolish the law or the prophets. I have come . . . to fulfill. Amen, I say to you, until heaven and earth pass away, not even the smallest letter or the smallest part of a letter will pass from the law, until all things have taken place" (Matthew 5:17–18). In him all of God's promises are fulfilled and we have the promise of eternal life. Through him our inheritance is the kingdom of God. (See Hebrews 9:15.)

At the Last Supper, Jesus took the cup of wine, showed it to his disciples, and said,

"This cup is the new covenant in my blood."

1 CORINTHIANS 11:25

Every time the Church celebrates the Eucharist, we profess our belief that all God's promises are fulfilled in Jesus Christ. He is the New Covenant. He is the Savior promised by God through the prophets. Jesus, then, is the center of **salvation.** In him all God's promises are fulfilled. He is the Savior of all people.

But what about those who have not heard of Jesus? What about those who have heard of Jesus but have chosen not to place their faith in him? The answer to these questions is very important.

Above all, God is a God of love. He has created everyone out of love and wants everyone to share in the life and love of God forever.

[Salvation] holds true not only for Christians, but for all men of good will in whose hearts grace works in an unseen way. For, since Christ died for all men . . . we ought to believe that the Holy Spirit in a manner known only to God offers everyone the possibility of being associated with this paschal mystery.

CHURCH IN THE MODERN WORLD, 22

Through the good graces of the Holy Spirit, Christ saves all who believe in him and live his message. He saves all those who seek to serve and love God with all their hearts.

To Help You Remember

1. What are some of the events in the story of God's covenant with humanity?

2. Why is Christ important to all members of the human race?

3. What do you do that shows you believe Jesus is the Savior of the world?

Salvation Is for Everyone

Write the names of Christians and non-Christians you know who are signs of God's love. Tell what they did.

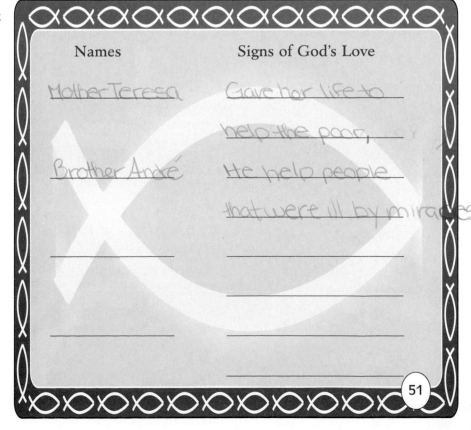

Names	Signs of God's Love
Mother Teresa	Gave her life to help the poor,
Brother André	He help people that were ill by miracles

51

Faith Vocabulary

Incarnation. A word meaning "take on flesh"; it is the term the Church uses to name our belief that the Son of God "took on flesh," or became man. Jesus is true God and true man.

With My Family

Talk about some of the choices your family has made. How are they signs of your faith in Jesus?

Pope John Paul II presiding over the Eucharist in St. Louis, Missouri, January 1999.

The Church's Faith in Jesus Christ

Each Sunday at Mass we profess our faith in Jesus Christ. We stand and with the whole Church pray aloud:

> We believe in one Lord,
>   Jesus Christ,
>   the only Son of God,
>   eternally begotten of the
>   Father,
>   God from God, Light from
>   Light,
>   true God from true God,
>   begotten, not made, one in
>   Being with the Father.
> Through him all things
>   were made.
> For us men and for our
>   salvation he came down
>   from heaven:
> by the power of the Holy Spirit
>   he was born of the Virgin
>   Mary, and became man.

This is part of our profession of faith in Jesus that is found in the Nicene Creed. It was written over three hundred years after Jesus lived on earth, died, was raised from the dead, and ascended to his Father in heaven.

The Confession of Peter

While Jesus lived on earth and did the work his Father sent him to do, not everyone came to believe he was the Messiah. Some people were confused and hesitant to believe. Others were hostile. On one occasion he had a conversation with his disciples:

> When Jesus went into the region of Caesarea Philippi he asked his disciples, "Who do people say that the Son of Man is?" They replied, "Some say John the Baptist, others Elijah, still others Jeremiah or one of the prophets." He said to them, "But who do you say that I am?" Simon Peter said in reply, "You are the Messiah, the Son of the living God."
>
> MATTHEW 16:13–16

Only Peter spoke out and confessed his faith in Christ. Perhaps the others simply hesitated and waited for Peter to speak.

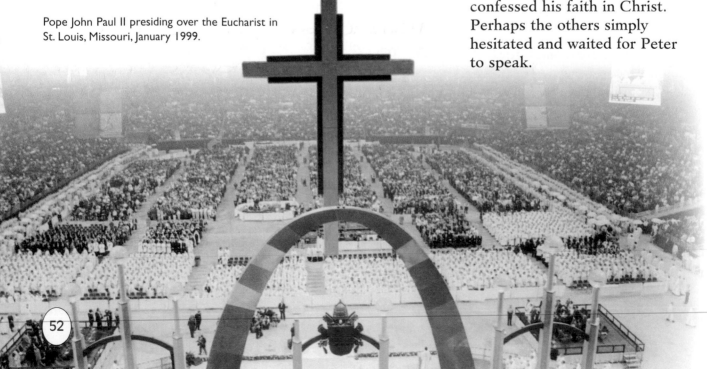

Each Sunday, moved by the grace of the Holy Spirit and drawn by the Father, we profess our faith in Jesus Christ and confess with Peter, "You are the Messiah, the Son of the living God" (Matthew 16:16).

We Believe in One Lord, Jesus Christ

The gospel story of Simon Peter's confession of faith in Jesus is the foundation of what the Holy Spirit has led the Church to believe about Jesus:

1. Jesus is Lord. From the beginning of Christian history, Christians have called Jesus Lord. Paul the Apostle wrote, "And no one can say, 'Jesus is Lord,' except by the holy Spirit" (1 Corinthians 12:3). When we say, "Jesus is Lord," we are expressing our faith that Jesus is truly God.

2. Jesus is the Son of the living God. He is the second Person of the Holy Trinity. Jesus is truly God. Jesus is intimately one with his heavenly Father in the Holy Spirit. Jesus says:

   "Whoever believes in me believes not only in me but also in the one who sent me, and whoever sees me sees the one who sent me."
   JOHN 12:44–45

3. Jesus is true God and true man. He is like us in all things but sin. Jesus, the Son of God, became human. We call this the mystery of the **Incarnation**. The Letter to the Hebrews says:

   For we do not have a high priest who is unable to sympathize with our weaknesses, but one who has similarly been tested in every way, yet without sin.
   HEBREWS 4:15

4. Jesus is the Messiah, the Savior whom God promised to send. He is the One in whom all God's promises come true. As true God and true man, Jesus Christ is the one and only mediator, or "go-between," who links God and the human family. He alone reconciles the human family with God.

   For there is one God.
   There is also one mediator between God and the human race,
   Christ Jesus, himself human, who gave himself as ransom for all.   1 TIMOTHY 2:5–6

To Help You Remember

1. What did Peter confess to Jesus?

2. Briefly describe the Church's main teachings about Jesus.

3. In what ways can you profess your faith in Jesus?

A Meditation

1. Find a quiet place. Close your eyes and relax.
2. Imagine yourself at the Jordan River at the Baptism of Jesus. (Read Matthew 3:13–17.)
3. Describe the scene.
4. Imagine Jesus talking to you after his baptism. Share your thoughts with Jesus.
5. Record some of your thoughts.

_____

_____

_____

_____

_____

_____

_____

Faith Focus

Why are the death and resurrection of Jesus so important to us?

Faith Vocabulary

Paschal mystery.
The Passover events of Jesus' death, resurrection, and ascension.

The Paschal Mystery

The center of Jesus' work on earth as our Savior and Redeemer is called the **Paschal mystery.** The word *paschal* comes from a Hebrew word meaning "the passing over." The Paschal mystery of Christ is his passing over through death to new life and his return to the Father. There he reigns gloriously at the right hand of his Father until he comes again in glory at the end of time. We profess this faith in the Apostles' Creed when we pray:

He suffered under Pontius Pilate,
was crucified, died, and was
buried.
He descended into hell.
On the third day he rose again.
He ascended into heaven
and is seated at the right
hand of the Father.
He will come again to judge
the living and the dead.

The dead Christ went down to the dead and opened the gates of heaven for the just who had gone before him and for those who would come after him. Three days later he was raised from the dead. Christ's Resurrection is the fulfillment of the promises of the Old Testament and the promises Jesus made while he was on earth.

This great mystery of God's love for us is at the center of the Gospel. Jesus often preached of this mystery as he taught near the Sea of Galilee. And on the first Pentecost, Peter, filled with the Spirit, proclaimed that God's love was revealed in Jesus. He said:

"You who are Israelites, hear these words. Jesus the Nazorean was a man commended to you by God with mighty deeds, wonders, and signs, which God worked through him in your midst, as you yourselves know. This man, delivered up by the set plan and foreknowledge of God, you killed, using lawless men to crucify him. But . . . God raised this Jesus; of this we are all witnesses. Exalted at the right hand of God, he received the promise of the holy Spirit from the Father and poured it forth, as you [both] see and hear."
ACTS OF THE APOSTLES 2:22–23, 32–33

The Gospel clearly teaches us that the Resurrection of Jesus took place. The disciples went to the tomb and the body of Jesus was not there. Then, the Risen Jesus appeared to them. He spoke to them and ate with them. Jesus' Resurrection is so important for Christians that Paul the Apostle, who was alive when Jesus was raised from the dead, wrote:

For I handed on to you as of first importance what I also received: that Christ died for our sins in accordance with the scriptures; that he was buried; that he was raised on the third day in accordance with the scriptures; that he appeared to Kephas, then to the Twelve.
1 CORINTHIANS 15:3–5

The death-resurrection-ascension-exaltation of Jesus is the sign of God's everlasting love for us. Through Christ's Paschal mystery, his passing over from death to new life, all things have been justified, or made right with our relationship with God. Christ is the first-born from the dead. Through him we are saved and will also rise to life everlasting.

Christ's ascension and exaltation in glory marks the entrance of Christ's humanity into heaven, God's domain. Through Christ's ascension and exaltation, we have been given an unbreakable promise of everlasting life and happiness with God and with all the angels and saints forever. From there, Christ, who is now hidden from our eyes, will come again in glory at the end of time.

Sharing in the Paschal Mystery

Through Baptism we are joined with Christ. Entering the waters of Baptism, we die to sin. Rising from them, we rise to new life. What happened to Christ happens to us. Christ's journey through life, death, resurrection, and return to the Father is our journey too.

We are making this journey in many ways each day. Think of the times you were successful or failed at something. Recall how you felt when you were complimented. How do those feelings compare with the feelings you had when you were insulted?

There are also times you may choose to do something you know is wrong. Then you realize what you have done and try to fix it. You admit your wrongdoing, ask for forgiveness, receive it, and are reconciled, or made friends again with others.

These are just a few of the ways we live our life in Christ. With God at our side, we make our journey knowing that God has made an unbreakable covenant with us in Jesus Christ. What a difference that makes for us— and for the world!

To Help You Remember

1. What is the Paschal mystery?

2. Describe the importance of the Paschal mystery.

3. How do we share in the Paschal mystery?

God Always Helps Us

Write a prayer you can pray when you are experiencing failure or great sadness.

God, I ask you to help me in what I'm going through. I would like you to help me get over what I'm going through. thank you! ⊞

55

Jesus Christ is Savior of the world. He is the Son of the living God, who took on flesh and became like us in all things but sin. Through his passion and death we have been reconciled with God. Through his resurrection and return to his Father, we hope to live with God and the saints forever in heaven.

Sharing and Living the Gospel

From Peter's speech to the present day, the Holy Spirit has worked through the people of the Church to bring the Gospel to others. Saint Charles Lwanga (ca. 1860–1886) was one of those Christians.

Charles lived in Uganda, which is located in Africa. He was a member of the king's household where he and other young men worked. Many of these young men had become Christians because of the work of missionaries who preached and lived the Gospel in Uganda.

Hearing that his people were joining this new religion, the king ordered two Christians who were members of the royal court to be killed. The king was amazed by the reaction of the others. More and more young men in his court decided to become Christians.

Finally, the king ordered all those who were Christians or preparing to become Christians to make themselves known. Among these young men was twenty-two year old Charles Lwanga. After hearing the king's order, Charles and the others bravely suffered death because of their faith in Christ. As he was led away, one of Charles' friends was heard saying, "A fountain fed from many springs will never dry up. When we are gone, others will rise in our place." Today there are more than six million Christians in Uganda.

Who helps you come to know Jesus? Who helps you live your faith as a follower of Jesus?

Victoria Nile flowing into Murchison Falls, Uganda.

Each day you have many opportunities to profess and live your faith in Jesus Christ. Sometimes this is easier to do than at other times. Always the Holy Spirit is with you to help you.

Who Do You Say That I Am?

You are a reporter for a magazine and have been asked to write an article about Jesus. Write notes for your article on the pages of this planner. In your notes be sure to include how your faith in Christ affects the choices you make.

My Faith Decision

When I must make a difficult decision about living my faith, I will remember that Jesus died and was raised from the dead. I will remember how much God loves me. I will ask myself what Jesus would do in this situation and try my best to do it.

And now we pray.
Lord, by your cross and resurrection you have set us free. You are the Savior of the world.
Memorial Acclamation
Eucharistic Prayer

Complete each sentence with a word or words from this chapter.

1. The Church teaches that ___salvation___ is for all people.

2. Jesus is the ___new___ ___convenant___ . In him all God's promises are fulfilled.

3. The events of Jesus' death, resurrection, and ascension are called the ___paschal___ ___mystery___ .

4. ___Incarnation___ is the term the Church uses to express its belief that the Son of God took on flesh and became human.

Explain the following statements.

1. The Bible can be called "The Story of the Promise."

    ___The bible tells us the stor(c)is about God promises to the people.___

2. Jesus Christ is true God and true man.

    ___Jesus Christ is the son of God. He brought on the human flesh, became human and was amoung us.___

3. The Paschal mystery of Jesus stands at the center of the Gospel.

    ___Jesus center of work on earth His death, reserection.___

Discuss with your family.

What can we do as a family to share our faith in Jesus Christ?

Visit our
web site at
www.FaithFirst.com

God's Plan of Salvation

A Scripture Story

We Pray

Lord our God,
encourage us through the
prayers of Saints Peter
and Paul.
May the apostles who
strengthened the faith
of the infant Church
help us on our way of
salvation.

OPENING PRAYER
VIGIL MASS
PETER AND PAUL, APOSTLES

The letters, or epistles, of
Paul tell us that we, as
believers in Jesus Christ,
should show others what it
means to be Christian.
How can we use the New
Testament letters to deepen
our faith and become living
letters in our own time?

*The Great Theatre in Ephesus,
Turkey. In New Testament times,
Ephesus was a wealthy city and a
chief port of Asia with a population
of 250,000 people.*

Bible Background

Saint Paul Arriving at Malta by the Dutch painter Peter Mulier (1637–1701).

Faith Focus

Why were the letters in the New Testament written?

Faith Vocabulary

epistle. A longer, more formal type of letter.

From the first drawings found in caves to the latest gadgets that deliver E-mail anywhere anytime, people have always communicated with one another with drawings and symbols. Letters have been the most common form of written communication throughout history. Some letters have become famous. A young Jewish girl hiding from the Nazis in Holland wrote an extraordinary series of letters during the Holocaust. We know these letters as *The Diary of Anne Frank*.

The New Testament Letters

Some of the greatest letters ever written are found in the New Testament. The New Testament letters are sometimes called **epistles.** In fact, "letters" and "epistles" represent a similar kind of writing, but there is a difference. When someone had an idea and wanted to explain it in detail, they might call their letter an epistle. The school principal or our great-aunt Doris might write us epistles.

Letters are usually more personal and are exchanged between people who know each other well. Our friends normally write us letters. They may want to send their good wishes and keep in touch or they simply may want to write a letter because they need our advice on a specific matter.

The Letters of Paul

Paul the Apostle wrote very lovingly to the early Christians. Often these people were his converts who came to believe in Jesus Christ through Paul's preaching.

Paul wrote to encourage, support, and instruct his friends. He felt very close to these people. Read Philippians 1:3–7. It is an example of a personal note from Paul.

Paul's letters sometimes addressed a problem that a particular Christian community was facing. For a good example of this, read Paul's First Letter to the Corinthians 11:17–34.

At other times Paul used his letters as a means to remind people of the faith that he preached to them—especially if they were in danger of falling away from the truth. Read Galatians 4:8–11 for an example of Paul reminding people about the truth about God.

There are other letters in the New Testament not written by Paul, such as the three letters of John, the letter of James, and the letters of Peter. The teachings of all the letters in the New Testament are important for deepening our understanding and living our faith in Jesus Christ. We will now study the Letter to the Ephesians in more detail.

To Help You Remember

1. What is the difference between a letter and an epistle?

2. Explain some of the reasons Paul the Apostle wrote letters to the early Christians.

3. How can reading the letters in the New Testament help us today?

Reading a New Testament Letter

Look up and read the New Testament letter to Philemon. What does it tell you?

_____

_____

_____

_____

_____

_____

_____

_____

_____

_____

Reading the Word of God

Faith Focus

What is the message of the opening part of the Letter to the Ephesians?

Faith Vocabulary

Ephesians. The people who lived in the city of Ephesus, which today is in the nation of Turkey.

The Letter to the Ephesians

In New Testament times, Ephesus was the capital of the Roman Empire's province of Asia. It was a great commercial center, teeming with merchants, tradespeople, and sailors from all over the world. Into this noisy crossroads of a city came Paul.

Paul stayed there for two years before the local silversmiths forced him to flee. They were angry that their trade in shrines to a pagan goddess had suffered due to the growth of the Christian faith.

Read and discover the opening words to the **Ephesians.**

Paul, an apostle of Christ Jesus by the will of God, to the holy ones who are [in Ephesus] faithful in Christ Jesus: grace to you and peace from God our Father and the Lord Jesus Christ.

Blessed be the God and Father of our Lord Jesus Christ, who has blessed us in Christ with every spiritual blessing in the heavens, as he chose us in him, before the foundation of the world, to be holy and without blemish before him. In love he destined us for adoption to himself through Jesus Christ, in accord with the favor of his will, for the praise of the glory of his grace that he granted us in the beloved.

In him we have redemption by his blood, the forgiveness of transgressions, in accord with the riches of his grace that he lavished upon us. In all wisdom and insight, he has made known to us the mystery of his will in accord with his favor that he set forth in him as a plan for the fullness of times, to sum up all things in Christ, in heaven and on earth.

In him we were also chosen, destined in accord with the purpose of the One who accomplishes all things according to the intention of his will, so that we might exist for the praise of his glory, we who first hoped in Christ. In him you also, who have heard the word of truth, the gospel of your salvation, and have believed in him, were sealed with the promised holy Spirit, which is the first installment of our inheritance toward redemption as God's possession, to the praise of his glory.

EPHESIANS 1:1–14

This letter shares with the Ephesians Paul's most precious possession. It shares with them the faith in Christ that Paul preached to others.

To Help You Remember

1. Describe what the city of Ephesus was like in New Testament times.

2. What was God's plan for us since before the foundation of the world?

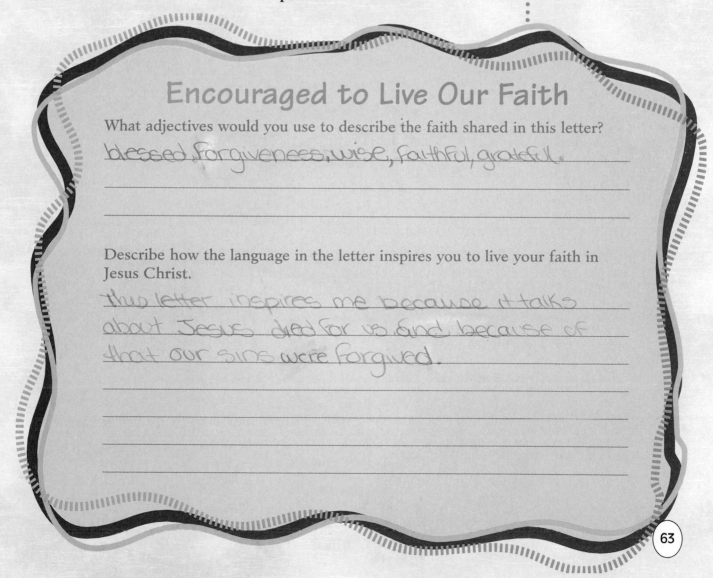

Encouraged to Live Our Faith

What adjectives would you use to describe the faith shared in this letter?

blessed, forgiveness, wise, faithful, grateful.

Describe how the language in the letter inspires you to live your faith in Jesus Christ.

this letter inspires me because it talks about Jesus died for us, and, because of that our sins were forgived.

Understanding the Word of God

Have you ever written a thank-you note to a friend? Did you have a special name for your friend? Did you want to make sure that your friend understood exactly what you wrote? Did you want your letter to mean something special to your friend—a letter that he or she would never forget? The writer of the letter to the Ephesians wanted his letter to have an impact. He followed an order, or plan, when writing his letter to make that impact.

Faith Focus

How can we apply the teachings of the Letter to the Ephesians to our lives today?

With My Family

Write a letter to a family member or friend whom you have not been in touch with for a while. Be sure to include a message of thanks for their friendship.

The Writing Style

The first two verses of the Letter to the Ephesians are the greeting. The writer of the letter is identified—"Paul, an apostle of Christ Jesus by the will of God." Many today acknowledge that Paul did not write this letter. They believe that it might have been written by a disciple of Paul who used Paul's name to get his readers' attention. Then those who are receiving the letter are named: "to the holy ones who are in Ephesus." The greeting closes with a prayerful wish: "grace to you and peace from God our Father and the Lord Jesus Christ."

Notice that the prayerful wish is sometimes used in a slightly different form at the beginning of the Mass. This occurs when the priest greets the people, "The grace and peace of God our Father and the Lord Jesus Christ be with you."

The next verses, verses 3 to 14, are a long prayer of praise and thanksgiving to God. The letters in the New Testament and other letters in the ancient world often began with a prayer of thanks.

• Verses 3–10. This section offers praise and thanksgiving to God for what he has done in Jesus Christ. It explains that God *chose* and *adopted* the Ephesians as his very own through Jesus. God *redeemed* them, or saved them from sin through the blood of Jesus. Finally, God *revealed* to them the plan that he had for them in Jesus.

- Verses 11–14. The last words of this passage tell us that the gift of the Holy Spirit is "the first installment of our inheritance toward redemption as God's possession." We believe that God's life in us has only just begun. In the future, we will share in God's life forever.

A Letter for Us Today

The Letter to the Ephesians was written two thousand years ago; but in a very real sense, it is also written to us today. We are part of God's plan. We are chosen by God. We are adopted as God's sons and daughters. We are redeemed. And we are shown God's plan for us.

The story of the Ephesians is our story. We too have heard God's good news proclaimed to us. We believe in Jesus Christ. And we have been sacramentally sealed with the promised Holy Spirit.

God continues to work with us as we proceed along life's bumpy road. In the end, the work that God has begun in us will be completed.

To Help You Remember

1. What are the major parts of the letter-writing style in Ephesians?

2 According to Ephesians, what has God accomplished in us?

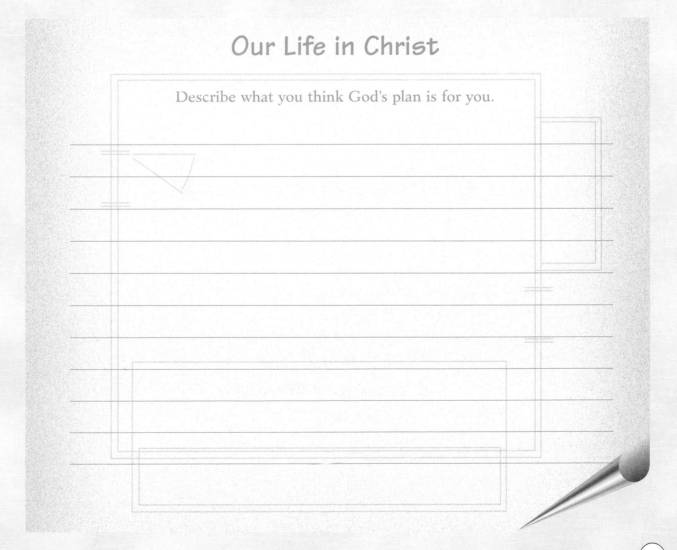

Our Life in Christ

Describe what you think God's plan is for you.

Paul and the other apostles were chosen by Jesus to follow him in a special way. They would continue the work of Jesus after he returned to his Father. One of the ways Paul shared his faith in Jesus was through his letters.

Letters Go a Long Way

Maria Rodriguez always liked sharing family letters with her grandmother Rosa. She didn't mind the hour drive across town to visit the senior citizens' home where her grandmother had a little cozy apartment. "I may be ninety, but I can still make my tea and watch my soaps," her grandmother would laugh. Then she would turn a little sad and say, "I wish my friends could get such lovely letters. They mean so much to me. It would make their day as well."

That's when Maria got an idea. She explained it to her sixth-grade class at Saint Mary's Parish. "Most of us have E-mail at home. And we can use the computers in the media lab. Let's say each of us sends a letter about all the things happening in our lives to the seniors in my grandmother's complex. Just think how we could make their day a little happier."

Soon the E-mails were flying to Maria's E-mail address at home—thirty-seven of them in total. Maria printed them out, and then she and three other volunteers rolled each one up and tied it with a gold ribbon. The next Sunday, Maria gave out her letters to her grandmother's friends. "You should have seen their faces," she later reported to her class.

How can you correspond with elderly or ill members of your parish who live alone?

Like Paul, you too share your faith in Jesus by your words and by your actions.

Sharing Our Faith in Jesus

Make a list of several things you can say or do that show others you are a follower of Jesus.

_____

_____

_____

_____

_____

_____

_____

My Faith Decision

This week I will choose one of the things I just wrote about. This week I will try to do what I have written.

And now we pray.

God our Father, you taught the gospel to all the world through the preaching of Paul your apostle. May we who follow him bear witness to your truth.

FROM OPENING PRAYER, MASS, CONVERSION OF PAUL, APOSTLE

CHAPTER REVIEW

Define the following by using each word in a sentence.

1. epistle

   It is a longer more formal leter found in the new testament.

2. redemption

   Being saved from sin threw the blood of Jesus.

3. Ephesians

   the people how lived in the city of Ephesus whit today is in turkey.

Answer the following questions.

1. What are some reasons that the New Testament letters were written?

   to teach, support and encourage people

2. What does Ephesians say God has done for us in Jesus Christ?

   He redeemed us, he adopted us and blessed us

3. What does it mean to say that Ephesians was written for us today?

   Means we are part of Gods plan and he continues to work in us.

Discuss with your family.

How can we help each other discover God's plan for us?

Visit our web site at www.FaithFirst.com

The Church: The Age of the Spirit

We Pray

God our Father,
may your Church
always be
your holy people,
united as you are
one with the Holy Spirit.
May it be
for all the world
a sign of your unity
and holiness,
as it grows to perfection
in your love.

*OPENING PRAYER
MASS FOR THE
UNIVERSAL CHURCH*

At Baptism you were joined
to Christ and received the
gift of the Spirit. If you
were asked to talk about
what it means to belong to
the Church to younger
students, what would you
tell them?

*World Youth Day, Paris, France,
August 1997.*

The Work of the Spirit in the World

Faith Focus

Why is Pentecost called the birthday of the Church?

Has your school ever held a spirit day? Students and faculty dress in school colors and wear school ribbons. Brightly colored posters filled with catchy sayings decorate

Present-day city of Jerusalem in Israel.

Faith Vocabulary

Pentecost. The feast on which the Church remembers and celebrates the coming of the Holy Spirit upon the apostles and the opening of the Church to all peoples. On that day over three thousand people were baptized.

Church. The Body of Christ, the people God the Father has called together in Jesus Christ through the power of the Holy Spirit.

the hallways. Everything around the school seems to shout out messages about what it means to belong to the school. Spirit days are days filled with enthusiasm. The message is always the same: It is great to belong to Saint Rita's or Armstrong Middle School. The day ends with everyone feeling proud to belong to such a great community.

The Holy Spirit

When we think of the Holy Spirit, we mostly think of the story of the first Christian **Pentecost**. We might think that the Holy Spirit waited until Pentecost to begin his work among us. The truth is that the Holy Spirit has always been at work in the world.

We read about the Spirit in the story of creation and the Spirit's work with the Old Testament prophets. We read about the work of the Holy Spirit in the life of Mary in the gospel story of the Annunciation.

The work, or mission, of the Son and the Spirit always go together and cannot be separated, one from the other. At Jesus' baptism in the waters of the Jordan River, the Spirit is present. After his baptism, the Gospel according to Luke tells us, "Filled with the holy Spirit, Jesus returned from the Jordan and was led by the Spirit into the desert" (Luke 4:1). When Jesus begins his public ministry, he announces in the synagogue in Nazareth that the words of the prophet Isaiah are fulfilled in him, "The Spirit of the Lord is upon me" (Luke 4:18). Before the Risen Lord returned to the Father, he promised the Spirit would come to his disciples.

Pentecost

Fifty days after Jesus was raised from the dead the disciples were suddenly filled with enthusiasm. The word *enthusiasm* means "filled with spirit" or "filled with God." This is how the New Testament describes that day.

> When the time for Pentecost was fulfilled, they were all in one place together. And suddenly there came from the sky a noise like a strong driving wind, and it filled the entire house in which they were. Then there appeared to them tongues as of fire, which parted and came to rest on each one of them. And they were all filled with the holy Spirit and began to speak in different tongues, as the Spirit enabled them to proclaim.
>
> ACTS OF THE APOSTLES 2:1–4

The Holy Spirit came upon the disciples as Jesus had promised. From every nation under heaven people listened to Peter, were moved by the Spirit, and were baptized. The **Church** was born. Pentecost is the birthday of the Church.

On this first Pentecost, the Holy Spirit brought very different people together. Through faith and baptism they were joined with Christ and one another. The promise made to Abraham had come true in Christ. The Holy Spirit began the work of gathering people of all races and cultures into the one People of God.

The Church born on Pentecost is a sign and instrument of God's communion with all humanity. It is a sign in the world of the unity of the whole human race. That mission, which began on that first Pentecost, continues today and will continue until Christ comes in glory at the end of time.

To Help You Remember

1. What happened to the disciples of Jesus on Pentecost?

2. Describe how the pilgrims in Jerusalem responded to Peter.

3. What can you do or say to show your belief that the whole human race is one family?

One People of God

Read Acts of the Apostles 2:5–11. Circle the places the Jewish pilgrims in Pentecost came from.

Faith Focus

What do the four marks of
the Church tell us about
the Church?

Faith Vocabulary

marks of the Church.
Essential features
of the Church and
her mission. The marks
of the Church are one,
holy, catholic, and
apostolic.

With My Family

Choose one of
the marks of the
Church. Talk
about ways it is
characteristic of
your family.

The Marks of the Church

Christians living in every nation around the world gather and take part in the celebration of Mass. We celebrate that we are one with Christ and with each other. We are the Body of Christ, the People of God.

At Mass we profess what we believe about the Church. Standing, we pray aloud:

> We believe in one, holy, catholic, and apostolic Church.

One, holy, catholic, and apostolic are called the four **marks of the Church.** They mark, or identify, the essential features of the Church that Jesus Christ has given to us.

One

The night before he died Jesus prayed to his Father for the disciples who were with him and for all those who would one day become his followers. He said:

> "I pray not only for them, but also for those who will believe in me through their word, so that they may all be one, as you, Father, are in me and I in you, that they also may be in us, that the world may believe that you sent me."
>
> JOHN 17:20–21

The Church of Jesus Christ is one Church. For there is:

> one Lord, one faith, one baptism; one God and Father of all, who is over all and through all and in all.
>
> EPHESIANS 4:5–6

How can that be? We see so many Christian churches: Catholic, Episcopalian, Lutheran, Methodist, and many more. What we see is the one Church founded by Jesus separated into many parts. We, who are the Church, must work to be one, as Jesus and the Father are one.

Holy

The members of the Church are not only one with each other. We are one with each other because we are one with Christ and the Spirit and the Father. Because we are one with Christ and have received the gift of the Spirit, we live in communion with God. We are:

> "[A] holy nation a people of his own."
>
> 1 PETER 2:9

Each day the Spirit helps us live the life God shares with us. He helps us live holy lives.

Catholic

The story of the first Pentecost helps us understand what the third mark, catholic, tells us about the Church.

Jesus Christ is the Savior of all people, the Savior of the world. The Spirit through the Church reaches out to and embraces the whole human family. We are people with a mission. Working with the Holy Spirit, we share the good news of Jesus with everyone without exception. With enthusiasm we live our faith wherever we are.

Apostolic

The fourth mark of the Church, apostolic, tells us that the Church traces itself all the way back to the apostles, whom Jesus sent out to teach in his name. There is an unbroken connection between the apostles and their successors, our bishops. The pope, who is the successor of Saint Peter the Apostle, and the bishops, in communion with him, govern the Catholic Church.

Our faith and all that we believe is rooted in what the apostles preached and taught in the name of Jesus. Today that work is continued and will continue to the end of time through the bishops of the Church. Called by the Spirit, our bishops are the successors of the apostles. As the apostles did, they too teach us today in the name of Jesus.

Signs of the Church for Others

Decorate this banner with symbols that show that the Church is one, holy, catholic, and apostolic.

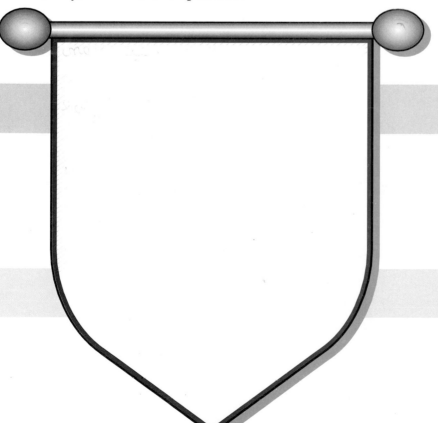

To Help You Remember

1. Name the four marks of the Church.

2. Explain each mark of the Church.

3. What can you do to show that the Church is one, holy, catholic, and apostolic?

The Popes of the 20th Century

Leo XIII	1878–1903
St. Pius X	1903–1914
Benedict XV	1914–1922
Pius XI	1922–1939
Pius XII	1939–1958
John XXIII	1958–1963
Paul VI	1963–1978
John Paul I	Aug. 26– Sept. 28, 1978
John Paul II	1978–

Pope John Paul II is the 262nd pope. He is the most traveled pope in history. He has crisscrossed the globe, traveling over 670,000 miles, in his work of bringing the Christian message to all.

Faith Focus

Why do we use images to help us understand what the Church is?

There are many images that Christians use for the Church. These images, like the marks of the Church, help us understand the mystery of the Church. People of God, Body of Christ, and Temple of the Holy Spirit are three images for the Church that you have heard many times. What do these images tell you about the Church?

The Bride of Christ

Another image the Scripture uses for the Church is the Bride of Christ. In the New Testament we read:

Husbands, love your wives, even as Christ loved the church and handed himself over for her to sanctify her, cleansing her by the bath of water with the word, that he might present to himself the church in splendor, . . . that she might be holy and without blemish. . . . This is a great mystery, but I speak in reference to Christ and the church.

EPHESIANS 5:25–27, 32

Christ's relationship with the members of his Church is like that of a husband and wife. It is a relationship built on the love promised and shown to one another. Jesus himself described his love for us this way:

"No one has greater love than this, to lay down one's life for one's friends."

JOHN 15:13

Christ loves the Church with a love that has no limits. His love for us will never end.

Mother

We also use the image of a mother for the Church. This image helps us understand that we receive the gift of our life in Christ through the Church. The Church teaches us the language of our faith and how to live as a child of God and follower of Christ. The Church nourishes us as we gather around the table of the Eucharist.

As our faith teacher, the Church passes on to us what God has revealed to us. Jesus gave this responsibility to the Church, commanding his disciples:

"All power in heaven and on earth has been given to me. Go, therefore, and make disciples of all nations, baptizing them in the name of the Father, and of the Son, and of the holy Spirit, teaching them to observe all that I have commanded you. And behold, I am with you always, until the end of the age."

MATTHEW 28:18–20

Through the gift of the Holy Spirit, the Church faithfully passes on to us and teaches us what God has revealed to us as Jesus himself promised:

"The Advocate, the holy Spirit that the Father will send in my name—he will teach you everything and remind you of all that [I] told you."

JOHN 14:26

To Help You Remember

1. Why does Saint Paul call the Church the Bride of Christ?

2. Explain what the image of a mother helps us understand about the Church.

3. What can you do to help someone understand Christ's love for the Church?

Picturing the Church

Create an image or symbol that helps you understand the Church. Draw and explain that image in this space.

The Church is the sign and instrument of God's communion with all peoples. The Church has four marks, or essential qualities, that identify it. They are one, holy, catholic, and apostolic.

Letters from the Church

Since its very beginning, the Church has written letters to help us understand our faith. Beginning with Paul the Apostle and the other writers of the New Testament letters, the Church has a long tradition of letter writing. That tradition continues in the Church today.

One of the most important types of letters in the Church is called encyclical letters. The word *encyclical* literally means "circular" letter. An encyclical is a formal letter written by or authorized by the pope. Encyclical letters are addressed to all church members, much like a principal's letter is addressed to the whole student body.

Encyclicals are official letters of the Church. They spotlight issues on doctrine, morality, or discipline, such as war and peace, social justice, and moral behavior, and the meaning of the truths of our faith.

In what other ways does the Church teach us?

Pope John XXIII

Peace on Earth

Pope Paul VI

Progress of Peoples

Mother of the Redeemer

Pope John Paul II

The choices you make and the things you do and say tell others about the Church. All your actions and words tell others about you and the values that are important to you.

The People of God

Create a bulletin board announcement that invites people to join with you in telling others about the Church.

My Faith Decision

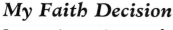

I am a sign or image of the Church. When others see me, they see the Church. This week I will try to be a clear image of what the Church is by

_____

_____ .

And now we pray.

Lord, may the world be filled with the light of your Spirit and believe in Jesus whom you sent.

FROM OPENING PRAYER, MASS FOR UNITY OF CHRISTIANS

Match the terms in Column A with their meanings in Column B.

Column A

_____ 1. Pentecost

_____ 2. marks of the Church

_____ 3. catholic

_____ 4. apostolic

_____ 5. Church

Column B

a. A word meaning "linked to the apostles"

b. The feast that commemorates the Holy Spirit's descent upon the apostles and the opening of the Church to all peoples

c. The essential features of the Church and her mission

d. The Body of Christ, the People of God whom God has called together in Jesus Christ through the power of the Holy Spirit

e. A mark of the Church that tells us Jesus is the Savior of all people

Answer the following questions.

1. What does the story of Pentecost tell us about the work of the Spirit in the Church?

_____

_____

2. Explain the four marks of the Church.

_____

_____

_____

_____

3. Why do we use images for the Church?

_____

_____

Discuss with your family.

How can the image of family help us understand what the Church is and what its work in the world is?

Visit our web site at www.FaithFirst.com

The People of God

We Pray

God our Father,
keep the Church faithful
to its mission:
may it be a leaven
in the world
renewing us in Christ,
and transforming us
into your family.

*OPENING PRAYER
FROM MASS FOR THE
UNIVERSAL CHURCH*

We speak of the Church in
many ways. It is the Body
of Christ, the People of
God. What is the work of
the Church in the world?

"You are my people."
Hosea 2:25

The Church

Faith Focus

Why do we call the Church the People of God?

Remember how God promised that Abraham's descendants would be as numerous as the stars? Each one of us is one of those stars.

Remember how God led Moses and his people out of slavery? God is now leading us from our own personal forms of slavery.

Remember how God promised Moses' people a land for their inheritance? God now promises us eternal life and heaven as our inheritance.

Remember how God asked his people to abide by his words and commandments? He now asks the same of us. What do all these things tell you about God and his relationship with us? We are his people. He is our God through thick or thin. We are the People of God.

The New People of God

Everything that the Old Testament tells us about God and our relationship with him is fulfilled in Jesus. Jesus Christ, by the power of the Holy Spirit, is the New and Everlasting Covenant. In him and through him God calls all peoples to be brought into the People of God. This is how the Second Vatican Council teaches us this truth of our faith:

> "Christ instituted . . . the new covenant in his blood . . . he called a race made up of Jews and Gentiles which would be one . . . in the Spirit, and this race would be the new People of God . . . That messianic people has as its head Christ."
>
> DOGMATIC CONSTITUTION ON THE CHURCH, 9

We belong to the Church, the People of God, whom God has chosen in Jesus Christ as his very own. Like our Old Testament ancestors in faith, who journeyed from slavery in Egypt to freedom, we, the new People of God, are also on a journey of faith. Our destination is the kingdom of God.

This is the kingdom announced and begun in Jesus Christ. It is our work now to prepare for the coming of that kingdom, which will be brought to completion by God himself "at the end of time when Christ our life will appear" (*Constitution on the Church*, 9). While we, the People of God, journey through the world and through time, we are to do whatever we can to prepare for the coming of the kingdom of God.

The Communion of Saints

The Church, the People of God, is a communion of saints. The word *communion* comes from a Latin word meaning "sharing something in common." Through Baptism all the members of the Church share in the life of Christ. We are a communion in "holy things" and "holy people."

Holy Things

The Church is a communion of holy things. We share in the faith passed on to us from the times of the apostles. We share in the sacraments, above all the Eucharist, by which the unity of believers, who form the Body of Christ, is both represented and brought about. We share in the charisms, or gifts, of the same Spirit. We share with others the goods that God has blessed us with.

Holy People

The Church is a communion of holy people. The Holy Spirit invites everyone to holiness, to live in communion with the Holy Trinity now and forever in heaven. The communion of saints includes all the faithful members of the Church who are alive and those who have died.

Saints are holy people who have died and are living with God in heaven. We pray to them and honor them throughout the year at liturgy. Other members of the communion of saints are not yet ready to receive the gift of eternal happiness at the moment of their death. We pray for them, especially on All Souls' Day, asking God that they may join all the saints in heaven.

To Help You Remember

1. What do the terms *People of God* and *communion of saints* mean?

2. Why do we call the Church the new People of God?

3. How can you prepare for the coming of the kingdom of God?

The Church

Describe five ways God is working in and through the Church.

81

Faith Vocabulary

vow. A solemn promise binding a person to a particular act, service, or condition.

The Body of Christ

The Church is also called the Mystical Body of Christ, the Temple of the Holy Spirit. The Spirit is the source of the Church's life and of its unity as the one People of God, which is made up of many diverse members. The Spirit is also the one source of the richness of the Church's many gifts and charisms. Charisms are graces of the Holy Spirit that are given to build up the Church and to help the Church fulfill its work in the world.

Christ is the Head of the Body and we are its members. The Church lives from him, in him, and for him. He lives with the Church and in the Church. All salvation comes from Christ, the Head, and through the Church, which is his Body.

The Church is both visible and spiritual. The Church is formed of two parts, human and divine. The Church is made up of many parts, each one with a particular responsibility and function. Here are some of the groups of people who make up the visible Church on earth.

Lay Faithful

The largest group of people in the Church are called the *lay faithful,* or laity. The laity are the baptized and confirmed members of the Church who carry on Jesus' mission, especially where they work and live. They make Christ present in the world through their words, actions, and worship.

Consecrated Religious

There are men and women in the Church who belong to religious communities. They take vows or promises of poverty, chastity, and obedience. They are consecrated to support one another and live as witnesses of the Gospel in the world and in the Church.

Ordained Ministers

The *ordained ministers*—bishops, priests, and deacons—serve us in the name of Christ. They serve the whole Church by proclaiming God's word, celebrating the sacraments, and caring for the life of the Church.

The Ministry of the Pope

Within the Catholic Church there is a special ministry, or service, that keeps the Church faithful to the teachings of Jesus. It is the ministry of Peter, also known as the *Petrine ministry*.

Jesus gave Peter a special task. He said to Peter:

"[Y]ou are Peter, and upon this rock I will build my church, and the gates of the netherworld

To Help You Remember

1. Name three groups of baptized people who make up the Body of the Church.

2. Describe the ministry of the pope in the Church.

shall not prevail against it. I will give you the keys to the kingdom of heaven. Whatever you bind on earth shall be bound in heaven; and whatever you loose on earth shall be loosed in heaven." MATTHEW 16:18–19

The Petrine ministry is continued today in the Church by the bishop of Rome, the pope. The pope is the immediate and universal pastor, or shepherd, of the whole Church on earth. His ministry includes the responsibility to:

- keep the Church together as one,
- keep it faithful to the truth of Jesus, and
- strengthen and encourage his brothers and sisters.

All the members of the Church contribute, each in their own way, to the Church's one mission. All of them make up the Body of Christ, his holy people. In this way, *everyone is equal* in the eyes of God.

Everyone in the Church is reborn through the sacrament of Baptism. Everyone is joined to Christ in his Church. Everyone shares in Christ's new life. And everyone is guided by the Holy Spirit in this new life.

We each have a different part to play in the Church. But each part is important. Just as Paul says about the members of the human body, each member of the Church contributes to the good of the whole Body of Christ.

What Role Will You Take?

Describe three roles you can play in today's Church. Be imaginative.

1. _____
_____
_____

2. _____
_____
_____

3. _____
_____
_____

Faith Focus

Why is the kingdom of God so important to the teaching of Jesus?

Faith Vocabulary

kingdom of God. All people and creation living in communion with God. The kingdom will be fully realized when Christ comes again in glory at the end of time. Then all people will live justly, peacefully, and lovingly with God and each other.

All the people of the Church join together to continue the work of Christ in our world. This includes preparing for the coming of the **kingdom of God.** This is how the Gospel describes this work of Jesus:

> Jesus came to Galilee proclaiming the gospel of God: "This is the time of fulfillment. The kingdom of God is at hand. Repent, and believe in the gospel."
>
> MARK 1:14–15

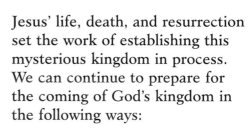

All throughout his work on earth Jesus described the kingdom, or reign, of God. At its core, it is:

- a kingdom of truth, mercy, and eternal life;
- a kingdom where holiness and grace will prevail;
- a kingdom where justice, love, and peace triumph over injustice, hatred, and war.

Jesus' life, death, and resurrection set the work of establishing this mysterious kingdom in process. We can continue to prepare for the coming of God's kingdom in the following ways:

1. *We pray for the coming of the kingdom of God.* Each time we pray the Lord's Prayer, we say, "Thy kingdom come." Every time we celebrate the Eucharist, we pray for the coming of the Lord Jesus to fulfill his work and to bring about the kingdom of God on earth.

2. *We prepare the way for the coming of the kingdom.* We do not make the kingdom of God happen. It is God's work. We, however, prepare a way for the coming of the kingdom by bringing the truth of God to those who have not heard it. We do this by being forgiving, just, and compassionate to all people. Whenever we do these things, God is creating the kingdom through our work.

3. *We live in a way that looks ahead to the kingdom of God. We live the Beatitudes.* We are to seek first the kingdom of God. We are to live lives of simplicity, sharing what we have, not letting anything get in the way of fully living our friendship with God. Living the Beatitudes guides us in our efforts of living for the kingdom. The Beatitudes are:

"Blessed are the poor in spirit,
for theirs is the kingdom of
heaven.
Blessed are they who mourn,
for they will be comforted.
Blessed are the meek,
for they will inherit the land.
Blessed are they who hunger
and thirst for
righteousness,
for they will be satisfied.
Blessed are the merciful,
for they will be shown mercy.
Blessed are the clean of heart,
for they will see God.
Blessed are the peacemakers,
for they will be called
children of God.
Blessed are they who are
persecuted for the sake
of righteousness,
for theirs is the kingdom of
heaven."

MATTHEW 5:3–10

The Beatitudes fulfill all God's promises to his people. They respond to our desire for happiness that God has placed in our hearts. Living them will help us reach our final goal, which is the kingdom, eternal life with God the Holy Trinity. When the kingdom of God is finally established, there will be great joy and peace. God's way will be the way of life for all people.

To Help You Remember

1. What is the kingdom of God announced by Jesus?

2. Describe ways we can prepare for the coming of the kingdom of God.

With My Family

Invite all of your family members to write a list of the top ten things they are doing in their lives to prepare for the coming of God's kingdom.

Preparing for the Kingdom

Work together in groups to plan a project that promotes the kingdom of God. Describe three things you will do to prepare for God's kingdom. Describe three things that might slow up or block our preparation for the kingdom.

_____
_____
_____
_____
_____
_____
_____

The Church is the community of the People of God. Joined to Christ in Baptism, we receive the gift of the Holy Spirit to continue Christ's work among us until he comes again in glory at the end of time.

Scholastica and Benedict

Christians have always looked to one another and needed one another to live the Gospel. While this is always true, it is especially true when we live in times and places where so many forces are trying to move us away from God. Scholastica (died in 543) and Benedict (480–546) lived in such a time. However, this did not deter Scholastica and Benedict from living their lives like lights that clearly guided others through dark times.

Scholastica and Benedict lived in Italy. There they dedicated their lives to helping others live the Gospel. Benedict wrote a rule of life that spelled out a clear way to live the Gospel. His rule of life was so helpful that people came from all over to live together to follow it.

Scholastica was the first woman to choose to follow Benedict's rule of life. Soon other women came to live together to follow the same rule.

Who helps you to live the Gospel? How do you help others?

ST. BENEDICT.

You are a member of the Body of Christ, the People of God, the Church. You have received the Spirit and work with the Spirit to continue the work Jesus began while he lived on earth.

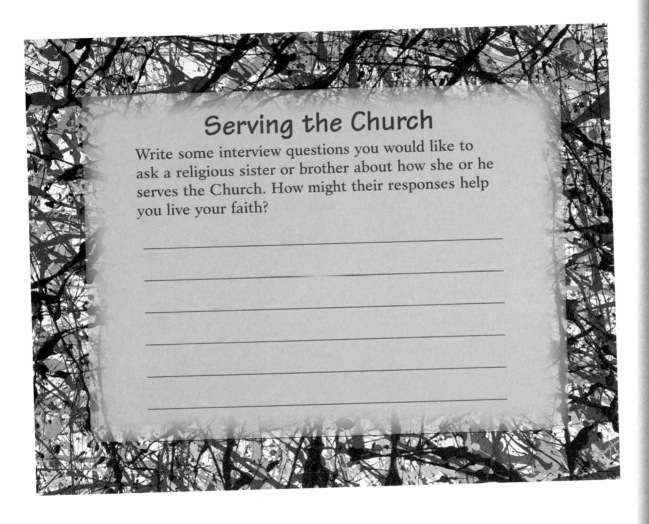

Serving the Church

Write some interview questions you would like to ask a religious sister or brother about how she or he serves the Church. How might their responses help you live your faith?

_____

_____

_____

_____

_____

_____

My Faith Decision

I am a member of the Body of Christ, the Church. I will use the gifts and talents with which God has blessed me. This week I will share my talents by

_____

_____ .

And now we pray.

Sing praise to the LORD, you faithful; give thanks to God's holy name.

PSALM 30:5

Complete each sentence. Use the words in the word box.

ordained ministers	lay faithful	kingdom of God
Petrine ministry	vow	

1. The _____ are the baptized members of the Church who carry on the mission of Jesus.

2. A _____ is a solemn promise which binds a person to a particular act, service, or condition.

3. The _____ is the special ministry of the pope, the bishop of Rome.

4. Bishops, priests, and deacons are _____ .

5. The _____ is all people and creation living in communion with God.

Explain these statements.

1. The Church is the People of God.

_____

_____

2. The Church is the Body of Christ.

_____

_____

3. All the baptized share in the work of preparing for the kingdom of God.

_____

_____

Discuss with your family.

What things are you doing as a family to prepare and promote the kingdom of God?

Visit our web site at www.FaithFirst.com

Mary, Mother of Christ, Mother of the Church

We Pray

Father,
may Mary's prayer,
the gift of
a mother's love,
be your people's joy
through all ages.
Grant this through Christ
our Lord. Amen.

PRAYER OVER THE GIFTS
SOLEMNITY OF MARY,
MOTHER OF GOD

Christians honor Mary
as the Mother of God.
In what other ways do we
show our honor and respect
for Mary?

"Behold, you will conceive in your
womb and bear a son, and you
shall name him Jesus."

Luke 1:31

Mary, Woman of Faith

Faith Focus

Why do Christians look to Mary as a model of faith?

Faith Vocabulary

Annunciation. The announcement made to the Virgin Mary by the archangel Gabriel that she was chosen by God to become the mother of Jesus by the power of the Holy Spirit.

We all know people of faith. Their faith in God seems so strong and unwavering that they hang in there when almost everyone else would throw in the towel. People of this kind of faith are at the center of the story of God's people. Their names fill the pages of the Bible. Many women stand out among these people of faith.

Old Testament Women of Faith

The Bible opens with the story of Eve. At first you might ask, How is Eve a woman of faith? Didn't she disobey God?

While that is true, Eve first heard God's promise of a Savior. She first heard and trusted in the promise that her descendants would eventually be victorious over the evil one. After Eve comes a long line of our ancestors in faith whose stories teach us about placing our trust in God.

Sarah, the wife of Abraham, shared in God's promise to him. She was promised that through her child God would establish a great nation. Other women such as Hannah, Deborah, Ruth, Judith, and Esther, also trusted in God's word and promises to them.

Looking back over the faith story of God's people, we have come to see that all of these women of faith in the Old Testament prepared the way for Mary. It is through Mary's great act of faith in God's word to her that God's promise of a savior would be fulfilled.

Mary's Faith

The Gospel according to Luke tells us that the archangel Gabriel spoke to Mary, a virgin who lived in the town of Nazareth in Galilee. The angel said to her:

"The holy Spirit will come upon you, and the power of the Most High will overshadow you. Therefore the child to be born will be called holy, the Son of God." Mary said, "Behold, I am the handmaid of the Lord. May it be done to me according to your word." LUKE 1:35, 38

We call this the story of the **Annunciation.** Now put yourself in Mary's place. You are engaged to an honest man, a carpenter in the village, who is respected by all. So, how do you answer the angel if you answer at all?

Mary says, "May it be done to me according to your word." Mary does not understand how this will happen. Yet she does not hesitate. Mary gives her trust to God completely. Wherever God leads her, she will go. Her yes changes the course of human history.

Mary is revered by the Church as our great model of faith. She listened, she freely believed, and she generously said, "So be it." There will come times in our lives when we too will be confronted with what seems to be impossible or unbelievable. If you want to know how to respond, look to Mary's example to guide you.

To Help You Remember

1. Who were some of the women of faith in the Old Testament who prepared the way for Mary's life of faith?

2. Explain the gospel story of the Annunciation.

3. How can Mary be a model of faith for you?

Walking with Mary

Take a moment. Be still and:

1. Think of some situations where we might require a faith as strong as Mary's.

2. Place yourself in the gospel story as you read Luke 1:31–38.

3. Have a conversation with Mary.

4. Write words or draw a picture to remind you of your conversation with Mary.

Faith Focus

Why do we honor Mary as the Mother of God and the mother of the Church?

With My Family

Ask some older members of your family how they honored Mary when they were young.

Mary, Mother of God

Jesus, the son of Mary, is true God and true man. When the angel Gabriel announces to the virgin Mary that she is to be the mother of Jesus, he says to her:

> "Behold, you will conceive in your womb and bear a son, and you shall name him Jesus. He will be great and will be called Son of the Most High."
>
> LUKE 1:31–32

Jesus, the child to whom the virgin Mary will give birth, is the Son of the Most High, the Son of God. He is the Son of God who took on flesh and became a human being. Jesus is one person who is both truly man and truly God. That is why we believe the virgin Mary is the Mother of God. God chose the virgin Mary to be the mother of his Son. She is the handmaid of the Lord, who was a virgin her whole life long.

So special was Mary's role in God's plan, she was free from original sin from the very first moment of her existence, or conception, and remained pure of all personal sin her whole life long. We call this the Immaculate Conception of Mary.

When her life on earth ended, the Most Blessed Virgin Mary was taken up, or assumed, body and soul, into the glory of heaven. There she already shares in the glory of her Son's Resurrection, to which all the members of the Body of Christ look forward. We call this the Assumption of Mary.

Mother of the Church

Mary, the mother of Jesus, is our mother too. She is the mother of all who believe and follow her son,

Jesus. In the Gospel according to John, we read:

> Standing by the cross of Jesus were his mother and his mother's sister, Mary the wife of Clopas, and Mary of Magdala. When Jesus saw his mother and the disciple there whom he loved, he said to his mother, "Woman, behold, your son." Then he said to the disciple, "Behold, your mother." And from that hour the disciple took her into his home.
>
> JOHN 19:25–27

The "beloved disciple" who is at the foot of the cross stands for all of us who are Jesus' disciples. From the cross, Jesus gives us his mother as our mother. She is forever the mother of all the followers of Jesus who are joined to him through faith and baptism. And just as the beloved disciple took her into his home, we too take Mary as our mother into our homes and lives.

When the disciples scattered in fear after the death of Jesus, Mary remained with them. We know that she was with them in the upper room on that first Pentecost.

> When they entered the city they went to the upper room where they were staying, Peter and John and James and Andrew, Philip and Thomas, Bartholomew and Matthew, James son of Alphaeus, Simon the Zealot, and Judas son of James. All these devoted themselves with one accord to prayer, together with some women, and Mary the mother of Jesus.
>
> ACTS OF THE APOSTLES 1:13–14

You can almost picture Mary, calm and prayerful, nurturing the apostles in those perilous early days.

Mary continues to be our mother today. She watches over us from her place of honor in heaven with her Son. We look to her, as she expects us to, for prayerful guidance.

Honoring Mary

Create a poster with words and pictures that tells others about your love and respect for Mary.

Devotion to Mary

Why does Mary play such an important role in our faith lives? To put it simply, she is the mother of Jesus, the Son of God, and the Mother of God. Jesus has asked her to be our mother and asked us to accept her as our mother too.

Mary was also Jesus' very first disciple, the one who heard his word and kept it. She is a path to him, who is our Savior and our Lord. Because of her close relationship with Jesus, Mary teaches us how to praise, thank, and petition God.

While we honor Mary as the greatest of saints and most revered member of the Church, we do not think that she is greater than her son. Jesus is the only one who can save and redeem us. But because Mary is Jesus' mother, God has given her a special honored role in his plan of salvation. We ask her to help us live as loyal and faithful followers of her son, Jesus.

Liturgical Year

Catholics honor Mary and express their devotion to her throughout the year. We do this in many ways. During Advent we remember her as the one who brings Jesus into the world. During Lent and Holy Week, we remember Mary, the mother of Sorrows, who shares in the suffering of her son and who understands our suffering as well. All throughout the year we celebrate special feasts of Mary. By celebrating these feasts we remember her great faith and trust in God and loving faithfulness to her son.

The Eucharist

At every Mass we bless and thank God for Mary. We pray:

> In union with the whole Church we honor Mary, the ever-virgin mother of Jesus Christ our Lord and God.
> EUCHARISTIC PRAYER I

The Eucharist is the Church's greatest prayer of thanksgiving and praise to God the Father. We believe that Mary joins with us and her Son in giving God our praise and thanksgiving. We recognize her presence with us and honor her.

During our celebration of the Eucharist, we also look forward to joining Mary and the saints in heaven. We pray:

> Father, in your mercy grant also to us, your children, to enter into our heavenly inheritance in the company of the Virgin Mary, the Mother of God.
> EUCHARISTIC PRAYER IV

The Liturgy of the Hours

As a Church we also honor Mary each and every day as we pray the Liturgy of the Hours. At Evening Prayer we join with Mary in singing her great song of praise, the Magnificat. We join with her to thank God for his many gifts and to look forward to the fulfillment of all his promises.

The Rosary

One of the most cherished ways Catholics express their devotion to Mary is by praying the rosary. The rosary is a prayer of meditation on the life of Jesus and Mary. While praying the rosary, we place ourselves with Mary and Jesus in the main mysteries of the story of our salvation. The rosary is a wonderful prayer that puts us in touch with the heart of our faith.

All these different ways of showing our devotion deepen our relationship with Mary and with her son, Jesus Christ.

To Help You Remember

1. Why has the Church, since its beginning, been so devoted to Mary?

2. Describe some of the ways the Church expresses its devotion to Mary.

3. How can you include Mary, your mother, into your life?

Learning More About Mary

In your own words write a short biography of Mary. Use the gospel stories or the mysteries of the rosary to develop your biography.

_____

_____

_____

_____

_____

_____

_____

_____

_____

We honor Mary as the Mother of God and as our mother too. We express our devotion to her throughout the year in many ways.

Feasts Honoring Mary

Mary, our mother, is remembered throughout the year by celebrating feast days in her honor.

January 1 brings us the Solemnity of Mary, the Mother of God.

On February 11 we celebrate the feast of Our Lady of Lourdes, a remembrance of Mary who, with her son, wants our healing of mind, body, and soul.

On March 25 we celebrate the feast of Annunciation, when Mary received God's invitation to be the mother of Jesus.

On May 31 we celebrate the feast of the Visitation, or visit of Mary to Elizabeth.

July 16 is the feast of Our Lady of Mount Carmel. We are reminded of our need to dedicate ourselves to prayer.

August 15 is the feast of Mary's Assumption, when Mary was taken body and soul to heaven.

October 7 is the feast of Our Lady of the Rosary.

December 8 is the feast of the Immaculate Conception, which celebrates that Mary was free from original and personal sin throughout her entire life.

On December 12 we celebrate the feast of Our Lady of Guadalupe, the patroness of the Americas.

In what ways does your parish honor Mary?

Mary is your mother too. Mary cares for you. Mary cares about you. She is and wants to be a very important person in your life.

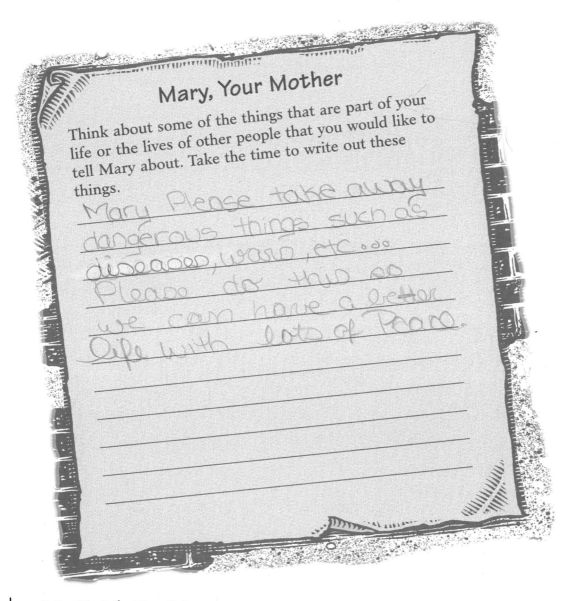

Mary, Your Mother

Think about some of the things that are part of your life or the lives of other people that you would like to tell Mary about. Take the time to write out these things.

Mary Please take awny dangerous things such as diseases, ware, etc... Please do this so we can have a better life with lots of Peace.

My Faith Decision

This week I will spend time with Mary, my mother, in prayer.
I will _____
_____
_____ .

And now we pray.
Hail Mary, full of grace,
the Lord is with you!

Circle the term in the parentheses that best completes each statement.

1. (Sarah, Clopas, Mary of Magdala) was the wife of Abraham and a woman of great faith in the Old Testament.

2. The (Creed, Magnificat, Hail Mary) is Mary's great prayer of praise and thanksgiving.

3. An important devotion to Mary is the (rosary, Mass, Stations of the Cross).

4. The angel (Michael, Gabriel, Raphael) announced to Mary that she would be the mother of Jesus.

5. The (Visitation, Nativity, Annunciation) is when the angel told Mary that she was to become the mother of Jesus.

Answer the following questions.

1. Why is Mary a model of faith for all believers?

   Mother of Christ, believed in
   Freely believed and said 'so be it'

2. What do we mean when we say that Mary is the mother of the Church?

   She is the mother
   Mary watches over us and cares for
   us

3. Why are Catholic Christians so devoted to Mary?

   she is the mother of Christ

Discuss with your family.

How can we include our devotion to Mary into our family life?

Visit our web site at www.FaithFirst.com

And the king will say to them in reply, 'Amen, I say to you, whatever you did for one of these least brothers of mine, you did for me.' Then he will say to those on his left, 'Depart from me, you accursed, into the eternal fire prepared for the devil and his angels. For I was hungry and you gave me no food, I was thirsty and you gave me no drink, a stranger and you gave me no welcome, naked and you gave me no clothing, ill and in prison, and you did not care for me.'

Then they will answer and say, 'Lord, when did we see you hungry or thirsty or a stranger or naked or ill or in prison, and not minister to your needs?'

He will answer them, 'Amen, I say to you, what you did not do for one of these least ones, you did not do for me.' And these will go off to eternal punishment, but the righteous to eternal life."

MATTHEW 25:31–46

Jesus clearly teaches us that we are to do the things that he did while he was on earth. We are to love one another as he did. We are to reach out and help people in need.

To Help You Remember

1. Who does Jesus say will be invited to live in the kingdom of God?

2. Describe the actions of those who will be invited into the kingdom.

Living the Gospel

What are some of the ways you can be like the people blessed by God in the story Jesus told?

_____

_____

_____

_____

_____

_____

_____

_____

Understanding the Word of God

Faith Focus

What does the Gospel tell us about how we are to live and what happens to us after death?

Faith Vocabulary

compassion. Sharing in the sufferings of others and often expressed by giving some form of aid or comfort.

The good news proclaimed in this gospel passage is that God invites all people to live with him forever. And while this is true, we believe that there is a clear warning in this passage too. It is this: much will depend on how we respond to God's invitation while we are alive on earth. How we live on earth will have a great impact on how we will live after we die.

Life After Death

We live in hope, trusting in Christ's promise of eternal life with God and with Mary and the saints. We profess our belief in eternal life in the Nicene Creed. We pray:

> We look for the resurrection of the dead, and the life of the world to come.

Death was not part of the original plan of God the Creator. Bodily death entered the world as a result of original sin. By death, our soul is separated from our body. Christ has conquered death and turned it into a doorway that gives us entrance into a more wonderful and blessed life than we can imagine.

As Jesus teaches in the parable of the sheep and goats, God will judge each of our lives when we die. We call this the particular judgment. On the last day, at the end of time, the lives of everyone will be judged. We call this the Last Judgment. On that day, God will give incorruptible life to the bodies of all God's faithful. Our bodies will be reunited with our immortal souls and we will rise from the dead just as Christ is risen and lives forever.

Heaven is our everlasting enjoyment of living a life in communion with God, the Holy Trinity. It is living forever with the virgin Mary, the angels, and all the holy men and women who have lived before us. It is the fulfillment of all our deepest longings and desires for happiness. It is to live with Christ, who will reign in glory.

Some people who die are not ready to receive the gift of eternal life. While they are living as children of God at the moment of their death, their choice to do so is a weak one. After death, they are purified of their weakness and given the opportunity to grow in their love for God. This opportunity is called purgatory.

Sadly, some people choose to turn themselves completely away from God's love. They do this by sinning seriously and not asking

God for forgiveness. When people do this and die, they choose to stay separated from God forever. We call this eternal separation from God hell.

Preparing for the Kingdom

The Holy Spirit guides us and helps us while we are on earth to prepare for the kingdom of heaven. Matthew gives us clear advice to help us do this. To put it simply, we are to act with **compassion** toward others.

- We are to give food to the hungry, drink to the thirsty, and clothing to the needy.
- We are to offer hospitality to those who are alienated and care for those who are sick or imprisoned.

When we do these things, especially for people most in need, we are doing it for Christ. We are, in a sense, doing our part in creating a bit of heaven on earth. We are preparing for the kingdom.

But Matthew also gives us a warning. It is the kind of advice we sometimes do not want to hear. He tells us that we can also choose to live separated from Christ forever. We can neglect the needy, turn our backs on society's outcasts, and simply look out for Number One—ourselves. By such neglect and selfishness, we effectively separate ourselves from Christ.

To Help You Remember

1. What is the connection between our life on earth and our life after we die?

2. Describe what we mean by heaven, or living in the kingdom of God.

With My Family

Jesus teaches us that we are to reach out and help others in need. Discuss the ways your family can follow this teaching of Jesus.

Those Blessed by God

Jesus talked about the hungry, thirsty, naked, ill, imprisoned, and the stranger. What other people could you add to that list? What is something that you can and will do to act with compassion toward these people?

The four accounts of the Gospel share with us the good news of Jesus Christ. In the Gospel Jesus promised that all who live by his teachings will be invited by his Father to live in the kingdom. The Gospel according to Matthew gives us very clear advice on what this promise means.

Caring for Others

Since the first days of the Church, Christian communities have treated others with hospitality and compassion. Called together by God in the name of Christ, we help one another as Jesus asked us to do. We reach out to one another, especially those in need.

The people of Saint Elizabeth parish take this work very seriously. Their ministry puts into practice exactly what Matthew wrote about. No one in need is left out.

You all know how important it is to be comfortable and nicely dressed for school. When the people of Saint Elizabeth's heard about the children in another parish who needed shoes for the start of school, they saw to it that every child who needed shoes received them. This is certainly the work of the "Blessed" that Matthew wrote about.

How can you help your parish follow the teaching of Jesus that Matthew shares with us?

Each day you have many opportunities to help others. Some of those choices are easy and some are difficult. Every time you reach out to help, you are among the "sheep," the people blessed by God. Every time you help someone, Jesus says that you are helping him.

Preparing for a Place in the Kingdom

Describe some of the ways you help others. Next time you help someone, remember that you are helping Jesus too.

_____
_____
_____
_____
_____
_____
_____
_____
_____
_____
_____
_____
_____

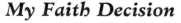 *My Faith Decision*

This week I will try to remember what I am doing when I help someone. I am not only helping a friend or neighbor. I am really treating Christ with kindness.

And now we pray.

One thing I ask of the LORD; this I seek: To dwell in the LORD's house all the days of my life.

PSALM 27:4

Write a sentence to explain the meaning of each term.

1. Gospel

_____

_____

2. kingdom of God

_____

_____

3. evangelist

_____

_____

4. heaven

_____

_____

5. compassion

_____

_____

Answer the following questions.

1. Name the three stages during which the writing of the Gospel took place.

_____

_____

2. Describe the people Jesus says will be invited to enter the kingdom of God.

_____

_____

3. How can we live with Christ now?

_____

_____

Discuss with your family.

What is something our family can and will do to show compassion for the needy?

Visit our web site at www.FaithFirst.com

Celebrations of the Whole Church

Every celebration of a sacrament is a celebration of the whole Body of Christ. We join with Christ and we share in his saving work. In the sacraments, it is Christ himself who presides over, or leads, the Church in its celebration.

- At Baptism, for example, when the priest says, "*I* baptize you," he speaks in the name of Jesus, who baptizes.
- In the Eucharist when the priest says, "This is *my* body," he speaks in the name of Jesus, who gives us his Body and Blood under the forms of bread and wine.

Because Jesus acts in the sacraments, we can say that the sacraments effect what they signify. In other words, the sacraments really do what they say they do. They unfailingly allow us to share in Christ's saving work and make us sharers in the life of God. The sacraments anticipate the coming of the kingdom of God and give us grace to get there.

Understanding Jesus Through the Liturgy

What are some of the things that you see and hear during the liturgy? How do these things help you better understand what is really happening?

_____

_____

_____

_____

_____

_____

_____

Faith Focus

What are some of the signs and symbolic actions used in the sacraments?

Faith Vocabulary

Paschal mystery. The "passing over" of Jesus from death into a new and glorified life through his death-resurrection-ascension.

Sacramental Signs

Sacramental celebrations combine words with signs and symbolic actions such as immersing in water, breaking bread, anointing with oil, and imposing of hands. It makes sense that the Church would use words, signs, and symbolic actions—things that we can see, touch, and hear—in the celebration of the sacraments. We live and grow in a world filled with physical signs of God's love for us. Through these signs, Jesus brings us into the mysteries of his life and into the very life of God, who is Father, Son, and Holy Spirit.

Jesus used a variety of different signs and symbolic actions during his life on earth. He anointed people and placed his hands on them. He talked about the basic signs of water, darkness, and light to point to the mystery of God and our life with God. He gave deeper meaning to such basic human activities as eating and drinking, washing and anointing.

What happens when we use these words and signs in the celebration of the sacraments? What is the work of Jesus when his Church, the Body of Christ, gathers with him for the celebration of the sacraments? He makes his **Paschal mystery**, his death and resurrection and ascension, present to us so that we can share in it and let it move us toward God's kingdom. The celebration of the sacraments helps us take part in Jesus' passing from life to death and reminds us that we also shall pass from death to eternal life.

Christ's Paschal Mystery

Christ died once and was raised once. So how do we share, here and now, in the Paschal mystery? How does Christ make his forgiveness and life-giving power present to us today?

Christ gave the Holy Spirit to his Church. Until the end of time when Christ will come again in glory,

the Spirit brings Christ's Paschal mystery to all people through the sacraments. When the Church celebrates the sacraments, we join Christ in his dying and rising to new life.

Promise of Eternal Life

The sacraments also give us a glimpse at the fullness of life that God has prepared for us. Throughout the Old Testament, God revealed himself as the God of life. He prepared the way for all to receive the great gift of new and resurrected life in Jesus, who said:

"I am the resurrection and the life; whoever believes in me, even if he dies, will live, and everyone who lives and believes in me will never die."

JOHN 11:25–26

At the end of time, there will be no need for sacraments. They will have led us to our celebration of fullness of life with God.

On the last day, just as Christ, we will rise bodily and see God face-to-face. We will see God as he is.

Beloved, we are God's children now; what we shall be has not yet been revealed. We do know that when it is revealed we shall be like him, for we shall see him as he is.

1 JOHN 3:2

Now, *that* is something to work for and look forward to.

Symbols of Life

Create a bookmark with symbols that point to our life with God.

To Help You Remember

1. Why do Christ and his Body, the Church, use signs and symbolic actions to celebrate the sacraments?

2. Describe some of the signs and symbolic actions used in the celebrations of the sacraments.

Faith Focus

How can we use the seasons of the liturgical year to celebrate Christ's life and grow closer to him?

Faith Vocabulary

liturgical year. The cycle of seasons and feasts that makes up the Church's year of worship.

Epiphany. An appearance or manifestation of God. The feast of the Epiphany commemorates the magi's visit to Jesus and the first manifestation of Jesus as Savior of all people.

With My Family

What season of the Church year are we now celebrating? Discuss the ways your family can celebrate that season in your home.

The Liturgical Year

For Christians, each year is not simply the passing of time. Each year is a time of grace. Each year is a celebration, a yearlong celebration of our life in Christ. The Church's year of celebration is called the **liturgical year**.

Advent-Christmas

The liturgical year begins with the season of Advent. Advent begins on the last Sunday in November or the first Sunday in December and lasts about four weeks. It culminates in the celebration of Christmas. Advent is a time of preparation for Christ's coming among us.

The Christmas season includes **Epiphany** and celebrates the birth of Jesus and his "epiphany," or manifestation as the Savior of the whole world. The Christmas season reminds us that the Son of God came among us for the whole human family.

Ordinary Time

After Epiphany, which is celebrated around January 6, there are several weeks of Ordinary Time. During the remaining weeks of January and up to the beginning of Lent, we focus on the events of Jesus' public ministry, or the work his Father gave him to do on earth.

Lent-Easter

The season of Lent begins on Ash Wednesday, which is about forty days before Easter, not counting Sundays. The season calls us to change our hearts, seek God's forgiveness, and renew our commitment to live our baptism.

The center of the whole liturgical year is the Easter Triduum, or "the three days" of celebration beginning on Holy Thursday evening, continuing on Good Friday, and ending with the celebrations of the Easter Vigil and Easter Sunday.

The fifty days of the Easter season are a time of appreciating the mystery of the new life that we have in Christ, who was raised from the dead. On the fortieth day after Easter, the Church celebrates the Ascension of the Lord. Ten days later we celebrate the great feast of Pentecost.

Ordinary Time

After Pentecost and until the beginning of Advent, from late spring and through the summer and fall, there is a longer period of Ordinary Time. During this time we hear the story of Jesus from one of the four accounts of the Gospel—Matthew, Mark, Luke, or John. We learn about and work at growing as disciples of Jesus.

Sundays and Weekdays

Every Sunday is really a celebration of Easter. It is the Lord's Day, the day of the Lord's resurrection.

Celebrating All Year Long

How is the liturgical year like a year in your family? In the circle write or draw the seasons and special days that have meaning in your family.

We gather around the Risen Lord, who is truly present with us, drawing us into new life with God.

During the liturgical year, the Church also honors the saints. These feast days of the saints provide us with models of trust and loving kindness.

Among the saints, Mary has a special place. She is the Mother of God and the mother of the Church. We remember the apostles, martyrs, and other holy men and women. Throughout the liturgical year, we praise God for what he has done for them and is doing for us.

Jesus lived and died and was raised from the dead over two thousand years ago. He gave us the sacraments to share in his life and work. From Advent to Christmas, from Lent to Easter, from Pentecost to Advent we celebrate and take part in God's loving plan of salvation.

One Faith, One Lord

No matter where you go throughout the world the Catholic Church celebrates the sacraments. The look of the churches may be different. Some churches are massive cathedrals filled with statues and stained-glass windows. Others are simple huts. Some are modern and some are not. But in each church, we gather to proclaim the same Gospel and share the same Eucharist.

The language may be different. The music may be different. The people may even dress differently, but what is essential to our liturgy is always the same: Christ is with us as we celebrate once again his death and resurrection.

We are all joined to Christ in Baptism. We are all members of the Body of Christ, the Church. We celebrate one Lord and one faith.

Have you ever attended Mass in a Catholic church in another state or country? How was the celebration the same as the way Mass is celebrated in your parish? How was it different?

You have taken part in the celebration of several sacraments. Which of the seven sacraments have you celebrated with your family and parish? Remember Jesus is always there. He is always leading you in the celebration.

Celebrating with Jesus

What are some of the things we do at the celebration of the Eucharist that are signs of our belief that we are celebrating with Jesus? How do these things help you and others take part in the celebration?

We receive the host which is the body of Jesus and blood of Jesus. Then go back to our seats and pray.

My Faith Decision

Before Mass this week I will try to spend a few moments to remember that we are joining with Jesus in our celebration. I will

_____

_____ .

And now we pray.
Through him,
with him,
in him,
in the unity of the
Holy Spirit,
all glory and honor
is yours,
almighty Father,
for ever and ever.
FROM EUCHARISTIC PRAYER

Match the terms in column A with their meanings in column B.

Column A

_E_ 1. liturgy

_B_ 2. Paschal mystery

_D_ 3. sacraments

_A_ 4. liturgical year

_C_ 5. Epiphany

Column B

a. The Church's yearly cycle of seasons and feasts that make up the Church's year of worship

b. Christ's passing over from death to new and glorified life

c. The celebration of the manifestation of Jesus as Savior of the world

d. The seven main celebrations of the Church's liturgy

e. The Church's work of worshiping God

Explain these statements.

1. The sacraments are celebrations of the whole Church.

   We all the church. We are the Church.
   We join with Christ to share the saving
   work of the sacraments.

2. We use words and symbolic actions to celebrate the sacraments.

   We live and grow in a world filled with signs
   and of Gods lover for us, we use these signs in
   the celebration of the

3. The Church remembers and takes part in God's saving plan of love for us throughout the whole year.

   We celebrate the liturgical year, which we celebrate
   with different feasts and cycle of season.

Discuss with your family.

What can we do as a family to make every Sunday a celebration of Easter?

Visit our
web site at
www.FaithFirst.com

Passover and the Sabbath

A Scripture Story

We Pray

One thing I ask of the
    LORD;
   this I seek:
To dwell in the LORD's
    house
   all the days of my life,
To gaze on the LORD's
    beauty,
   to visit his temple.

PSALM 27:4

The Old Testament shares
many stories about what it
means to worship God.
What Old Testament stories
help you to worship God?

*"You shall make an ark of acacia
wood. . . . In the ark you shall put
the commandments which I will give
you. Make two angels from gold
with their wings spread for each end
of the ark. There I will meet you."*
Exodus 25:10, 16–22

121

Bible Background

Faith Focus

Why is the Book of Leviticus important?

Faith Vocabulary

Leviticus. The third book of the Pentateuch. It centers on the call to holiness and the laws and rituals of worship used by the Israelites.

Ancient Hebrew Scripture scroll.

Limestone tablet, found in Gezer in Palestine, that dates from time of Solomon (961–922 B.C.). It contains a simple song to teach children the seasons of the year.

What would you think of celebrating Christmas in August? Having a birthday pizza with candles? Easter eggs for Thanksgiving? Getting all dressed up and going someplace where everyone else will be dressed in play clothes? At first you might think it would be fun. If you really did do one or two of those things, it would probably feel very strange to you.

Why? Because special days and celebrations are kept special by observing certain rules and customs. Usually these rules and customs have been set up for years and years before you were born, and people have practiced them for generations.

Rituals

The same is true with our religious feasts and celebrations. Over the years, people develop rituals. A ritual is made up of the words and actions we use to celebrate our faith in God. These words and actions sometimes come out of the practice of men and women who lived long before us.

Some of the things Christians use to worship God and celebrate our faith have come out of the traditions and laws of people who lived in Old Testament times. That is why reading the Old Testament can help us learn a great deal about the liturgy of our Church.

Leviticus

The preparation and celebration of the religious rituals in Jesus' time, as well as our own religious rituals, have their roots in the stories in the books of the Old Testament. One of those books is **Leviticus**, which is the third book of the Pentateuch.

The Book of Leviticus served as a liturgical handbook for the priests of the Israelites. In it are gathered many of the rituals and laws of worship of the Israelites. By reading Leviticus we can discover the law of sacrifice and the ceremony of ordination of the Israelite priests. We can read about the Israelite year of worship, including the feasts of Passover and Unleavened Bread, Pentecost, New Year's Day, Day of Atonement, and Feast of Booths. Following rituals in the celebration of their feasts taught the Israelites the necessity of holiness in every aspect of their lives. It made them aware that observing the laws of the Lord provided a way of life that leads to holiness.

> The LORD said to Moses, "Speak to the whole Israelite community and tell them: Be holy, for I, the LORD, your God, am holy." LEVITICUS 19:1–2

To Help You Remember

1. What is a ritual?

2. What information does the Book of Leviticus contain?

3. Why is it important to obey the laws of the Lord?

Special Celebration

Name your favorite celebrations of the Church. Circle one and describe how you and your family celebrate it. What things do you do over and over again each year?

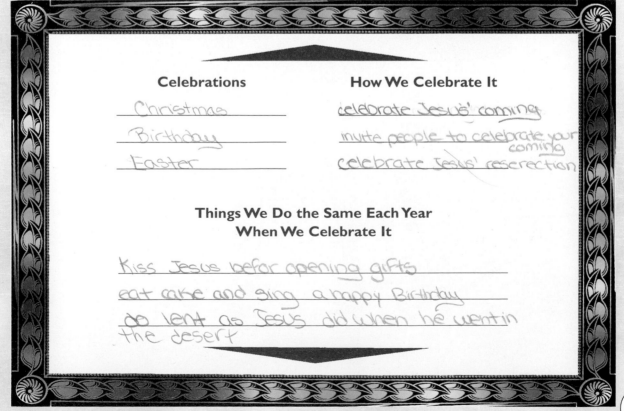

Celebrations	How We Celebrate It
Christmas	celebrate Jesus' coming
Birthday	invite people to celebrate your coming
Easter	celebrate Jesus' reserection

Things We Do the Same Each Year When We Celebrate It

Kiss Jesus befor opening gifts
eat cake and sing a happy Birthday
do lent as Jesus did when he went in the desert

Reading the Word of God

Faith Focus

What does the Book of Leviticus tell us about celebrating the Sabbath and Passover?

Faith Vocabulary

Sabbath. In Hebrew the word means "to cease or desist from labor, to rest." For the Israelites the day of rest was a day dedicated to God.

Passover. The feast of the Israelites that celebrated their passage from slavery in Egypt to freedom.

Holiness Code

The Book of Leviticus contains a section called the Holiness Code. This section of Leviticus contains the rituals and rules for celebrating the liturgical year of the Israelites. The celebration of the **Sabbath** and **Passover** are included in this code.

Sabbath

The Holiness Code begins with the Sabbath. We read:

The LORD said to Moses, . . . "For six days work may be done; but the seventh day is the sabbath rest, a day for sacred assembly, on which you shall do no work. The sabbath shall belong to the LORD wherever you dwell." LEVITICUS 23:1, 3

Passover

We next read about the feasts of Passover and Unleavened Bread, which are joined together in Leviticus. We read:

"The Passover of the LORD falls on the fourteenth day of the first month, at the evening twilight. The fifteenth day of this month is the LORD's feast of Unleavened Bread. For seven days you shall eat unleavened bread. On the first of these days you shall hold a sacred assembly and do no sort of work. On each of the seven days you shall offer an oblation to the LORD. Then on the seventh day you shall again hold a sacred assembly and do no sort of work." LEVITICUS 23:5–8

The writer of Leviticus then describes the celebration in more detail. We read:

The LORD said to Moses, "Speak to the Israelites and tell them: When you come into the land which I am giving you, and reap your harvest, you shall bring a sheaf of the first fruits of your harvest to the priest, who shall wave the sheaf before the LORD that it may be acceptable for you. On the day after the sabbath the priest shall do this. On this day, when your sheaf is waved, you shall offer to the LORD for a holocaust an unblemished yearling lamb. Its cereal offering shall be two tenths of an ephah of fine flour mixed with oil, as a sweet-smelling oblation to the LORD; and its libation shall be a fourth of a hin of wine. Until this day, when you bring your God this offering, you shall not eat any bread or roasted grain or fresh kernels. This shall be a perpetual statute for you and your descendants wherever you dwell."

LEVITICUS 23:9–14

Knowing and keeping these celebrations and their rituals was important to the Israelites. It helped them remember and celebrate their faith in God. It helped them remember God's great love for them and that they were God's people.

To Help You Remember

1. What is the Holiness Code in the Book of Leviticus?

2. Describe how the Israelites were to celebrate the Sabbath and Passover.

3. How do Catholics celebrate Sunday, the Christian Sabbath?

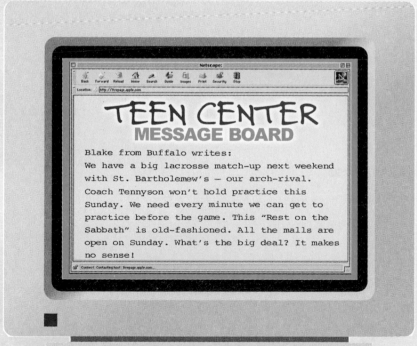

TEEN CENTER
MESSAGE BOARD

Blake from Buffalo writes:
We have a big lacrosse match-up next weekend with St. Bartholemew's — our arch-rival. Coach Tennyson won't hold practice this Sunday. We need every minute we can get to practice before the game. This "Rest on the Sabbath" is old-fashioned. All the malls are open on Sunday. What's the big deal? It makes no sense!

Observing Our Laws of Worship

Read this E-mail. How would you respond to it? Share your response with someone in your class.

Understanding the Word of God

Faith Focus

How does observing special feasts help us live holy lives?

Faith Vocabulary

unleavened bread. Bread made without yeast.

With My Family

Discuss your favorite family foods and holiday customs. Find out how they started. Does your family have any "laws" about special celebrations?

Holiness Is . . .

Okay, so what's the big deal? Why did the Jewish people need to have a particular kind of bread, an exact counting of days, a yearling, their first fruits? How would this make them holy? Put simply, it helped them focus on three things:

- faith in God,
- gratitude to God, and
- remembrance of God.

The painstaking time devoted to observing these feasts was time devoted to God and to God's covenant with them.

Faith. The Passover feast celebrated the Israelites' faith in God who delivered them from slavery. The sabbath expressed their belief in God who gave them all things.

Gratitude. By fasting and prayer during the time of Passover, the people showed their gratitude to God, who was their true source of freedom. By preparing meals in a special way and by sacrificing their best livestock, they gave thanks to God, who provided for them.

Remembrance. The use of **unleavened bread** at Passover reminded the Israelites that their ancestors had to flee Egypt so quickly that they were not able to bake bread made with yeast. By sacrificing lambs, rams, goats, and the fruit of the earth, the people paused to remember not only what God had done to care for them but also what he was doing now. God was still beside them, present with them, helping them journey through life's hardships.

Christian Liturgy

Christians worship God by celebrating the sacraments. We remember all that God has done for us in Jesus. We remember in faith that Jesus died and was raised for us. Out of gratitude, we lift up our hearts and voices and sing out God's praise. We recognize how much we owe God for the wonders of his grace. Jesus has truly redeemed us from sin and death and given us new life.

Like the Israelite people in the Old Testament, we worship God and celebrate the mysteries of our faith. Like the Israelite people, we believe that our journey toward God and the promised kingdom continues. We need to keep remembering the Paschal mystery of Jesus and his victory over sin and death. We need to keep the sabbath holy.

We need to celebrate and acknowledge that God—Father, Son, and Holy Spirit—is the center of our lives. God is both the source of our life and the end of our life.

To Help You Remember

1. How did celebrating rituals and feasts help the Israelites attain holiness?

2. Describe the importance of faith, gratitude, and remembrance in our life of worship.

3. Why do we, as a community of faith, worship God today?

My Prayer of Gratitude

Look at this outline of a young person. Make it into your self-portrait. But instead of drawing eyes, a nose, and a mouth, draw those things that you are most grateful to God for. Then take a moment and thank God for all his gifts to you.

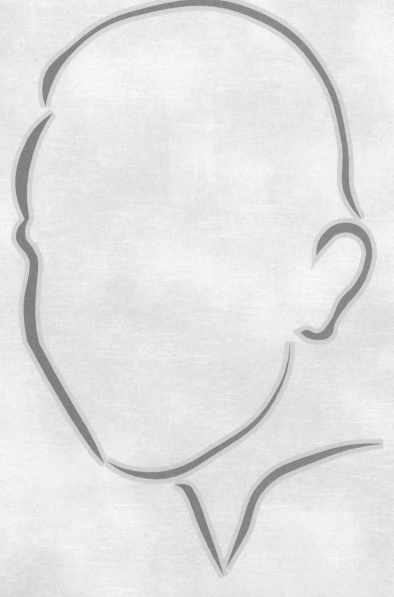

127

The Old Testament Book of Leviticus describes for us the laws and rituals the Israelites used to celebrate their liturgy and liturgical year.

Rites of the Church

The Church also has developed rituals and rites for the celebration of our liturgy. We use many books to help us celebrate the liturgy.

The *Sacramentary* (or *Roman Missal*) contains the prayers and rites we use for the celebration of Mass. The *Rite of Marriage*, the *Rite of Penance, Rite of Christian Initiation of Adults,* and other similar books contain the prayers and rites for other liturgical celebrations. The *Lectionary* and *Book of the Gospels* contain the Scripture readings we use in the celebration of the liturgy.

Deacon proclaiming the Gospel from the *Book of the Gospels*.

Priest presiding at Mass, using the *Sacramentary*.

Name the rites of the Mass. What are some of the things we do every time we celebrate Mass? What are some of the things that change?

Priest witnessing the exchange of marriage promises, using *Rite of Marriage*.

Each week you take part in the celebration of Mass. You celebrate your faith. You give thanks, or show your gratitude, to God. You remember how much God is part of your life.

Telling the World

It is one of those sunny warm days at the beach—one of those days when the whole wide world seems to be in one place at one time. And right overhead comes a plane trailing one of those advertisement slogans. Everyone looks up. Write the slogan that best expresses how we all need to thank and celebrate God.

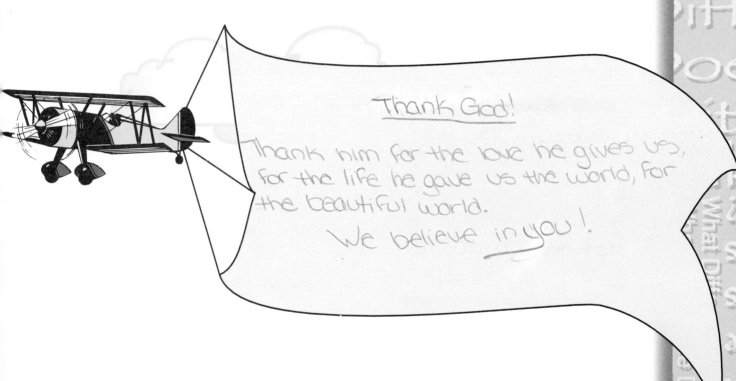

Thank God!
Thank him for the love he gives us, for the life he gave us the world, for the beautiful world.
We believe in you!

My Faith Decision

I will try to celebrate Sunday as a holy day—all day long! I will do this by

_____

_____ .

And now we pray.
It is good to give thanks to the LORD.
PSALM 92:2

Complete each statement with a word found in this chapter.

1. ___Rituals___ helped the Jewish people celebrate their faith in God.

2. ___Passover___ is the Jewish feast of thanksgiving for God's delivering them from slavery in Egypt.

3. ___Unleavened bread___ is the name for bread made without yeast.

4. ___Sunday___ is the Christian sabbath.

Answer the following questions.

1. What is one important message contained in the Book of Leviticus?

   Moses thaught the Israelites how to do their prayers

2. Describe why we celebrate the sabbath.

   The time contains

3. Use the words *faith*, *gratitude*, and *remembrance* to describe how we worship God.

   We remember god by his gratitude which gives us faith.

Discuss with your family.

In what ways do we as a family work together to become holy?

Visit our web site at www.FaithFirst.com

Baptism and Confirmation

We Pray

Lord,
fulfill your promise.
Send your Holy Spirit
to make us witness
to the world
to the good news
proclaimed by
Jesus Christ.

*OPENING PRAYER
MASS FOR CELEBRATION
OF CONFIRMATION*

Baptism and Confirmation
initiate us into Christ's life.
What do you know about
Baptism and Confirmation?

*I will sprinkle clean water
upon you to cleanse you. . . .
I will give you a new heart
and place a new spirit within you.*
Ezekiel 36:25, 26

131

Baptism

Faith Focus

What do we celebrate at Baptism?

Faith Vocabulary

Baptism.
The sacrament in which we are joined to Jesus Christ, become members of the Church, and are reborn as God's children. In Baptism we receive the gift of the Holy Spirit, and original and personal sins are forgiven.

With My Family

Water can symbolize many things. Talk about what water symbolizes to you. How can water help you understand what is really happening in Baptism?

What was it like the first time you joined a new group? What were the steps you followed to become a member of that group? What did you have to learn? What did you have to do? When a person wants to join the Church, there are steps to follow, and things to learn and to do.

Initiation into the Church

Baptism, Confirmation, and Eucharist are called the Sacraments of Initiation. Baptism is the beginning of our new life in Christ. Confirmation is its strengthening. Eucharist nourishes us with the Body and Blood of Christ.

Baptism, Our New Life Begins

Since the earliest days of the Church, both adults and children have been baptized. Baptism is a grace, or gift, of God. It is the gateway, or doorway, to life in the Spirit and to salvation in Christ.

Jesus commanded that his disciples go forth and baptize all people and make them his disciples. (Read Matthew 28:19–20.) It is

through Baptism and becoming a follower of Christ, a member of the Church, that we come to salvation. That is why the Church teaches that Baptism is necessary for salvation for all to whom the Gospel is proclaimed and who have had the opportunity to ask for this sacrament.

What about infants who die without being baptized? The Church trusts in God's great love. We believe that God will welcome unbaptized children to share in the eternal life of happiness won for all people by Christ.

What happens to us when we are baptized?

1. Baptism is our new birth in Christ. We are joined to Christ in his dying and rising.
2. Through Baptism we become members of the Church, the Body of Christ, and the People of God, and are made sharers in the priesthood of Christ.
3. Baptism frees us from sin—original sin and any personal sins that we may have committed.
4. Through Baptism, we become God's adopted daughters and

6. We will be witnesses for Christ by our words and actions.

7. We are given the strength to remain witnesses, even in the face of ridicule, suffering, and misunderstanding.

Witnesses for Christ

Confirmation confers on its recipients some extremely important powers and responsibilities. But those who are confirmed are not left alone to meet those responsibilities. The Spirit is always at their side. At the sacrament of Confirmation the candidates receive the **Gifts of the Holy Spirit:** wisdom, understanding, right judgment, courage, knowledge, reverence, and wonder and awe. You will find confirmed Catholics living these gifts by teaching the poor, nurturing their children and grandchildren, and leading lives of heroic integrity. They prophesy and witness to Christ by their loving kindness. Their goodness may even cause them to be ridiculed.

By the world's standards, they may not be considered rich, famous, or successful. But by God's standards, they are rich in the grace of the Holy Spirit.

To Help You Remember

1. What does the Church celebrate at Confirmation?

2. Describe how Confirmation strengthens us to live our faith.

Living Confirmation

Think of someone you know who is truly living the gifts of Confirmation. Write a description of that person and how she or he is living as a "confirmed" Christian.

Who can be confirmed? The Church in its wisdom asks that a person meet certain requirements before being confirmed.

Faith

First of all, the person who is to be confirmed must be baptized. Baptism is the doorway to the other sacraments. During the rite of Confirmation the bishop asks the candidates:

> Now, before you receive the Spirit, I ask you to renew the profession of faith you made in baptism or your parents and godparents made in union with the whole Church.
>
> RITE OF CONFIRMATION

Candidates must profess their faith with the Church. Those who are confirmed take on the special responsibility of witnessing to their faith and even defending it when necessary. They must be willing to share what they believe.

Age

Throughout the history of our Church, infants, school-age children, and high school students, as well as adults, have received the sacrament of Confirmation. Today, in some

WHAT DIFFERENCE DOES IT MAKE IN MY LIFE?

Through Baptism you were joined to Christ and became a member of the Church. Each day you join with Christ and other members of the Church to continue the work of Christ in the world today.

My Mission

Look at your life right now. Write a mission statement explaining what you want to do today to make the world a better place.

I would want to help the make peace in the world.

My Faith Decision

This week I will reread my mission statement and put it into action. I will especially try to

_____

_____.

And now we pray.

God, our Father, keep the Gifts of the Holy Spirit alive in our hearts to help us live the Gospel.

BASED ON
RITE OF CONFIRMATION

Write a sentence explaining each of these terms.

1. Baptism

a sacrament.

Baptism is when we become part of the church, join Jesus Christ and when our original sins are forgiven.

2. Confirmation

the celebrate the gifts of the Holy Spirit.

Confirmation is the sacrement that completes the Baptism. Where the bishop prays that those who are confirmed receive many gifts. such as wisdom, right, courage, knowledge and more.

3. sacramental character

It is a character that Jesus Christ gives us, that allows us to share a life with God. A spiritual mark, that cannot be repeated which marks us forever

Answer the following questions.

1. What are some things that happen through, or are the effects of, Baptism?

Is our new birth in Christ, we join to Jesus in his dying an rising, we become members of the church, frees us from various sins. we are reborn as God children and are spiritually marked as belonging to Christ.

2. What are some of the effects of Confirmation?

We commit to join Christ in his mission to announce and help prepare for the comming of god's kingdom. etc...We receive the Holy Spirit,

3. How might you prepare yourself for Confirmation?

We can read the bible, go and listen is cathecisme, go to church.

Discuss with your family.

How can we show others that we are committed to sharing our faith with others?

Visit our web site at www.FaithFirst.com

David, King of Israel

A Scripture Story

We Pray

Father,
may the ministers
of our Church
perform their ministry
with gentleness
and concern for others.

*From Opening Prayer
Mass for Ministers of the
Church*

The Bible tells us the
stories of the many men
and women who became
the leaders of God's people.
Who are the leaders of
God's people whose stories
you know about?

*Stained-glass window of David,
who was the king of the Israelites
from about 1000 B.C. to 962 B.C.*

Bible Background

Faith Focus

What do the historical books of the Old Testament tell about God and his covenant with the Israelites?

Alexander the Great was king of Macedonia from 336–323 B.C. He became the ruler of the largest empire ever led by one ruler. Alexander's army entered Jerusalem in 332 B.C.

You know that the Old Testament contains many different types of writing which can be divided into four groups. As we have seen, the first five books of the Old Testament are called the *Pentateuch*. The next group is called the *wisdom books*. These gather sayings, stories, and the psalm prayers that show a wise way of living and praying according to what God wants. The third group, the *prophetic books,* collects the writings of the prophets who called the people back to living their covenant with God faithfully. In this chapter we will study the *historical books*, the fourth group of writings in the Old Testament.

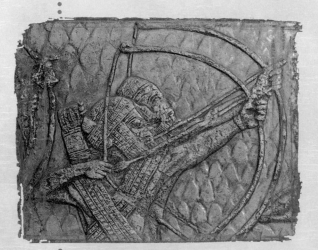

Mural of Assyrian archers found in the 209-room palace of Sargon II, emperor of Assyria from 722–705 B.C. Sargon II sent 30,000 Israelites to live in exile.

Victory and Defeat

The historical books of the Old Testament tell the story of the People of God from the time of Samuel to a time not long before the birth of Jesus. All together, the historical books cover about a thousand years of history.

The historical books include 1 and 2 Samuel, 1 and 2 Kings, 1 and 2 Chronicles, Ezra, Nehemiah, and 1 and 2 Maccabees. Shorter books that tell the stories of individuals are also added to the longer historical books. These are Tobit, Judith, and Esther.

The historical books begin with the time of the judges of Israel (ca. 1200–1050 B.C.). Then the spotlight of history shines on the monarchy, or office of the king, in Israel.

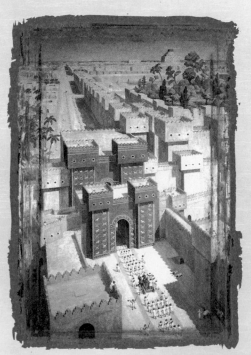

German archaeologists discovered and excavated ancient Babylon in the early 1900s. This painting shows the grandeur Babylon once had.

This part of the story begins with Saul (ca.1020 B.C.), David (1000–962 B.C.), and Solomon (961–922 B.C.). It continues with the stories of other kings until the destruction of Jerusalem and the exile of God's people in Babylon in the year 587 B.C.

Eventually God's people returned to their homeland, as the prophets promised, and they rebuilt their broken lives. The last historical books, 1 and 2 Maccabees, tell of the persecution of the Jewish people and their struggle to keep the faith.

Our Human History

The historical books are very important for Catholic Christian believers. They help us understand how God is active and involved in our history. Sharing this story of God's people, the Israelites, the historical books show us that God is able to draw good things out of difficult and even sinful situations. When we read the historical books today, we can begin to understand more clearly how God continues to be with us, guiding us and calling us to live lives of faith, hope, and love.

To Help You Remember

1. Name the four groups of books in the Old Testament.

2. Explain what the historical books tell us.

Some Important Events in the History of God's People

ca. 2000–1700 B.C.
Covenant with Abraham

ca. 1300–1050 B.C.
Exodus and Covenant with Moses

ca. 1200–1050 B.C.
The Period of the Judges

ca. 1020–539 B.C.
The Period of the Kings and the Exile

333–323 B.C.
Alexander the Great defeats Persians and rules Israel and other countries in Asia Minor

175–135 B.C.
The Revolt of the Maccabees

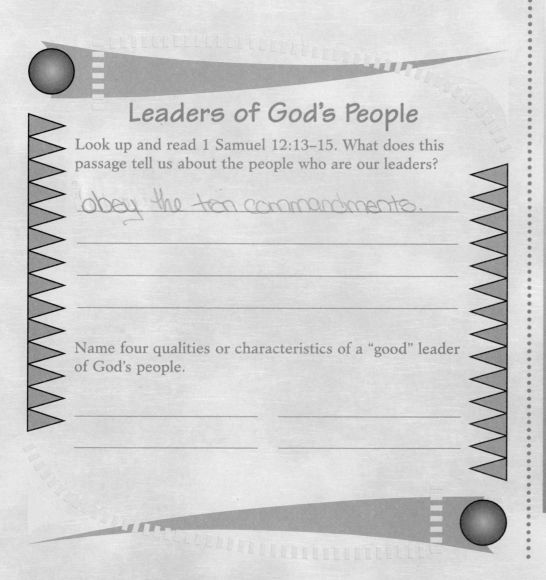

Leaders of God's People

Look up and read 1 Samuel 12:13–15. What does this passage tell us about the people who are our leaders?

obey the ten commandments.

Name four qualities or characteristics of a "good" leader of God's people.

Faith Focus

Who was David and how did he come to be anointed king?

In the books of Samuel we find the stories of prophets and kings. In the first book of Samuel we read the stories of Samuel the prophet and David the king.

David

The name *David* means "beloved." Born in Bethlehem, the son of Jesse, David was a man beloved of God. When he was a shepherd, he was chosen by God to be king of God's people. He ruled as king of God's people for nearly forty years. He is a model of one who tried to follow God's will. He wrote many of the Old Testament psalms. David was an ancestor of Jesus, who would be proclaimed Son of David, the Messiah-King (Matthew 21:9–11).

In Baptism the priest or deacon anointed the crown of your head with chrism. He said that God was now anointing you "with the chrism of salvation so that, united with his people, you may remain forever a member of Christ who is Priest, Prophet, and King" *(Rite of Baptism).*

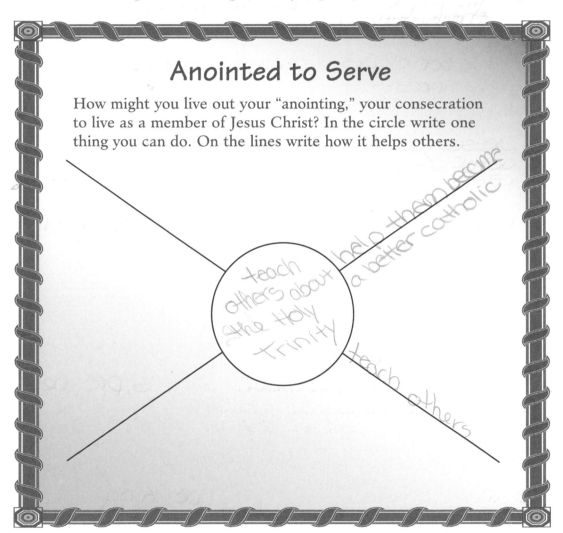

Anointed to Serve

How might you live out your "anointing," your consecration to live as a member of Jesus Christ? In the circle write one thing you can do. On the lines write how it helps others.

teach others about the Holy Trinity

help them become a better catholic

teach others

My Faith Decision

This week I will remember that I have been anointed and have received the Spirit of God to serve others. I will try to live out that anointing by

_____

_____ .

And now we pray.
You anoint my head with oil;
my cup overflows.
PSALM 23:5

Explain the following faith terms.

1. historical books of the Old Testament

   one of the books of the old testament, tells the story of the people of God from the time of Samuel to the birth of christ

2. David

   He is son of Jesse, King of Isreal and of god people Jesus ancestor

3. anointing with oil

   blesses you, brings the spirit of God upon them. act of concecration. used for healing and for celebrating sacrements.

4. chrism

   used at confirmation and is a sacred oil

Answer the following questions.

1. Into what four categories of writings can we group the books of the Old Testament?

   the pentateach, wisdom books, prophetic books and historical books.

2. What is the meaning of Samuel's anointing of David?

   he was chosen by god to be king

3. How does the Church use the ritual of anointing with oil?

   used for sacrements, used for healing, used to concecrate god's special services.

Discuss with your family.

In what ways can we as a family serve others?

Visit our
web site at
www.FaithFirst.com

The Eucharist

We Pray

Lord Jesus Christ,
we worship you among us
in the sacrament of your
body and blood.
May we offer to our
brothers and sisters a life
poured out in loving
service of that kingdom
where you live with the
Father and the
Holy Spirit
one God, forever
and ever.

*FROM ALTERNATIVE
OPENING PRAYER FEAST OF THE
BODY AND BLOOD OF CHRIST*

Holy Communion and Breaking of Bread are some of the many names we use to help us understand the Eucharist. In your own words tell what you know about the Eucharist.

Jesus said, "I am the bread of life; whoever comes to me will never hunger."

John 6:35

The Bread of Life

Faith Focus

How does the Old Testament help us understand the meaning of the Eucharist?

Faith Vocabulary

manna. A breadlike substance from a shrub.

prefigure. To suggest, indicate, or point to.

Passover table, set with unleavened bread, lamb, wine, and bitter herbs.

We use many words as symbols. When we do, they have a deeper meaning than we might at first suspect. For example, people sometimes use the expression "breaking bread together." This expression is a symbol. It can mean more than simply eating food. It also has the deeper meaning of enjoying the friendship of another person.

Manna

Many Old Testament stories point to and help us understand the meaning of the Eucharist. During the Exodus while the Israelites were in the desert, God promised and gave them **manna** to eat. This manna was more than food. It reminded the Israelites that they live by the bread of the word of God. We say that manna **prefigured** the Eucharist. It points the way to the Eucharist, the Bread of Life God gives us.

Melchizedek

The story of Melchizedek, king of Salem, also has a deeper meaning for Christians. The three elements in the story prefigure Christ's giving of himself to us in the Eucharist. The elements are (1) bread and wine, (2) the offering of bread and wine as gifts to God, and (3) grateful remembrance of what God has done for his people.

Passover

As you well remember, the Israelites did not have time to put yeast into their bread dough when they fled Egypt. They made *unleavened* bread and then ran for their lives. God commanded his people

Each time you
it strengthens y
members of the

Re
the
jou

greet and honor the Lord, w
present with us in the Script

The proclamation of the *Gos*
the last of the three readings
is the center of the Liturgy o
the Word.

The gospel readings, as well a
other Sunday readings, are or
three-year cycle—A, B, and C
year A, the Gospel according
Saint Matthew is read. On ea
Sunday in year A we move a l
more through the Gospel. Yea
is the year of Saint Mark. Sin
is the shortest Gospel, year B
includes parts of Saint John's
Gospel. Year C, finally, is the y
of Saint Luke. What year are y
in now?

to celebrate Passover each year
with unleavened bread, the
Passover lamb, bitter herbs, and
wine. When Jesus gave us the
Eucharist, he gave new meaning
to the blessing of the bread and
wine at Passover.

The Last Supper

Jesus gave us a new Passover
meal, the Eucharist, at the Last
Supper. Our celebration of the
Eucharist is both a perpetual
memorial of and a way of our
sharing in Christ's Paschal
mystery, in his passing over from
death to new life.

The Eucharist

The Eucharist, prefigured by
the manna, the offering of
Melchizedek, and the
Passover meal, is the great
sacrament of God's love for
us. Celebrating the Eucharist
recalls and makes present the
sacrifice, the complete love
that Jesus has for us—a love
so great that Jesus gave his
life for us. It is the same
kind of love the Eucharist
strengthens us to have for
one another.

"This is my commandment:
love one another as I love
you. No one has greater
love than this, to lay down
one's life for one's friends."
JOHN 15:12–13

At the celebration of the
Eucharist, the Church not
only remembers the sacrifice
of Jesus but joins with Christ
in offering ourselves to the

Father. In this way the one
sacrifice of Jesus will continue to
be offered until the end of time
when Christ comes again in glory.

At the Eucharist we join with
Jesus to remember how much we
are loved. We join with Jesus so
that we are more able to love God
and one another. We share more
fully in the Paschal mystery of
Jesus Christ, who is our true hope
in this world.

To Help You Remember

1. What stories in the Old Testament help us understand the Eucharist?

2. Describe what Jesus did at the Last Supper.

3. Why is it important for you to receive the Eucharist regularly?

Spea

Read Acts 1
20:1–9. Thes
with a partne
Then write a

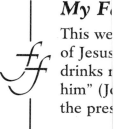

My F

This we
of Jesus
drinks r
him" (J
the pres

Breaking Bread

Name some of the ways we use the word *bread*.

_____

_____

Describe the things we do with bread.

_____

_____

_____

Write a prayer thanking God for the gift of bread!

_____

_____

_____

_____

Faith Focus

Why is the Liturgy of the Word celebrated at Mass?

With My Family

Talk about the readings that were proclaimed at Mass last Sunday. How can you apply their message to your family?

Use the following faith terms in a sentence.

1. prefigure

   Prefigure is to suggest, indicate, or point to.

2. Liturgy of the Word

   Liturgy of the word ~~one of the~~ first main parts of mass ~~where we is~~ the introductory rites of mass. follows

3. Eucharist

   Eucharist is when we recieve the body and blood of christ. what we share it with everyone

4. Liturgy of the Eucharist

   Liturgy of the Eucharist ~~of the~~ second main part of mass and is the prayer...

Answer the following questions.

1. How does the Passover help us understand our celebration of the Eucharist?

   When the Isrealites were freed from slavery

2. Describe the parts of the Liturgy of the Word.

   Responsorial psalm helps refect message of the first reading gospel acclamation, Homily, Creed and intercession

3. Describe what takes place during the Liturgy of the Eucharist.

   The bread and wine were changed to Jesus' body and blood.

Discuss with your family.

Take part in the celebration of Mass as a family. Talk about how this strengthens your family.

Visit our web site at www.FaithFirst.com

The Parable of the Great Feast

A Scripture Story

16

✠ THE FEAST IS READY ✠

We Pray

In this great sacrament
you feed your people
and strengthen them
in holiness,
so that the family
of mankind
may come to walk in the
light of one faith,
in one communion
of love.

PREFACE, HOLY EUCHARIST II

The word of God not only looks back but also looks forward. It points to the coming of the kingdom of God. What stories have you read in Sacred Scripture that tell us about what God has prepared for those who have been faithful to his covenant with them?

"Go out quickly into the streets and alleys of the town and bring in here the poor and the crippled, the blind and the lame."

Luke 14:21

161

Bible Background

Faith Focus

Why did Jesus use parables?

Faith Vocabulary

parables. Stories Jesus used to teach us. A parable compares one thing to another to help listeners or readers understand the main point of the story.

Feast at the House of Levi by Italian painter Paolo Veronese (1528–1588).

Have you ever been to a banquet? Banquets such as weddings or scouting and sports banquets are meals that celebrate a special event or an achievement of a person or a group of people. Usually only invited guests attend. People dress up and there is special seating at the tables.

Banquets and Meals

The people of Bible times celebrated banquets just as we do today. The most famous and important meal in the Gospel is the Last Supper. It is so important that all four evangelists—Matthew, Mark, Luke, and John—wrote about it.

The Gospel according to Luke includes many stories that center around meals. There are ten in all, beginning with a banquet at the house of Levi (5:27–39) and ending with a meal in Jerusalem just before Jesus' ascension.

Matthew and Luke both tell the story of another meal. It is called the **parable** of the Great Feast. Jesus used his listeners' experiences of meals and banquets in this parable to help them understand his message about the kingdom of God.

Parables

What are parables? In parables storytellers compare two things.

They use the words *like* and *as* to make their point. For example, Jesus said:

"What is the kingdom of God like? To what can I compare it? It is like a mustard seed that a person took and planted in the garden." LUKE 13:18–19

In the parable of the Mustard Seed, Jesus compared something his listeners knew about, the planting of the mustard seed, to help them understand something he was trying to teach them about, the kingdom of God.

In the parable of the Great Feast, as recorded in Luke's account of the Gospel, Jesus used his listeners' experiences of meals and banquets to help teach a lesson. Little by little, he helped them understand the meaning of the mystery of the kingdom of God, which he so often preached.

Fish and bread were widely used as food in New Testament times.

Pottery used at meals in New Testament times.

To Help You Remember

1. What is a parable?

2. Explain why Jesus used parables when he taught about the kingdom of God.

3. How can you help someone know more about our Catholic faith?

Listening to Jesus

Much of Jesus' teaching was done when he was at a meal. Choose and read one of these stories in Luke's account of the Gospel. Tell who was invited and what Jesus was teaching.

(Luke 5:27–35)   Luke 7:36–50   Luke 10:38–42   Luke 14:7–14

Who was invited?

Levi, tax collectors, prophets, sinners, disciples

What was Jesus' message?

they should all eat together and be nice even if they are not friends

Faith Focus

What does Jesus say about those people who were first invited to the feast?

The Parable of the Great Feast

In Luke's account of the Gospel, we often read about Jesus teaching at a meal. The Pharisees were sometimes present. They criticized Jesus about his sitting down at the same table "with certain people" whose behavior they did not approve. Jesus responded by telling parables and other stories. These forced his listeners to think about their own behavior.

Once Jesus was invited to the home of a leading Pharisee. The people were watching Jesus very carefully. Jesus also watched them as they tried to sit in places of honor at the table. Read this parable to discover what Jesus taught them.

One of his fellow guests on hearing this said to him, "Blessed is the one who will dine in the kingdom of God." He replied to him, "A man gave a great dinner to which he invited many. When the time for the dinner came, he dispatched his servant to say to those invited, 'Come, everything is now ready.' But one by one, they all began to excuse themselves. The first said to him, 'I have purchased a field and must go to examine it; I ask you, consider me excused.' And another said, 'I have purchased five yoke of oxen and am on my way to evaluate them; I ask you, consider me excused.' And another said, 'I have just married a woman, and therefore I cannot come.'

The servant went and reported this to his master. Then the master of the house in a rage commanded his servant, 'Go out quickly into the streets and alleys of the town and bring in here the poor and the crippled, the blind and the lame.' The servant reported, 'Sir, your orders have been carried out and still there is room.' The master then ordered the servant, 'Go out to the highways and hedgerows and make people come in that my home may be filled. For, I tell you, none of those men who were invited will taste my dinner.'" LUKE 14:15–24

While Jesus was one of the invited guests at the meal, soon the attention of all the other guests turned to him. He used that opportunity at the dinner to teach them about what it means to be invited to the "great feast," the kingdom of God.

To Help You Remember

1. Where does Jesus tell the parable?

2. Why do the people who were first invited not come to the dinner?

Banquet of Life

As a follower of Jesus how would you respond to this invitation? Fill in your RSVP.

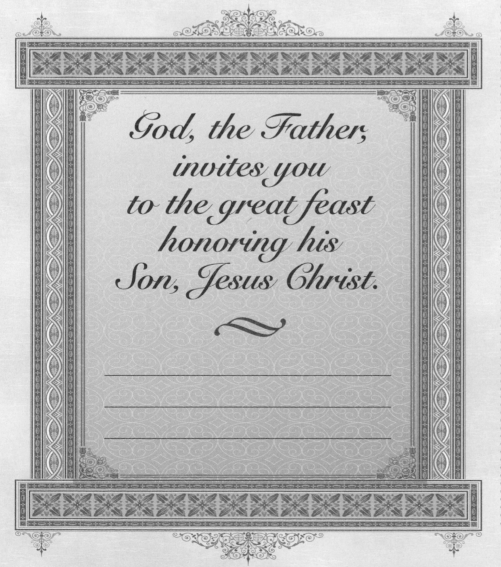

God, the Father, invites you to the great feast honoring his Son, Jesus Christ.

_____

_____

_____

Faith Focus

What does the parable of the Great Feast tell us?

The Meal in the Pharisee's Home

It is important to look at how and when Jesus told the parable of the Great Feast. Jesus was invited to a meal on the sabbath in the home of a leading Pharisee. It seems that people wanted to be with Jesus, and he used these times to make people think about God's love for them and all people.

Jesus noticed how the guests were trying to sit in the places of honor at the table. This clearly showed how important they thought they were. Jesus, seeing this, asked them to think about what they were doing. Jesus went on to talk about inviting the poor, the crippled, the lame, and the blind. These were people the Pharisees and their guests would have not usually invited—or even thought about inviting—into their homes. What might all this mean?

The Feast of the Kingdom

One of the guests seemed to understand that Jesus was talking about a meal in the kingdom of God. Unlike the guests who were invited to the meal in the Pharisee's home, everyone is invited by God to the great feast in the kingdom of God. In fact, Jesus goes on in the parable to say that many of those who are invited will refuse to come. And those who others believe should not be invited will take their place at the table.

How do we respond to God's invitation? When we share in the Eucharist with the church community, we are responding to God's invitation to come to the banquet. When we show God we are not "busy" about things we think are more important, like the guests in the parable who chose not to come, we are responding to God's invitation.

When we treat all others—without exception—with respect and compassion, we are accepting God's invitation. When we act in such a way that others can see that we believe God invites everyone to share in his life and love—the banquet in the kingdom of God—we are accepting God's invitation.

To Help You Remember

1. In this parable to what was Jesus comparing the "great dinner" the man was giving?

2. Describe some of the ways you can show that you have accepted God's invitation to come to the banquet.

A Promise of Future Glory

We believe that the Eucharist is a sign of God's invitation to the great feast in the kingdom of God. Use some of the imagery you have learned in this chapter to write a poem about the Eucharist.

The Eucharist

We receive the Eucharist because we want to join with Christ
We receive the Eucharist because we love Christ
We receive the Eucharist because we want to share in the goodness of Christ.

We receive the Eucharist with all our hearts when invited to the great feast in the kingdom of God.

God invites everyone to take their place in the kingdom of God. He asks us to go out and make sure everyone knows they are invited.

Catholic Campaign for Human Development

From the beginnings of our Church, Christians have brought that message to all. The Catholic Campaign for Human Development brings that message to people living in poverty. Established in 1969 the Catholic Campaign for Human Development has two purposes. The first is to raise funds to support "organized groups of white and minority poor to develop economic strength and political power." The second is to "educate the People of God to a new knowledge of today's problems . . . that can lead to some new approaches that promote a greater sense of solidarity."

Throughout its history, the Campaign has assisted more than three thousand self-help projects. The projects' successes have significantly changed the lives of the poor in our country.

Every parish in the United States is invited to take part in this work of the Church. One way Catholics do this is by contributing to a special collection at Mass on the Sunday before Thanksgiving.

How can you and your friends support the Campaign for Human Development?

You have received your invitation from God to share in the great feast in the kingdom of God. When you share in the Eucharist, you are showing God you have accepted his invitation.

All Are Invited

Describe how you and your friends might show others that God has invited them to share in the great feast in the kingdom of God.

What We Can Do	What Our Actions Tell Others
forgive	
go to church	
pray	
give donations	spend them
visit old people	they don't feel forgotten

My Faith Decision

This week I will remember the message of Jesus' parable of the Great Feast: God invites everyone and not just some people to the great feast in the kingdom. I will show that I believe this by

_____

_____ .

And now we pray.
Father,
in your kingdom
we shall sing
your glory with
every creature
through Christ our Lord.
FROM EUCHARISTIC PRAYER IV

Use these words and other words from this chapter to write your own parable about the kingdom of God.

parable **table**
banquet **Eucharist** **invitation**

While sitting around a table eating a banquet I noticed many people
a very misunderstand. He would
d.   No good

Answer the following questions.

1. What is a parable?

   It's a story that compairs one thing^something
   from another. That teaches people.

2. What lesson did Jesus try to teach his listeners by telling the parable of the Great Feast?

   He said it was like the the Kingdom of God
   and that the rich didn't care to come and the
   poor where there

3. How do we respond to God's invitation to come to the great feast in the kingdom of God?

   By helping, sharing, forgiving, etc...
   respond by showing

Discuss with your family.

What things do we do that show that we believe we have been invited by God to the great feast in the kingdom of God?

Visit our
web site at
www.FaithFirst.com

Sacraments of Healing

We Pray

Jesus,
come to me.
Jesus,
put your hand on me.
Jesus,
bless me.

FROM VISITS TO A SICK CHILD
PASTORAL CARE OF THE SICK

God promises us healing
and forgiveness. How does
God keep this promise
in Jesus Christ and the
sacraments of his Church?

*"Grace and peace be with you
from God the Father
and from Jesus Christ.*
From Rite of Penance

Receiving God's Forgiveness

Faith Vocabulary

sin. Freely choosing to say or do what we know is against God's law. Sin sets itself against God's love for us and turns our hearts away from it.

Making up is sometimes easy, sometimes difficult. Making up is sometimes embarrassing. It is not always easy to say, "I'm sorry." It is not always easy to say, "I forgive you." How long could a friendship last if we wouldn't or just couldn't make up?

Forgiveness of Sins

When we **sin**, God does not move away from us. We move away from God. Only God can forgive sin and bring us back to our senses. When we read the Scriptures, the message of God's faithfulness to us is very clear: God wants to give us every possible chance to renew our friendship with him. And note well, God will forgive any and all sins.

God gives the power to forgive sin to his Church. Baptism is the first and chief sacrament for the forgiveness of sin. Through Baptism original sin and all personal sins are forgiven. We are united to Christ, who died and was raised from the dead, and gave us the gift of the Holy Spirit.

Jesus also gave the Church the power to forgive the sins baptized people commit. This is normally done through bishops and priests in the sacrament of Reconciliation. In Reconciliation we celebrate God's love and forgiveness and our friendship with him.

Preparing for Reconciliation

The Church encourages us to prepare for the celebration of Reconciliation by making an *examination of conscience*. We do this by listening to God's word, praying over the commandments, and asking ourselves:

- How am I showing or not showing my love and respect for God?
- How am I showing or not showing my love for other people?
- How am I showing or not showing my love and respect for myself?
- How am I caring for or abusing the gift of God's creation?

Celebrating Reconciliation

The celebration of the sacrament of Reconciliation always includes five essential actions.

1. We must be *truly sorry,* or contrite, for what we have done. We express this through an *act of contrition.* Your own words will do just fine.
2. We must ask for forgiveness by *confessing* our sins to a priest, who stands in the place of Christ.
3. We *offer satisfaction* for our sins. We accept and agree to do a *penance.* This is usually a

prayer or a good deed that helps heal the wound caused by our sin.

4. We *make a firm purpose of amendment*. This means we decide not to sin again in the future. It means deciding, with God's grace, to live in a new way.

5. The priest prays the prayer of *absolution*, or forgiveness.

Celebrating the sacrament of Reconciliation regularly helps us deepen our friendship with God and with others. The word *reconcile* means "to make friends again." When we celebrate Reconciliation, we believe God forgives us and welcomes us as friends—with open arms.

What to Confess

The confession of our sins to a priest is an essential part of the sacrament of Reconciliation. In fact, many people often refer to this sacrament as "confession." But what exactly needs to be confessed?

The Church teaches that we must confess *all serious*, or *mortal, sins* that we have not already confessed. The priest who hears our confession will never tell anyone else what we have confessed to him. This absolute and sacred duty to keep what is confessed completely confidential is called *the seal of confession*.

The Church also encourages us to confess *venial sins*. This helps us strengthen our friendship with God and others. Even doing "little things" better is an important way for friends to show that their friendship counts. Confessing venial sins helps us do that.

To Help You Remember

1. Define sin in your own words.

2. What can you do to identify how you are living as a follower of Christ?

3. How can you prepare to celebrate the sacrament of Reconciliation?

Parable

Read Luke 18:9–14. Compare the Pharisee and the tax collector. What do we know about these two people? What insight about ourselves does Jesus give us in this parable?

Pharisee _He prayed to god to thank him that he was not like the others._

Tax Collector _He prayed to god for forgiveness._

My Insight _____

Faith Focus

What are the words of absolution?

Faith Vocabulary

absolution. The formal forgiveness of sin given by the priest during the sacrament of Reconciliation.

Absolution

Do you ever wonder what the words of **absolution** the priest says actually are? The priest says:

God, the Father of mercies,
through the death and
resurrection of his Son
has reconciled the world to
himself
and sent the Holy Spirit
among us
for the forgiveness of sins;
through the ministry of the
Church
may God give you pardon and
peace,
and I absolve you from your sins
in the name of the Father, and
of the Son, and of the
Holy Spirit.

What does that tell you? The priest in the name of God the Father, and God the Son, and God the Holy Spirit absolves, or frees, us from sin. The forgiveness of our sins is a work of the Holy Trinity. Through the words and actions of the priest we receive God's forgiveness. We are reminded once again of how much God loves us. We receive the gift of God's peace, God's love for us.

The Spiritual Effects of Reconciliation

Celebrating Reconciliation has some very important effects on our lives. Some of the more important effects are:

1. If we have turned our backs on God by sinning seriously, Reconciliation restores our friendship with him. We regain the life of grace, which sin caused us to lose.

2. Our sin not only affects our relationship with God but also hurts our relationship with the Church, the Body of Christ. Our sins, even the most personal ones, affect others. When we receive forgiveness in Reconciliation, our relationship with the Church is also healed. We become renewed members of the Body of Christ.

3. When we sin seriously, we turn our backs on God's love. Should we die with our hearts turned away from God, we would find ourselves separated from God forever. We call that separation from God hell. When we receive forgiveness for serious sin, we are once again reconciled with God. We are freed from the eternal separation from God.

4. When we sin, we cause damage to ourselves, to our relationship with God, and to others. Reconciliation helps us repair the damage and takes away the punishment that is rightfully ours.

5. After we have celebrated Reconciliation, we can expect to feel the gifts of peace and forgiveness. We have a renewed sense that God is with us.

6. Reconciliation also gives us the strength to do the right thing—even in the face of

difficulties. This sacrament gives us the grace to faithfully follow Jesus Christ.

Before the Risen Jesus returned to his Father, he appeared to his disciples and said:

> "Peace be with you. As the Father has sent me, so I send you." And when he had said this, he breathed on them and said to them, "Receive the holy Spirit. Whose sins you forgive are forgiven them, and whose sins you retain are retained."
>
> JOHN 20:21–23

What a wonderful gift! What a wonderful sacrament!

Freedom from the Punishment of Sin

When we sin, we turn our hearts away from God and toward something that, at the moment, we decide is more important than God. If we allow it, this attachment to sin might further move us to turn further away from God's love. We must free ourselves from this weakness either here on earth or after we die.

In Matthew 25, Jesus teaches that there is "punishment" connected with sin. That punishment may be eternal, or last forever. It may also be temporal, or temporary, which we are able to be released from through prayers and good works. Through indulgences the faithful can obtain remission, or the release from, the temporal punishment resulting from sin. They can do this for themselves and for the souls in purgatory.

To Help You Remember

1. What do the words of absolution tell us?

2. Describe the spiritual effects of the sacrament of Reconciliation.

Words of Reconciliation

Write a prayer expressing gratitude to God, who always is willing to forgive us.

God, Jesus I am truly sorry for what I have done. I am sorry and am asking for forgiver for what I have done is incorrect and I'm understand it's wrong. Thank you for forgiving me!

Faith Focus

Why does the Church celebrate the sacrament of Anointing of the Sick?

With My Family

Talk about the ways the members of your family care for someone in your family who is sick.

In the Old Testament Book of Numbers (21:4–9), we read the story of how the people of Israel became ill in the desert. At God's direction, Moses lifted up a bronze serpent, and all who looked on it were healed. The Church has understood that lifting up the bronze serpent prefigured the lifting up of Jesus on the cross. Jesus would be the source of healing for the whole human family.

The Healing Ministry of Jesus

Throughout his life on earth, Jesus often healed the sick. Matthew tells us:

Jesus went around to all the towns and villages, teaching in their synagogues, proclaiming the gospel of the kingdom, and curing every disease and illness.

MATTHEW 9:35

This work of Jesus invited people both to see how much God loves them and to place their trust and faith in God.

Anointing of the Sick

The Church continues Jesus' ministry of healing through the sacrament of Anointing of the Sick. Anointing of the Sick is the Church's second Sacrament of Healing.

From its very beginning the Church has ministered with the sick in this special way. In the New Testament, we read:

Is anyone among you sick? He should summon the presbyters of the church, and they should pray over him and anoint [him] with oil in the name of the Lord, and the prayer of faith will save the sick person, and the Lord will raise him up. If he has committed any sins, he will be forgiven.

JAMES 5:14–15

We celebrate Anointing of the Sick with those who are seriously ill, who are weakened by old age, or who are, in any way, in danger of death. Celebrating Anointing of the Sick strengthens their faith and trust that God is with them in their illness or weakness. God is with them to give them strength and hope. We believe that those who are anointed may also be healed of their illness.

Like the sacrament of Reconciliation, Anointing of the Sick may be received many times. Each time we become ill, we may receive this sacrament. We also may receive Anointing of the Sick more than once during the same illness if our sickness becomes worse. Some of the important effects of this sacrament are:

1. When we are suffering from illness, this sacrament unites us to the sufferings of Jesus. In this union we find strength and consolation because we believe and trust that the Lord is with us.

2. We receive peace and courage to face our sufferings.

3. If we are not able to celebrate the sacrament of Reconciliation, we can receive the forgiveness of our sins through Anointing of the Sick.

4. We may find that our health is restored.

5. When we are very ill and even dying, celebrating this sacrament helps us prepare for our final journey to God and to eternal life.

Celebrating Anointing of the Sick

Only the priest is the minister of the sacrament of Anointing of the Sick. Oil of the sick blessed by the bishop, or, if necessary, blessed by the priest himself, is used in this sacrament.

First the priest anoints the sick person's forehead, saying:
Through this holy anointing may the Lord in his love and mercy help you with the grace of the Holy Spirit.

Then he anoints the person's hands, saying:
May the Lord who frees you from sin save you and raise you up.

Through the celebration of Anointing of the Sick, Christ's work of healing continues in the world today. His healing presence helps the sick and dying find courage and strength and hope.

To Help You Remember

1. Why does the Church celebrate the sacrament of Anointing of the Sick?

2. Describe some of the effects of Anointing of the Sick.

Prayer of Faith

Saint James says that you should pray over those who are sick. Think of someone you know who is sick and in need of the prayers of the Christian community. Write a prayer of faith for that person.

God, Jesus, The Holy Spirit and all the others I'm asking all of you to help my Grandfather Lib Masala for he has many back paines and we don't know why or what it is. So I'm asking you to help him and look over him Please! Thank You!

We celebrate the forgiveness of our sins in the sacrament of Reconciliation. We turn our hearts back to God and God forgives us our sins. Reconciliation is an important part of our lifelong friendships, especially in our friendship with God.

Renewing a Friendship

When I was a child, I had a friend whose name was Keith. We did everything together. We ate at each other's house. Our families celebrated holidays together. We went on vacations together. We were good friends.

But as I grew older, Keith and I lost touch with each other. I went away to school and found new friends. He made new friends too. We sent cards to each other at Christmas, but that's about all. Our lives had changed.

One day I was thinking about Keith. I thought about all the times we had spent together and decided to call him. When I heard Keith's voice it felt as if we had just talked yesterday. Our friendship was renewed and better than ever.

The sacrament of Reconciliation is like that. It renews our friendship with God. God is always waiting to hear from us. Our friendship with God will be better than ever.

Why is celebrating the sacrament of Reconciliation an important part of being a member of the Church?

At times you need to step back from your life and simply look at it. You put your anger and irritations and failures on the table and you simply look at them. There is no need to be hard on yourself. Remember, Jesus is standing next to you and he is not wagging a finger to scold you. He is with you as a friend who supports you.

Examination of Conscience

Take a few minutes to put some of your actions, words, and feelings on the table. Use symbols that only you will understand so that no one else will know what you have written. This table and the symbols you put on it are good reminders of what things affect your life—and the lives of others.

My Faith Decision

What can I do this week to strengthen my friendship with God? I will

_____

_____ .

And now we pray.
Trust in the LORD and do good that you may dwell in the land and live secure.

PSALM 37:3

Fill in each blank with the term that correctly completes each sentence.

1. _The seal of confession_ is the sacred duty that the priest has to keep what is confessed to him completely confidential.

2. _Mortal sin_ is a serious violation of God's law.

3. _Venial sins_ are those sins that are not serious sins.

4. _Absolution_ is the forgiveness of sin given through the words and actions of the priest during the sacrament of Reconciliation.

5. _Confession_ is the term many people use to refer to the sacrament of Reconciliation.

Answer the following questions.

1. What are the five actions required by the sacrament of Reconciliation?

_p172-173_ We must be truly sorry, ask for forgiveness _ack of contrition_ by confessing, we offer satisfactions for our sins accept and agree to do a penance, we make a firm purpose of amendment, the priest prays the prayer of absolution

2. What are the effects of our celebrating the sacrament of Reconciliation?

_p174-175_ We regain the life of grace, we become renewed members of the Body of Christ, we are freed from eternal separation from God, helps us repare damages and takes away from punishment we can expect the gifts of peace and forgiveness gives us the grace to faithfully follow Jesus Christ

3. What are the effects of our celebrating the sacrament of Anointing of the Sick?

_p177_ We find strength and consolation because we believe and trust that the lord is with us, We receive peace and courage to face our sufferings, we can receive receive the sacrement of reconciliation if not able, we may find our health restored and helps us prepare for our final journey to God and to eternal life.

Discuss with your family.

How can we continue Jesus' work of forgiveness in our family?

Visit our web site at www.FaithFirst.com

Called to Serve the Church

We Pray

God our Father,
may your Church
be for all the world
a sign of your unity
and holiness
as it grows to perfection
in your love.

*OPENING PRAYER
FROM MASS FOR THE CHURCH*

In the Church there are
two Sacraments at the
Service of Communion—
Holy Orders and
Matrimony. How do
you think these sacraments
help the community of
believers?

*There are different kinds of spiritual
gifts but the same Spirit;
there are different forms of service
but the same Lord;
there are different workings
but the same God who produces
all of them in everyone.*

1 Corinthians 12:4–6

Sacraments at the Service of Communion

Faith Focus

What do we mean by service and communion?

Faith Vocabulary

communion. From two Latin words meaning "sharing with." The sharing of Christians in the life of Christ.

consecrate. To set apart someone or something as sacred, often dedicated for some specific holy purpose.

People very often measure success by accomplishments, power, wealth, titles, and social position. A person is considered successful if he or she has buckets of money, appears on the cover of *Rolling Stone*, drives an expensive car, or wields immense power. What would you say are the marks of a successful person? Would Jesus be considered successful if his life were evaluated by the qualities named on your list?

Service

Jesus does not seem to be too terribly impressed with many of the standards for success that we use. Sure, we can have great ambitions and strive to be first. But we must realize that being successful in Jesus' eyes means being a servant just as he was.

To serve as Jesus served means that we do not seek to be waited upon but that we strive to serve others. Furthermore, to be servants like Jesus means that we must be ready to give up our lives, just as he did. To serve in the Church implies giving the gift of ourselves to others.

To understand the meaning of service in the Christian community, read Mark 10:35–45. Christ sets a different standard for success for his disciples.

Communion

We are joined to Christ through Baptism and become members of the one Body of Christ, the Church. We belong to the Lord, and we belong to each other in the Lord. We live our life in **communion** with Christ and one another. Paul writes:

As a body is one though it has many parts, and all the parts of the body, though many, are one body, so also Christ. For in one Spirit we were all baptized into one body, whether Jews or Greeks, slaves or free persons,

his own body. He acts in the person of Christ, who is saying through the priest, "This is my body." Through their unique sharing in the priesthood of Christ, bishops and priests serve the Body of Christ, the Church.

When a bishop is ordained, he receives the fullness of the sacrament of Holy Orders. He serves the people of a diocese. The bishop is the visible head of the diocese and is a sign of its unity. Helped by the priests, their co-workers, and by the deacons, bishops have the duty of authentically teaching the faith, celebrating divine worship, above all the Eucharist, and guiding their Churches as true pastors.

At his ordination, a bishop becomes a member of the episcopal college, or the communion of bishops throughout the world. He shares in the responsibility for Christ's Church throughout the world. This responsibility includes concern for all the Churches, with and under the pope. He is united and is one with the holy father, the pope, and the other bishops.

The ministry or service of bishops is very important in the Church because the bishops continue the ministry of the apostles. Remember that the Church is built on the faith and witness of the apostles. The bishops, who are successors of the apostles, work in communion with the pope, the successor of Peter. They make certain that the Church remains faithful to the teachings of the apostles.

Sharing in the Priesthood of Christ

Describe some of the ways you might live out your baptismal call to share in the priesthood of Christ. Choose one of the ways and plan how you will do it.

_____

_____

_____

_____

_____

_____

A few of you reading this chapter may be feeling the first, quiet impulse of the Holy Spirit nudging you to consider Holy Orders. Nurture these impulses by talking with parents, teachers, priests, and whoever can give you guidance.

baptized woman join themselves to each other in a lifelong bond.

What does the sacrament of Matrimony have to do with a life of service and communion? Everything! If we marry to satisfy our own selfish needs, our marriage is liable to be either unsuccessful or unhappy—or both. If we celebrate the sacrament to serve God, our spouse, our family, and the Church, our marriage will become a true sign of Christ's life-giving love for his Body, the Church.

The Letter to the Ephesians (5:25–33) encourages husbands to love their wives, and wives to respect their husbands. This mirrors the love and respect that exists between Christ and his Church.

Faith Vocabulary

Matrimony. *The sacrament of the Church that unites a baptized man and a baptized woman in a lifelong bond of faithful love as a sign of Christ's love for the Church.*

Most of you will serve the community of the Church as husband and wife. You will be consecrated for that ministry in the sacrament of **Matrimony.**

Matrimony

While it is a bit too early to be making marriage plans, it is not too early to think about this sacrament. Matrimony takes place when a baptized man and a

Domestic Church

When husbands and wives nurture and cherish each other, they become a living sacrament. They are a living sign through which Christ works in the world.

Christian families form a domestic church, which is the "church of the home." They listen to God's word, pray together, and serve one another with generosity and compassion. These domestic churches are not isolated little islands. Joined one to another, they form a communion of generosity and compassion.

When selfishness and striving for riches or success replace service and communion, marriages and families are not successful. Sometimes spouses divorce and remarry without an annulment from the Church while their spouse is still living. When they do this, they still are members of the Church. They still are called to live Christian lives, but may not receive the Eucharist.

Christian married love, like Christ's love for the Church, is a faithful and lifelong love. It is a sign of the faithful and unbreakable love of God for people. Thus, Christ's followers are encouraged to be loving servants. Husbands are to love their wives. Wives are to love their husbands. Parents are to cherish their children and show by example how to live as Christ's followers.

To Help You Remember

1. How do a Christian man and woman become a sign of Christ's love for his Body, the Church?

2. Why do we call the Christian family a domestic church?

Signs of Christ's Love for His Church

What are some ways that married couples in your parish serve the Church?

_____

_____

_____

_____

_____

_____

_____

_____

Use the following terms in a sentence.

1. consecrate

   The preist was conseceated to become a bishop.

2. Sacraments at the Service of Communion

   When married couple give themselves to each othe when bishops, preist, deacons dedicate there lives to the schiplt of the Church.

3. Holy Orders

   ~~When you~~ Sort of like Matrimony but you get married to god (meaning you get closer to him forever)

4. Matrimony

   When you get married to a person you are willing to commit to, a person you love

---

Answer the following questions.

1. What do we mean by "service of communion?"

   _____

   _____

2. How are all baptized people priestly people?

   Because we are joined with Crist and are anointed to share in the work of Christ (the priest.

3. Why do we describe the Christian family as the domestic church?

   Because they listen to god's word, pray together and serve one another with generosity and compassion.

Discuss with your family.

How does our family form a domestic church?

Visit our web site at www.FaithFirst.com

Parent Page—Unit 3: We Live

Your Role

Leading a moral life is certainly a challenge today. It seems that things that used to be wrong aren't quite as wrong anymore. Our society seems to tolerate so much more than it used to. We as Christians often wonder if people believe there are any standards anymore. Those of us who still believe that there are standards often fight an uphill battle with our children about the decisions that they face. Our children say to us, "Why can't we do it? Everyone else is." As parents it becomes harder and harder to hold on to what we know is right. When we are challenged by the media, by our children, and by our leaders, it is important for us to remember that we are the primary educators of our children. We base our decisions on our experience, the wisdom of the Church, and our deep love for our children.

What We're Teaching

In this unit we are reviewing what it means to be holy. We teach the works of mercy and help the students see how they are called to put them into practice. We teach about choices, good and bad as well as good and better, and the role of our conscience in helping us discern what we should do. A study of the Ten Commandments and the wisdom writings in the Scriptures completes the unit.

Visit our web site at www.FaithFirst.com

What Difference Does It Make?

A billboard on a road in Dallas had stark white writing on it that said, "What was it about 'Thou shalt not' that you didn't understand?" It was signed, "God." It provoked much discussion among those who saw it, and newspaper articles were written about the anonymous donor who had the sign made. Many people were struck by the simplicity of the message. It was as though God were saying, "I was very clear in what I wanted of you. Did you really not understand what I was saying?" In these times, when so much seems to be relative and circumstantial, we do well to remind ourselves that God was very clear and direct in what he wants of us. Being clear on an issue makes all the difference. Are you clear with your sixth grader and with yourself on what is right and what is wrong?

Unit Opener Photographs: (top left) stained-glass window of the Bible, God's word of wisdom to us; (top right) living a life of holiness is a challenge and an uplifting experience; (bottom) living the Great Commandment.

Our Call to Holiness

We Pray

God our Father,
you alone are holy;
without you
nothing is good.
We ask you
to help us to become
the holy people
you call us to be.

*FROM OPENING PRAYER,
COMMON OF HOLY MEN
AND HOLY WOMEN*

We have studied the great mysteries of faith—the Trinity, the redeeming work of Jesus Christ, and the sanctifying work of the Holy Spirit. How do these mysteries of faith come alive and grow in us?

*Great is the LORD and worthy
of high praise;
God's grandeur is beyond
understanding.
One generation praises your deeds
to the next
and proclaims your mighty works.*
Psalm 145:3–4

Called to be Saints

Faith Focus

Why do we say everyone is called to live a holy life?

Faith Vocabulary

holiness. The characteristic of a person who is in the right relationship with God. Holiness refers to God's presence in us and our fidelity to this abiding God.

With My Family

Plan a "Practicing Holiness" family day. Write out a promise to try to live holy lives for that day and have your family sign it. Put it on the refrigerator door as a reminder.

Who would you describe as a very good person? What qualities would that person have? Why do you think that person comes to mind? Most likely it is someone living a holy life.

Be Holy

God created us with a body and a spiritual soul, with an intellect and a free will. He created us to know him, to love him, to serve him, and to live with him forever in eternal happiness. Our life's job description is to share in God's **holiness.** We are to strive to love him with our whole mind, heart, soul, and strength.

When we were baptized, we received one overriding order: be holy. Sure, we have responsibilities such as: studying, cleaning our rooms, raising children, and going to work. But these are some of the ways and means for living that holiness. At the same time, we can excel at school and keep spotless rooms; we can raise brilliant children and have successful careers. But if we end up as hateful, mean-spirited people, we will be big-time failures. If we wind up living lives that keep God far away or out of the picture completely, we have missed the whole point about what life and living our life is all about: being holy!

Living Holy Lives

At Baptism, God does not issue his orders to be holy and then just sit back, ignoring us, while we either sink or swim. No, God gives us lifelong support. The Holy Spirit is always with us, always at our side throughout our life.

Here is how God is always part of our life:

1. Through the death and resurrection of Jesus Christ, God accepts us with his grace. He shares his life with us and helps us live as his children.

2. Through the gift of the Holy Spirit, we receive the power to conduct ourselves in a way worthy of a Christian. Our bodies are temples of the Holy Spirit. In other words, the Holy Spirit lives in us.

3. Through the commandments, we have a surefire guide for achieving holiness. They show us how to live holy lives.

4. Through Jesus' example and help, we have the ability to remain holy in the face of misfortune, temptation, and betrayal.

5. Through Jesus' life of self-denial and service, we have a clear blueprint of how to conduct our lives. How often we are bombarded with TV commercials, urging us to buy, buy, buy—and buy more! Christ tells us to live with less: "If anyone wishes to come after me, he must deny himself and take up his cross daily and follow me" (Luke 9:23).

Living a holy life includes living a life based on the values revealed to us by Christ.

To Help You Remember

1. What is holiness?

2. Describe some of the ways God helps us live a life of holiness.

3. What can you do today to answer God's call to holiness?

My Wish List

Describe some of the things that you and your friends "absolutely must have" in your life. Review the list and place a + next to those things that will really help you live a holy life.

_____

_____

_____

_____

_____

_____

_____

Every Christian is called to live a life of holiness. This includes reaching out to others, as Jesus did, with mercy and compassion.

The Gleaners

Heroes and saints are not the only ones to take up the challenge to feed the poor. Ordinary people in parish communities are working to help those in need.

Individuals from Saint Philip the Apostle parish in Bakersfield, California, took the opportunity to love their neighbors. They saw that many people in their community were without food.

They also saw that their fertile region produced an abundance of crops, such as tomatoes, oranges, onions, and carrots. Some of this food went to waste.

Remember Ruth in the Old Testament who stood by her mother-in-law, Naomi? The Gleaners chose their name to honor Ruth, who gleaned the fields for unharvested crops to support herself and Naomi.

The Bakersfield group contacted local farmers, who helped them collect the unused crops. The Gleaners grew larger and larger, involved members of other churches, and purchased their own buildings. They now bring in fresh produce and canned goods from grocery stores and from food drives in the community. Currently, they are capable of distributing food not just to people in Bakersfield but to the needy throughout the county.

What can you do to help feed the hungry?

WHAT DIFFERENCE DOES IT MAKE IN MY LIFE?

God calls you to share in his life and love. He calls you to a life of holiness. God's gift of his life and love to you is not for you alone. God calls you to treat others in a way that they know God's love for them too.

Signs of a Holy Life

Develop a list of activities that help you work with others to live a holy life.

____

____

____

____

____

____

____

____

____

____

My Faith Decision

I believe I am called to live a life of holiness. This week I will

____

____.

And now we pray.

All powerful God,
fill us with your light
and love.

FROM PRAYERS
AFTER COMMUNION
MASS FOR HOLY WOMEN

Match each term in Column A with its meaning in Column B.

Column A

_e_ 1. holiness

_b_ 2. virtues

_f_ 3. faith

_d_ 4. hope

_a_ 5. charity

_c_ 6. theological virtues

Column B

a. The virtue by which we love God above all else and love our neighbor as ourselves

b. Strengths and habits that enable us to grow stronger in the God-life that dwells within us

c. Strengths or habits given to us by God

d. The virtue by which we believe in God

e. God's presence in us and our fidelity to God

f. Trusting that God is looking after us

Answer the following questions.

1. What are some ways God helps us live a holy life?

Point 1 to 5 on P 195 At our Baptism: he gives us long life support. through

2. Name and explain the theological virtues.

_P197_ Faith: we believe in God & everything revealed to us
Hope: trust that God looks after us
Charity/love: where we love God and everyone including ourselves

3. Why is living the works of mercy part of living a holy life?

_P198_ Because we grow in holiness. It's called the practice of Spiritual and Corporal of Mercy

Discuss with your family.

How does our family treat others with mercy and compassion?

Visit our web site at www.FaithFirst.com

Making choices

We Pray

LORD, who may abide in
your tent?
Who may dwell on your
holy mountain?
Whoever walks without
blame,
doing what is right,
speaking truth from
the heart.
PSALM 15:1–2

Living a life of holiness
sometimes involves a
struggle to do what is right
and good. Our path to God
involves making proper
choices. How can we make
good choices?

*Keep me safe, O God;
You will show me the path to life,
abounding joy in your presence.*
Psalm 16:1, 11

203

Morality

Faith Focus

Where can we find guidance for making moral decisions?

Faith Vocabulary

moral decisions. The things we choose to say and do, or not to say and do, to live as children of God and followers of Jesus Christ.

morality. A means of evaluating whether our actions are good or evil; a way of judging whether our actions lead us to God or away from God.

conscience. The gift of God that is part of every person that helps us judge what is right and what is wrong.

Where do we go when we want to find someone's phone number? A telephone book is a practical starting place. What would it be like if you just started dialing numbers, hoping to dial the right one?

Where do we go when we need information about **moral decisions?** Here are some practical starting points:

1. the Bible, especially the Ten Commandments;
2. the life and teachings of Jesus;
3. the teachings of the Church; and
4. the laws inscribed in creation, or the natural law.

The greater knowledge and respect we have for these four sources, the better our moral decision making will be.

The Sources of Morality

Knowing what determines the **morality**, that is, the goodness or evil of human acts, will also help us make good moral decisions. Well, there are three things that determine the morality of human

acts. We call these *the sources of morality*. They are:
- *the object* of the act,
- *the intention* of the act, and
- *the circumstances* surrounding the act.

Let's look at each one individually.

Object

The *object* of the act is what we do, a good deed or a bad deed. Our **conscience** can help us know whether the object of our act is good or evil. Before we even make a decision, some things we can choose are good in themselves, such as praying. Other things, such as endangering the lives of others by speeding past someone who is driving too slowly on a crowded highway, are evil in themselves.

Intention

The *intention* of the act is what we *want* to do, or our purpose for doing something. The intention of an act is inside of us. A good intention cannot change an evil act into something good. For example, if we steal money to buy someone a gift, the act of stealing is still wrong, even though we had good intentions.

Circumstances

The *circumstances* of the act are those things that surround the decision we make. Circumstances can make an act better or worse. For example, we might tell a lie because we do not want to hurt someone's feelings. The circumstance for lying is kindness. That may make the act of lying less evil than it otherwise would be. The better choice, of course, is not to lie.

These three sources of morality sound complicated, but they really are not. Simply put, we need to remember:

- what we do,
- why we want to do it, and
- what circumstances there are that might make a difference.

To Help You Remember

1. Name four sources of moral truth and wisdom.

2. What three things determine the morality of our choices?

Making Moral Choices

Making a good choice is not always easy. What circumstances might make it difficult for people to choose to do something they know is right?

_____

_____

_____

_____

_____

_____

_____

_____

///////////

With My Family

Discuss with your family the difference between the many voices that compete for our attention and the one voice of our conscience. Together list three ways you will work on listening to your God-given gift of conscience.

Our life is filled with so many things that compete for our attention. Look here! Buy this! Wear this! Eat here! Shop here!

There are voices all around us, all trying to tell us what to do. We have so many choices that perhaps we really do not know how to go about making a good choice. So the first thing we need to know is how to decide what is really the good thing to do.

Forming a Good Conscience

Every human being has the God-given gift of conscience. For centuries, people have known that the best way to make good decisions is to form a good conscience.

The more we use this gift wisely, the more it helps us judge what is good. The better we train our conscience to know what is good and what is evil, the better

we will be at making those decisions that help us live as followers of Christ.

We also know that not everyone forms a good conscience. We can have an erroneous conscience. We can have a conscience that does not know what is right or wrong or can make wrong decisions. Sometimes this is a person's own fault; sometimes it is not a person's fault. When an erroneous conscience is our own fault, we are responsible for the wrong caused by our actions and for their consequences.

Let's review four ways that we can develop a good conscience.

Study and Prayer

1. Reading, studying, and praying over the Scriptures is an important way of forming a good conscience. The Ten Commandments and the Sermon on the Mount are good places to look for guidance.

2. A second very important way of forming a good conscience is to pray for God's help. We can pray as the psalmist did:

> LORD, teach me the way of
> your laws;
> I shall observe them
> with care.
> Give me insight to observe
> your teaching,
> to keep it with all my heart.
> PSALM 119:33–34

Teachings and Advice

3. Learning and studying the teachings of the Church also help us form a good conscience. Jesus gave his Church the responsibility to teach his truth. He promised the Spirit would always be with the Church as its teacher and guide. So we can rely on the Church to guide us in making good moral decisions.

4. Sometimes it is difficult to tell what path we should take. When this happens, check in with people of faith, people you can trust.

Here is a rule to live by: Form your conscience with the Scriptures, pray the teachings of the Church, seek the advice of other believing people, and follow it. All will help you recognize the voice of God within you.

When you exercise wisely, you build up the muscles of your body and develop your athletic skills. When you form your conscience wisely, you build up an inner resource that will guide you throughout your life.

To Help You Remember

1. What is our conscience?

2. Name some ways we can develop and strengthen our conscience.

3. If you had difficulty making a moral decision, to whom would you go for help?

What to Do?

Your friend approaches you in the school yard and shows you a pack of firecrackers and a lighter.

1. What is your first reaction?

_____

_____

2. What will you do?

_____

_____

3. Why do you do it?

_____

_____

4. What might be the consequences of your decision?

_____

_____

Faith Focus

What happens when we sin?

Faith Vocabulary

capital sins. Seven sins named by the Church that are the sources of other sins. They are pride, greed, envy, rage, lust, gluttony, and laziness.

mortal sin. A serious failure in our love and respect for God, our neighbor, creation, and ourselves.

venial sin. A sin less serious than a mortal sin. It weakens our love for God and for one another.

The choices we make are not always easy. Sometimes we give in to our friends, or we take the easy way out of a tough situation. At other times, we come close to doing what we know is the good thing to do. At the last minute, we go along with the group as they get involved in doing what we know is just plain wrong.

Sin

The truth is we all know we can sin. That is the strange thing about God's love for us. We can turn away from him. When we deliberately turn away from God, offend God, we are choosing to sin. To help us understand more clearly what sin is all about, the Church speaks about sin in many ways. Here are three ways:

Capital sins are those that lead to other sins. There are seven of them: pride, greed, envy, rage, lust, gluttony, and laziness. For example, we may envy what someone else has and desire it for ourselves. Envy can then lead us to stealing, name-calling, and hatred. A false pride and wanting to appear better than others can lead us to telling lies or making things up about ourselves.

Mortal sins are serious offenses against God that break our relationship with God. If we die in this state of separation from God, we remain separated from God forever by our own choice. This terrible possibility of being forever separated from God is what we call hell. We can, of course, find forgiveness for mortal sins, usually through the sacrament of Reconciliation.

Venial sins are less serious offenses against God. Sins may be venial (1) if they do not involve grave or serious matter, (2) if we do not have full knowledge of the act's sinfulness, or (3) if we do not have complete freedom in making our choice. Because all sin turns our heart away from God's love, we should seek forgiveness of all sins, including venial sins.

Whenever we think about sins, especially our own, we must also remember that God wants to forgive us. If we are truly sorry for what we have done, we can always find forgiveness. Jesus died on the cross for our sins. As much as we must be aware of our sins, we must be even more aware of God's mercy and forgiveness.

Living Our Faith

Our moral life is a journey of faith. It begins with God's invitation to share in his life. We journey through life as a member of a faith community that guides us in making wise decisions to live as faithful followers of Jesus. When the journey ends, we will enjoy a life of eternal happiness with God.

Asking Forgiveness

Write a prayer to God telling of your sorrow and asking for mercy and forgiveness.

_____

_____

_____

_____

_____

_____

_____

_____

_____

Stained-glass window of
Don Bosco instructing youth.

Each day we make choices about living our faith. Some choices are easier than others. Our conscience and God's grace guide and help us in making our choices.

Saint John Bosco

The story of the Church is filled with people like John (Don) Bosco (1815–1888), who helped others learn to make good choices. After he was ordained a priest, Don Bosco studied the lives of people living in poverty in large cities. He tried to find out the answer to the question, How does living in poverty in a large city affect the moral decisions people make?

Don Bosco came to realize that people living in poverty in cities did not have the same chance for a good education and a good job as other people did. Because education is an important part of training ourselves in making good moral decisions, Don Bosco decided to create job training programs and professional schools. All the programs in the school founded by Don Bosco were founded on three values: reason, religion, and kindness.

Many religious priests, brothers, and sisters as well as volunteers carry on Don Bosco's work in the world today in over 200 schools. John Bosco was named a saint in 1934. His feast day is January 31.

Who helps you learn to make good moral choices?

God invites you to live a life of holiness. To help you do this, God has given you a conscience. Your conscience helps you know what is good and what is evil. This helps you do what is right and good.

Conscience Builders

Look over this list of conscience builders. Put a check (✓) next to those you use to help build your conscience.

Conscience Builders

- [ ] Read Sacred Scripture
- [ ] Pray for God's help
- [ ] Learn and study the teachings of the Church
- [ ] Ask people I trust for advice

How might using these conscience builders help you make good moral decisions?

_____

_____

_____

_____

My Faith Decision

When I have to make a decision, I will listen to what my conscience is telling me to do.

And now we pray.
Happy are those who observe God's decree, who seek the LORD with all their heart.
PSALM 119:2

211

Fill in each blank with a term that correctly completes each sentence.

1. _Choises_ are the things we choose to do or say to live as children of God and followers of Jesus.

2. _Conscience_ is our inner ability that helps us judge right from wrong.

3. _capital sins_ are those sins that lead to other sins.

4. _mortal sins_ are serious offenses against God that turn us away from God's love.

Answer the following questions.

1. What are the three things that determine the morality of an act?

   Object of the act
   intention " "
   circomstances " "

2. Describe the difference between mortal sin and venial sin.

   venial sins less serious but weeans our love
   for god

3. How does a well-formed conscience help us live a holy life?

   It helps us _make_ _cheese the good discision._
   Helps guide us.

Discuss with your family.

Where can we go for information about making good moral decisions?

Visit our
web site at
www.FaithFirst.com

Loving God

We Pray

The precepts of the LORD
are right,
rejoicing the heart.
The command of the
LORD is clear,
enlightening the eye.

PSALM 19:9

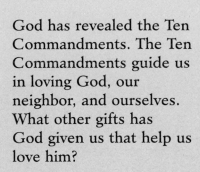

God has revealed the Ten
Commandments. The Ten
Commandments guide us
in loving God, our
neighbor, and ourselves.
What other gifts has
God given us that help us
love him?

*See what love the Father has
bestowed on us that we may be
called the children of God.*

1 John 3:1

Trust and Belief

Faith Focus

Why is faith at the heart of our living our covenant with God?

Faith Vocabulary

Faith. God's invitation to believe and trust in him. It is also our response to his invitation.

When we say we have faith in our dad or in our coach or in our best friend, what are we saying? We are saying many things.

First of all, we declare that we trust them and that we will entrust ourselves to them. Second, we state that we believe what they tell us. Third, we make a commitment to our relationship with them.

Faith in God

Now shift the focus to God. Why is faith in God similar to, yet very different from, our faith in people? The answer is simple: God is always faithful to us. God is Truth. God is Love. God always does what is best for us.

Our trust in people helps us understand our faith in God. We trust God. We believe that what he has revealed is true. We give ourselves to God the Father, Son, and Holy Spirit.

Faith in the Church

We describe living our life of faith in God as living our covenant with God. Our covenant with God includes our promise to follow the commandments and the teachings of Jesus.

God gave us the Church to help us know and understand the meaning of the commandments and Jesus' teachings. To help us live our faith truthfully and faithfully, the pope and the bishops teach us in Christ's name. To guide them in teaching us to live our faith correctly, the Holy Spirit gives the Magisterium of the Pastors of the Church the gift of infallibility. That means they are guided by the Holy Spirit to teach us without error the true meaning of what God has revealed about the Ten Commandments, the Beatitudes, and other moral teachings about loving God, our neighbor, and ourselves.

The Holy Spirit is always with the Church, guiding it to authentically teach. To believe in God is also to believe what the Church believes and teaches. To live our covenant with God is to listen to, study, and follow the teachings of the Church.

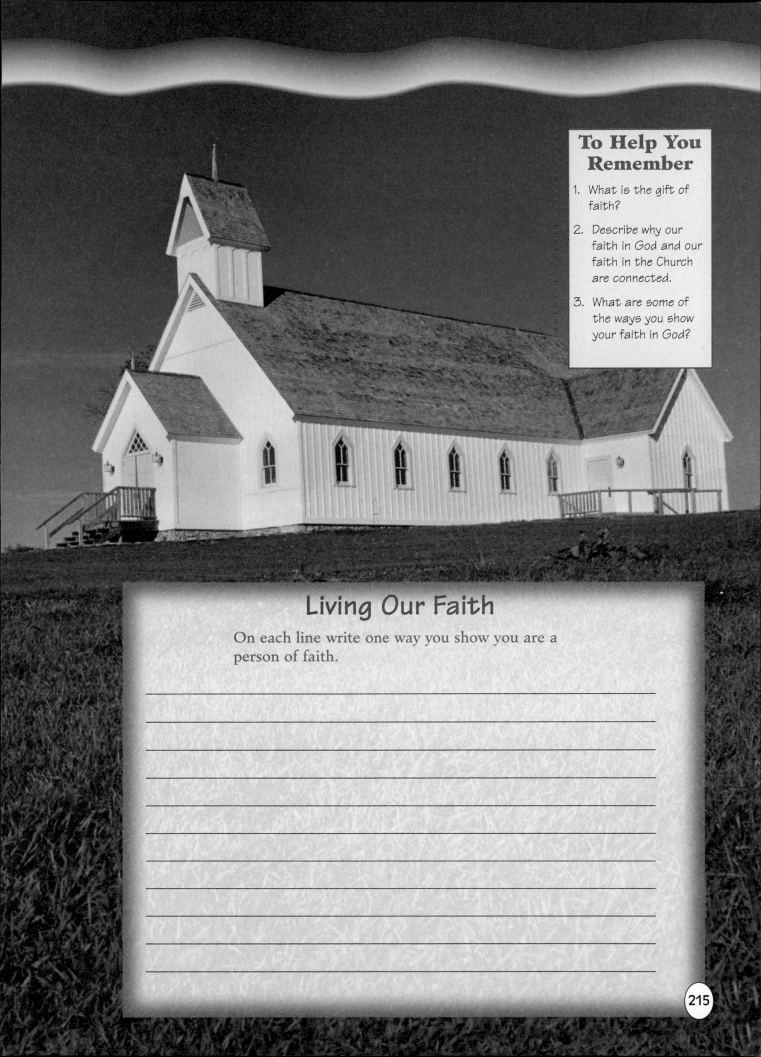

To Help You Remember

1. What is the gift of faith?

2. Describe why our faith in God and our faith in the Church are connected.

3. What are some of the ways you show your faith in God?

Living Our Faith

On each line write one way you show you are a person of faith.

_____

_____

_____

_____

_____

_____

_____

_____

_____

evil that leads us away from that happiness and away from God.

Our parents and teachers might be referring to that part of us when they tell us "to use the brains God gave you." The Church calls it the **natural law**. This is how the Church describes it:

> The natural law is written and engraved in the soul of each and every man and woman because it is human reason ordering him or her to do good and forbidding him or her to sin.

By teaching this truth about ourselves, the Church is really telling us what people have always known about themselves. There is something about the way God has created us that moves us naturally, or by nature, to choose what is good for us and others.

What are some of the principles, or **precepts**, of this natural law? Here are three.

- Do good and avoid evil.
- Tell the truth to each other.
- Be respectful toward one another.

What others can you think of?

Faith Focus

Why do we say that the basic rules for living as a good person are written in our hearts?

Faith Vocabulary

natural law. The original moral sense that is part of our very being and enables us, by human reason, to know good and evil.

precept. A rule or principle that imposes a particular standard of conduct.

We were just talking about faith as keeping our part of the covenant with God. What is that part? What do we want to do?

Natural Law

We have been created in the image and likeness of God. In God's fatherly love for us, he has etched into our hearts and minds a law, a pattern or design, that helps us live as images of God. This law helps us discover the way to the true happiness that God has promised us, and to recognize the

the New Law, using only one word—love.

- Third, he offered us, by his life and teachings, a clear idea of how to love.
- And finally, he gave us the Holy Spirit to help us keep our part of the covenant.

To Help You Remember

1. What is natural law?
2. Describe what the Ten Commandments have to do with natural law.

The Ten Commandments

To get a clearer picture of the precepts of the natural law, look at the Ten Commandments. When God made his covenant with his people, he spelled out what was expected of them. It was not as though God was telling them anything new, anything that their own good sense had not already told them. But this time the Bible says God chiseled the law into stone tablets and gave them to Moses. God obviously meant for them to be taken seriously.

When Jesus came to us, he taught us about the Ten Commandments.

- First, he did not arrive with an armful of new tablets, but rather reaffirmed the Old Law.
- Second, he pulled all of the Old Law into

Naturally!

Choose one of the Ten Commandments. Explain how that commandment makes good sense "naturally."

_____

_____

_____

_____

_____

_____

_____

_____

_____

_____

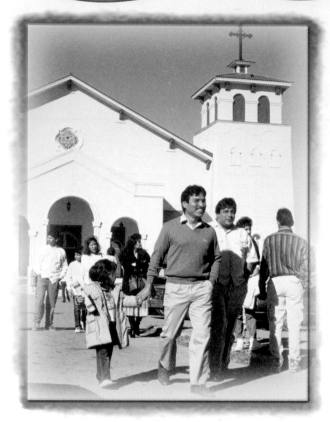

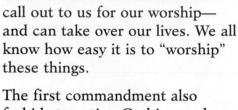

These are some of the idols that call out to us for our worship—and can take over our lives. We all know how easy it is to "worship" these things.

The first commandment also forbids tempting God in words or deeds. It also forbids sacrilege and simony. Sacrilege is profaning or treating unworthily the sacraments and other holy things. Simony is the buying and selling of spiritual things. (Read Acts 8:9–24.)

This commandment also counsels us to place our hope in prayer and God rather than in superstition and magic. The use of sacred images helps us in prayer and is not against this commandment.

Faith Focus

What do the first three commandments teach us about ourselves?

Faith Vocabulary

Idol. Something that takes the place of God in our life. It is something that takes over our life.

The first three commandments show us how to love God.

The First Commandment

I am the LORD your God; you shall not have strange gods before me.

Since most of us are not into worshiping **idols**, or other gods, what does this commandment tell us? It warns us about god "substitutes," such as drugs, alcohol, material possessions, power, and wealth.

The Second Commandment

You shall not take the name of the LORD your God in vain.

The Second Commandment forbids every improper use of the name of God. Blasphemy is the use of the name of God, of Jesus Christ, of the Virgin Mary, and of the saints in an offensive way.

This commandment also tells us, among other things, that we are only to take an oath when it is necessary, as in a court of law. It is a very serious thing to call on God to back up the truth of what we are saying. To casually say "I swear to God" is a pretty serious thing when we are trying to get out of a jam by avoiding the truth. Whenever we call God as our witness, we must tell the truth. As you might say today, it is a "no-brainer."

The Third Commandment

Remember to keep holy the LORD's Day.

In the Old Testament, the Lord commanded the seventh day to be the sabbath, or solemn day of rest (read Genesis 2:2–3). Christians observe Sunday as our sabbath. Sunday is to be observed as the foremost holy day of obligation. On Sunday and other holy days of obligation, the faithful are bound to participate in Mass.

Sunday is the day on which Jesus was raised from the dead—the first day of the new creation of the world in Christ. It stands to reason that we set aside at least one day of the week to pray, go to Mass, and focus on God. In view of what God has done for us, it is the least we can do.

Precepts of the Church

The Church has given us some practical helps for living our covenant relationship with God. They are called the precepts of the Church. They are:

1. You shall attend Mass on Sunday and holy days of obligation.
2. You shall confess your sins at least once a year.
3. You shall humbly receive Holy Communion at least during the Easter season.
4. You shall keep holy the holy days of obligation.
5. You shall observe the prescribed days of fasting and abstinence.

We also have the duty of providing for the material needs of the Church according to our ability.

You can see that these precepts are both reasonable and minimal. They present us with the practical building blocks of prayer, penance, fasting, and generosity. On their foundation, we can build a life of faith and loving service.

To Help You Remember

1. What are the first three commandments?
2. Describe the precepts of the Church.
3. How can the commandments and precepts of the Church help you show your love and respect for God?

With My Family

Discuss ways you can make Sunday a family day.

Make Sunday Special!

Think of some creative ways that you can keep the Lord's Day holy. Use them to design this placard.

SUNDAY

In the early days of the Church, wealthy people gave money to the Church. Others brought cheese, hand-woven cloth, grain, animals, vegetables, bread, and other goods. After gathering at the entrance of the Church, they walked in procession to an area near the altar where they left their gifts. The ancient tradition called for using some of the offerings to help the needy.

God has entered a covenant with us. He is our God and we are his people. We live that covenant by living the commandments and the teachings of Jesus. We strive to love God and others as Jesus taught us.

Today this practice is continued in many local parishes to provide outreach to the poor. Funds given by the faithful during the liturgy are used to support the Church and its work.

The Collection

By taking part in the celebration of Mass, we show our love both for God and for others. The collection at Mass is one sign of that love. It is an ancient tradition of the Church.

What can you contribute for the support of your church and for the needs of the poor? What do you do now? What more can you do?

God invites you to place your faith in him. This may not always be easy to do. There are many things that try to take the place of God in your life. It is important that you recognize what these things might be.

Name That Idol

On the pedestal, describe something that could make it hard for you to place your trust in God.

My Faith Decision

I will make God number one in my life. If there is something in my life that is turning my heart away from God, I will

_____

_____ .

And now we pray.
O God, you are my God—
for you I long!
PSALM 63:1

Use each of the following terms in a sentence.

1. faith

_____

2. natural law

_____

3. Ten Commandments

_____

4. precepts of the Church

_____

Answer the following questions.

1. What does it mean to have faith in God?

_____

_____

_____

2. What is the connection between the natural law and the Ten Commandments?

_____

_____

_____

3. How do the precepts of the Church help us build a life of faith?

_____

_____

_____

Discuss with your family.

How can we as a family make the sabbath a holy day?

Visit our web site at www.FaithFirst.com

Loving One Another

We Pray

Bless the LORD,
    my soul! . . .
How varied are your
    works, LORD!
In wisdom you have
    wrought them all.

PSALM 104:1, 24

Jesus told his disciples,
"This is my commandment:
love one another as I love
you" (John 15:12). How do
the last seven of the Ten
Commandments teach us
how to show love for
ourselves and for others?

Trust in the LORD and do good.
Psalm 37:3

223

Loving Others and Ourselves

Faith Focus

What do the Fourth and Fifth Commandments teach us about showing love for ourselves and for others?

Faith Vocabulary

respect. The feeling of esteem and the willingness to demonstrate it by acts of consideration and courtesy.

The Fourth Commandment

Honor your father and your mother.

This simple six-word commandment conceals many nuggets of good advice. Here are some of them:

- Children, even as they become adults, are to honor and **respect** their parents. When parents are in need, their children must offer appropriate assistance.
- Parents are to care for the physical and spiritual needs of their children.
- Parents should respect and encourage their children's vocations. They should remember and teach that the first calling of a Christian is to follow Jesus.

- Family members—parents and children—are to love and respect each other.
- All family members are to contribute to the family's well-being.
- When family fighting or discord erupts, efforts toward peace and forgiveness must be made.

The Fourth Commandment also includes, in a general way, the authority of government. For society to work, there is a need for authority, which is the ability to make laws and keep good order. Ultimately, authority comes from God. As long as the authority follows God's law, which is the first and most important law, it must be obeyed for the common good of everyone.

The Fifth Commandment

You shall not kill.

This law is huge and its implications are many.

- We must not take innocent life.
- We are to respect our own lives and bodies and those of others.
- We must not misuse food, alcohol, tobacco, or drugs.
- We are not to put ourselves or others in danger.
- We are not to drink and drive. It is seriously wrong to endanger one's own safety and the safety of others because of drunkenness or love of speed.

necessary to stop a person or people from unjustly harming him or her. Legitimately defending the lives of people and the common good is also a grave duty for those who have that responsibility. All people have the right to live safely and securely.

- We are not to directly and intentionally kill, or murder, another human being.
- We are not to end the life of a child before it is born by direct abortion.
- We are not to intentionally put an end to the lives of handicapped, sick, or dying persons. Intentional euthanasia is gravely wrong.
- We are not to end our own life by suicide.
- We are not to engage in acts of terrorism or hostage-taking.

This command "not to kill" does not prohibit the legitimate defense of human life. This means that a person may use the force

The underlying principle here is that all life is sacred. All life belongs to God. In the Sermon on the Mount, Jesus recalls the Fifth Commandment and then adds warnings about anger, hatred, and vengeance. Going even further, Jesus asks us to love our enemies and to turn the other cheek.

To Help You Remember

1. Besides honoring and obeying our parents, what does the Fourth Commandment teach?

2. Describe the principle that underlies the Fifth Commandment.

3. What are some ways you can keep the Fourth and Fifth Commandments?

All Life Is Sacred

Write an E-mail message to encourage a friend to join with you in living the Fifth Commandment. Be specific about ways you and your friend can live the commandment.

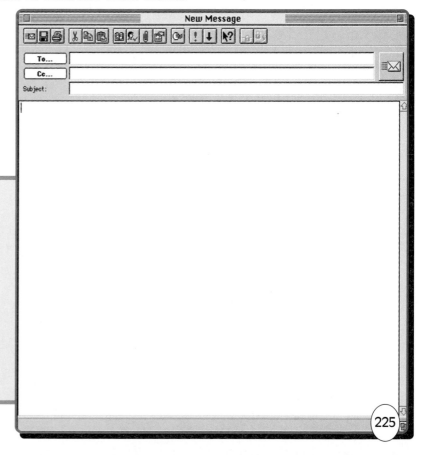

Faith Vocabulary

sexuality. The gift of being male or female—a boy or a girl, a man or a woman.

The Sixth Commandment

You shall not commit adultery.

Sexuality is one of God's gifts to us. It affects all aspects of our life. It concerns our capacity to love and to produce children. It concerns our ability to form bonds and be in communion with others.

This commandment calls *everyone* to live a chaste life. The virtue of chastity guides us in respecting and honoring our sexuality and sharing our love with one another in appropriate ways, following Christ as our model.

Among the sins gravely contrary to the Sixth Commandment are masturbation, fornication, pornography, and homosexual practices. This commandment also forbids adultery. Sexuality is a source of joy and pleasure. When a husband and wife have sexual intercourse, they join their souls and their bodies. This expresses the deepest love and spiritual commitment to each other.

When a married person has sexual relations with someone other than his or her spouse, he or she commits adultery. In their marriage commitment, a man and a woman promise to be faithful to each other until death.

This fidelity is at the heart of the marriage commitment, or marriage covenant. Adultery is an act of infidelity, or unfaithfulness, in a marriage. When adultery occurs, injustice, distrust, and injury often replace love. The marriage covenant breaks down and is seriously weakened. The family is damaged, children are hurt, and society suffers.

The Ninth Commandment

You shall not covet your neighbor's wife.

The Ninth Commandment calls us to respect and honor the promises a man and a woman make to one another in marriage. But, it means much more.

To covet means "to desire." Our actions begin in our hearts and thoughts. So, if we want to live loving and honorable lives, we have to train ourselves to be pure in mind and heart, as well as in our actions. Purity of mind and heart requires modesty. Modesty means refusing to unveil what should remain hidden. Modesty is decency. It protects who we are and our love. It encourages patience and moderation in our friendships and loving relationships with others.

Thoughts or temptations to misuse our sexuality happen. But God's grace is always there to help us deal with these temptations. To dwell on these thoughts and desires can easily lead us to a misuse of our sexuality.

We need to be careful about what we look at, what we read, and how we talk with one another about sexual matters. We need to do those things that help us respect and honor others.

To Help You Remember

1. What is adultery?

2. Describe why it is important to honor and respect our own sexuality and the sexuality of others.

3. How can young people honor and respect their own sexuality and the sexuality of others?

Television Families

Think about some of today's popular TV shows. Name one that depicts people in a healthy marriage. What are some of the qualities of that marriage? How are others affected by that marriage?

Faith Focus

How can the Seventh, Eighth, and Tenth Commandments help us imitate Jesus?

Faith Vocabulary

reparation. The process of righting a wrong; making amends; doing something or paying something to make up for damages we have caused.

The Seventh Commandment

You shall not steal.

The Seventh Commandment asks us to live out justice and charity in our relationships with other people. It forbids stealing, cheating, misusing or damaging another's property, paying unjust wages, and treating people as if they were objects to be bought and sold.

The Seventh Commandment also calls us to use the goods of the earth responsibly. As good stewards of creation, we know that how we treat the environment will have an impact on future generations.

Whenever we break the Seventh Commandment by stealing or cheating, we need to seek forgiveness from God. We have the obligation to make **reparation,** or restitution. We need to repair whatever damage we have caused or to restore what we have unjustly taken.

The Eighth Commandment

You shall not bear false witness against your neighbor.

The Eighth Commandment is about the truth. It asks us to live honest and truthful lives. It teaches us to be truthful in all things and to respect the good name of others.

The Eighth Commandment forbids "bearing false witness," which covers a multitude of sins. Here is a list of some actions that are against the Eighth Commandment:

- Lying
- Saying what is false and trying to make people believe it is true
- Damaging the reputation of other people
- Gossiping
- Breaking secrets or confidences, unjustly bringing harm to others
- Putting others down to make ourselves look good
- Speaking negatively about others
- Shifting the blame for the wrong we have done from ourselves on to others
- Breaking professional secrets

An offense against the truth requires reparation. Breaking this commandment weakens our trust and respect for others. If we break this commandment, we have the obligation to make a serious effort to repair the damage that our misuse of the truth has caused.

The Tenth Commandment

You shall not covet your neighbor's goods.

The Tenth Commandment calls us to treat others fairly and justly. It also tells us to share the blessings God has given us with others. We are to avoid greed and envy.

The Tenth Commandment reminds us to be thankful and generous with what we have. All our blessings and the blessings others enjoy are all gifts from God.

To Help You Remember

1. How do you observe the Seventh Commandment?

2. How do you observe the Eighth Commandment?

3. How do you observe the Tenth Commandment?

Let's Be Honest!

What do we mean by the expression "Honesty is the best policy"?

Jesus told his disciples, "This is my commandment: love one another as I have loved you" (John 15:12). The Fourth through the Tenth Commandments guide us in loving others as Jesus taught us.

Pacem in Terris

The Church helps us to understand the true meaning of the commandments. In 1963 Pope John XXIII wrote an encyclical called *Pacem in Terris,* which means "Peace on Earth." Pope John was very concerned about how human life was being abused around the world. In this encyclical Pope John XXIII called us to live the commandments as Jesus' life on earth taught us to live them.

Pope John emphasized that human life is sacred. Warfare, unjust wages, the misuse of authority, and poverty violate human dignity. He challenged Catholic individuals and nations to promote peace. Peace, Pope John said, is based on loving our neighbor as ourselves and acting justly toward one another.

We can live up to Pope John's challenge in many ways.
- Being truthful in all our dealings with others
- Seeking peaceful solutions rather than fighting
- Respecting the property of others
- Treating everyone in a courteous and honorable way

The Golden Rule, "Do unto others as you would have them do unto you," is another way to summarize the last seven of the Ten Commandments. It is also a blueprint for building peace on earth.

How might doing some of the things Pope John XXIII taught in the encyclical help people live in peace?

Each day you show respect for yourself and others in many ways. Making these choices builds friendships, families, and safe communities.

Living the Golden Rule

The Golden Rule is "Do unto others as you would have them do unto you." Write several ways you would like others to treat you. Then use them as a guide to the way you treat others.

_____

_____

_____

_____

_____

_____

_____

_____

_____

My Faith Decision

This week I will have the opportunity to live the Golden Rule. One thing I will do to show respect for others is

_____

_____ .

And now we pray.
Make known to me your ways, LORD; teach me your paths.
PSALM 25:4

Describe each of the following faith terms.

1. respect

   _____

2. sexuality

   _____

3. adultery

   _____

4. reparation

   _____

5. bear false witness

   _____

Explain how the commandments guide us in living each of these values.

1. All life is sacred.

   _____

   _____

2. Sexuality is a gift from God that we honor and respect.

   _____

   _____

3. Justice and faithfulness and truth are signs of our love for others.

   _____

   _____

Discuss with your family.

How can our family show love and respect for our neighbors?

Visit our web site at www.FaithFirst.com

The Wisdom Books

A Scripture Story

23

We Pray

How varied are your
works, LORD!
In wisdom you have
wrought them all;
the earth is full of your
creatures.

PSALM 104:24

Wisdom is a gift of the
Holy Spirit. It is also the
name given to seven books
in the Old Testament.
How does wisdom guide
us to live as faithful
followers of Jesus?

*The fear of the LORD is the
beginning of wisdom;
prudent are all who live by it.
Your praise endures forever.*
Psalm 111:10

233

Bible Background

Faith Focus

What is the wisdom literature found in the Bible?

Faith Vocabulary

wisdom. The knowledge of how to do things according to God's plan of creation and salvation. Wisdom helps us see the world through the eyes of faith. We are helped to see the world as God sees it.

Pretend you are living in a time when there are few books or libraries. How do you pass on from one generation to the next the traditions, advice, and wisdom you have gathered?

The Oral Tradition

In Bible times people living in the Middle East before the time of Christ had an interesting way of gathering, preserving, and expressing common sense. They put their **wisdom** into forms they could learn by heart.

They collected and passed on their traditions, advice, and wisdom in stories, poems, chants, sayings, proverbs, and prayers. These insights were passed from one generation to the next by word of mouth.

This word-of-mouth way of doing things is called oral tradition. It is one generation repeating what the previous one had repeated to them, and on and on. The chief topics of wisdom were the problem of suffering, our origin and destiny, the meaning of happiness, good and evil actions, and death.

Eventually, many of the pieces of the oral tradition of the Israelites, like those of their neighbors, were collected and written down. Much of this wisdom literature was inspired by God and is found in the wisdom books of the Old Testament. God obviously was the focal point of these writings. Wisdom was a gift of God. Wise was the person who used that gift to live a holy and virtuous life.

The Wisdom Books

There are seven wisdom books in the Old Testament. They are Job, Psalms, Proverbs, Ecclesiastes, the Song of Songs, Wisdom, and Sirach.

The Book of Job is really a long poem that is like a play. In it, both Job and his friends try to understand the problem of human suffering. The wisdom of Job leads us to a sense of God's mystery and wonder. In other words, God has ways that neither Job nor we will ever understand.

The Book of Psalms, as you already know, is a collection of prayers in the form of poetry. The psalms spring from life experiences, such as suffering, a desire for God, a deep feeling of gratitude for what God has done, and a sense of awe before the beauty of God's creation. The wisdom of the psalms is to refer everything back to God—all our joy, all our sorrow, all our hope.

The Book of Ecclesiastes is a long reflection on the emptiness of life, an emptiness that can only be filled, in the end, by God.

The Book of Wisdom and the Book of Sirach help people understand the wisdom of staying faithful to God's law and walking in God's paths. This makes a practical difference in our daily lives. It enriches the way we live with one another in our families and work with one another in our communities.

To Help You Remember

1. What is oral tradition?
2. Describe the focus of the wisdom books.
3. How might you grow in using the gift of wisdom?

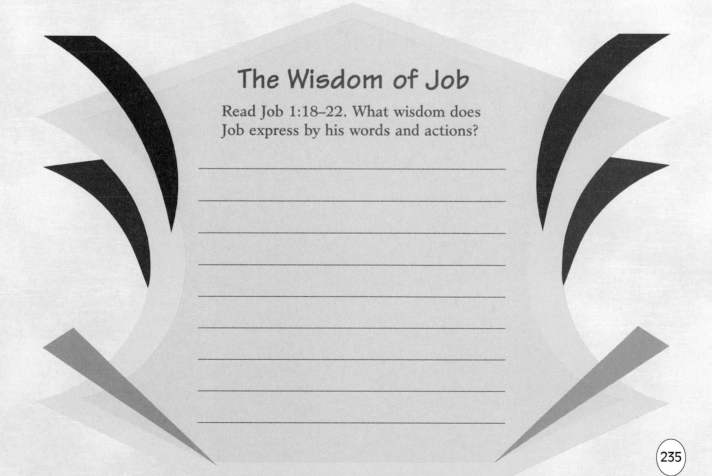

The Wisdom of Job

Read Job 1:18–22. What wisdom does Job express by his words and actions?

_____

_____

_____

_____

_____

_____

_____

_____

235

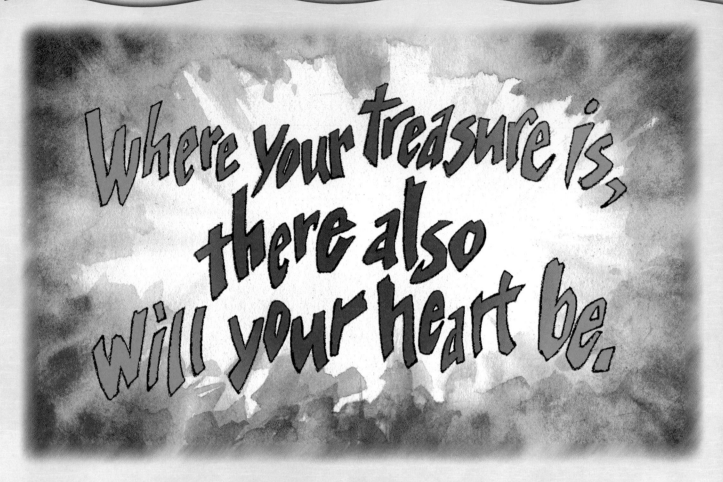

Where your treasure is, there also will your heart be.

Faith Focus

What do the sayings of the Book of Proverbs teach us?

Faith Vocabulary

proverb. A short, concise saying stating a well-accepted truth of fact. Example: Haste makes waste.

The Book of Proverbs

In the Old Testament, wisdom is also practical. It is a skill in action. The Book of Proverbs is a collection of relatively brief sayings, called **proverbs,** that are meant to guide people through life. These sayings are examples of "skills in action."

This is how the Book of Proverbs describes wisdom:

Wisdom has built her house,
she has set up her seven
columns;
She has dressed her meat,
mixed her wine,
yes, she has spread her table.

She has sent out her maidens;
she calls
from the heights out over
the city:
"Let whoever is simple turn
in here;
to him who lacks
understanding, I say,
Come, eat of my food,
and drink of the wine I have
mixed!
Forsake foolishness that you
may live;
advance in the way of
understanding." . . .

The beginning of wisdom is the
fear of the LORD,
and knowledge of the Holy
One is understanding.

If you are wise, it is to your
  own advantage;
  and if you are arrogant, you
  alone shall bear it.

PROVERBS 9:1–6, 10–12

Throughout the Book of Proverbs we are given a series of maxims, or rules of conduct, to make wise decisions. For example:

A mild answer calms wrath,
  but a harsh word stirs up
  anger.

PROVERBS15:1

You have probably already experienced the wisdom of that proverb.

Jesus used proverbs and other sayings much like this in his teachings:

"[W]here your treasure is, there also will your heart be."

LUKE 12:34

Jesus and his apostles were acquainted with the Book of Proverbs. Compare Luke 14:8–10 with Proverbs 25:6–7 or 1 Peter 4:8 with Proverbs 10:12.

To Help You Remember

1. What are proverbs?

2. What proverbs are found in the reading?

3. Give an example of a proverb of your own that helps you make wise choices.

Wise Person on Board!

Design a license plate, using your favorite proverb.

Understanding the Word of God

He is, according to Paul:

"The power of God and the wisdom of God."

1 CORINTHIANS 1:24

Jesus told this parable to help us understand true wisdom:

"Then the kingdom of heaven will be like ten virgins who took their lamps and went out to meet the bridegroom. Five of them were foolish and five were wise. The foolish ones, when taking their lamps, brought no oil with them, but the wise brought flasks of oil with their lamps. Since the bridegroom was long delayed, they all became drowsy and fell asleep. At midnight, there was a cry, 'Behold, the bridegroom! Come out to meet him!' Then all those virgins got up and trimmed their lamps. The foolish ones said to the wise, 'Give us some of your oil, for our lamps are going out.' But the wise ones replied, 'No, for there may not be enough for us and you. Go instead to the merchants and buy some for yourselves.' While they went off to buy it, the bridegroom came and those who were ready went into the wedding feast with him. Then the door was locked. Afterwards the other virgins came and said, 'Lord, Lord, open the door for us!' But he said in reply, 'Amen, I say to you, I do not know you.' Therefore, stay awake, for you know neither the day nor the hour.   MATTHEW 25:1–13

Faith Focus

How did God reveal wisdom most clearly to us?

With My Family

Brainstorm sayings that help you live the Gospel.

Wisdom

Wisdom enables us to decide well. It guides us in making decisions that will have lasting good effects. To grow in wisdom is to be open to the Spirit and to see all things in relationship to God's plan.

Jesus, the Wisdom of God

We believe that the key to God's wisdom is Jesus Christ himself.

Paul tells us that the Holy Spirit teaches us the gift of God's wisdom. He writes:

We have not received the spirit of the world but the Spirit that is from God, so that we may understand the things freely given us by God. And we speak about them not with words taught by human wisdom, but with words taught by the Spirit.

1 CORINTHIANS 2:12–13

When we keep our eyes fixed on Jesus who is the wisdom of God, we will live differently. We will make good and wise choices. We will love God and love each other. We will face difficult decisions and then do the right thing. Indeed, wisdom helps us see the "big picture."

To Help You Remember

1. Who do Christians believe is the key to understanding the wisdom of God?

2. Describe how wisdom guides us in living our lives.

3. What can you do to grow in wisdom?

True Wisdom

Read James 3:13–14, 17–18. Write a profile of a wise person.

_____

_____

_____

_____

_____

_____

_____

_____

_____

_____

Wisdom is a gift of God. We believe that Jesus Christ is the key to understanding true wisdom.

Seat of Wisdom

Christians also honor and respect Mary for her wisdom. She always kept God at the center of her life. Mary's love for God and her faith in him was the driving force behind all her decisions.

One of the titles Christians honor Mary with is Seat of Wisdom. Mary is called the Seat, or bearer, of Wisdom because she is the mother of Jesus, who is "the power and wisdom of God." We honor her as the Seat of Wisdom because she lived out her life according to the plan of God. She was eager to hear God's word and to act upon it. Even when she did not understand everything that God asked of her, she trusted and believed in him. She knew and believed in the larger plan of God's wisdom to save his people from their sins and to bring them the fullness of life.

We also use the title Mother of Good Counsel to honor Mary because of her wisdom. We turn to her for advice, or counsel. We ask her to help us make wise decisions.

Take a moment to talk to Mary in prayer. Ask her to help you make wise decisions that help you live as a follower of Christ.

You probably often hear the words *wise* and *foolish*. When might you say to someone, "That was a wise decision" or "That was a foolish thing to do"? There is a difference between acting wisely or foolishly. Remember the Holy Spirit blesses you with the gift of wisdom. Learn to use it well.

Our Actions Have Consequences

Think of someone in a movie or a television program who acts wisely or foolishly. Describe how this character's wise or foolish actions affect others.

_____

_____

_____

_____

_____

_____

_____

_____

My Faith Decision

This week I will begin each day by praying to the Holy Spirit who blesses me with the gift of wisdom. I will use this gift to help me make my decisions.

And now we pray.

Holy Mary, pray for us.
Mother of the Church, pray for us.
Mother of good counsel, pray for us.
Throne of wisdom, pray for us.
FROM THE LITANY OF THE
BLESSED VIRGIN MARY

Use each of the following faith terms in a sentence.

1. wisdom

   _____

   _____

2. wisdom books of the Old Testament

   _____

   _____

3. proverbs

   _____

   _____

Answer the following questions.

1. What are the main topics of the wisdom books?

   _____

   _____

2. How does the Book of Proverbs describe wisdom?

   _____

   _____

3. What is the difference between foolishness and wisdom?

   _____

   _____

Discuss with your family.

How do wise decisions affect our family? How do foolish decisions affect our family?

Visit our
web site at
www.FaithFirst.com

Parent Page—Unit 4: We Pray

Your Role

As a parent you have more influence on your child's prayer life than anyone else. In our hectic lives finding time to pray can be a challenge, but it is important to pray and we need to make prayer a priority. Your family may pray together either before eating a meal or in the evening before going to bed. You may say traditional prayers like the *Our Father, Hail Mary,* and *Act of Contrition,* or perhaps you simply talk to God. After all, that is what prayer is—talking and listening to God.

Take time to help your family be more aware of God's presence in their lives. Be a prayerful person yourself. Talk to God the way you would talk to your family or close friends. When you talk to them you don't weigh every word. You don't use stilted language. You don't read your words to them. You just say what is on your mind and in your heart. Sometimes your conversations are about significant things; at other times, they are just talks about the inconsequential things that are a part of our everyday life. Pray in the same way by speaking and listening to God. Remember that your child learns by example. By being a prayerful person, you can make your child aware of God's presence in their life.

What We're Teaching

In this unit we are teaching about not only prayers, but also how to pray. We use examples of prayers and discuss how Jesus is our model of prayer, who best shows us how to develop our prayer life. We examine many forms of prayer, including formal prayer and the prayer of meditation. In Chapter 26 the students deepen their understanding of the Lord's Prayer by exploring the meaning of its petitions. You will want to review these chapters with your child. Take the time to discuss the importance of prayer in your family life. And, better yet, pray together often.

Visit our web site at www.FaithFirst.com

What Difference Does It Make?

What if, at the end of a school day, your child didn't tell you what happened that day? What if your spouse stopped communicating with you? What if your friends never called or wrote to you? Or they only sent a greeting card with printed words on it? You would feel disconnected—and out of touch. So it is with God. The Church tells us that God is our Father. Jesus told us the same thing. And as a father, he wants to hear from us, to know how we're doing, to hear a thank you, or maybe a request. From us, not only from those who know us. Communication is essential to human relationships. It is essential to our relationship with God as well. When did he last hear from you? Remember, if you're not praying and if your family isn't praying, chances are that your sixth grader won't be praying either. If not, he or she will be missing out on building the most important relationship your sixth grader and your whole family has—your relationship with God.

Unit Opener Photographs: (top left) stained-glass window of Jesus; (top right) spending time alone listening to God; (bottom) enjoying the presence of God, who is always with us.

People of Prayer

24

We Pray

As morning breaks
I look to you, O God,
to be my strength
this day,
alleluia.

FROM *MORNING PRAYER,*
LITURGY OF THE HOURS

God is always with us. He is always inviting us to make him part of our lives. Praying helps us do that. What have you come to know and believe about prayer?

Blessed be God, who did not refuse me
the kindness I sought in prayer.
Psalm 66:20

Talking with God

We talk a lot and often to our closest friends. On the phone, as we walk down the school corridors, in the gym, we talk and we talk. Prayerful people do the same thing. To them, God is a very close and dear friend who is always available for a good chat.

Prayer

Prayer can be defined in many ways. It is the expression of our hearts to God. It is "lifting our minds and hearts to God." Another simple and accurate description is "talking with God."

Perhaps, more importantly, prayer is an invitation from God to encounter, or meet, him. God never gets tired inviting us to encounter him. As we read and reflect upon Scripture, we discover the real meaning of prayer. It is God calling us, and our calling upon God. (Read the story of God calling Samuel and Samuel calling God in 1 Samuel 3:1–10.)

With our friends, we do not always speak in complete sentences. The same is true for our conversations with God. We do not need to use fancy words.

We just need to talk from our heart. We do not need to impress God. He is always interested in what we have to say.

To vary our conversations with God, sometimes we might want to pray the Our Father, the Hail Mary, or another traditional prayer. At other times we might simply say "Abba" and silently repeat it over and over, while closing our eyes. God is our Father and it is good to realize he is near.

Prayer and the Trinity

Christians pray in a special way. We pray *to* the Father *through* the Son *in* the Holy Spirit. Our prayer is most often directed to the Father. Of course, we can and do also pray at times directly to God the Son and to God the Holy Spirit. But the ordinary pattern of our prayer is to address our prayer to the Father as Jesus did.

At that very moment he rejoiced [in] the holy Spirit and said, "I give you praise, Father, Lord of heaven and

earth, for although you have hidden these things from the wise and the learned you have revealed them to the childlike. Yes, Father, such has been your gracious will."

LUKE 10:21

As Christians, as followers of Jesus who are joined to him through Baptism, we go with him to the Father in the Holy Spirit.

In our prayer:

• Jesus joins us;

• the Holy Spirit moves in us; and

• the Father listens with loving attention.

Jesus leads us in prayer. He teaches us to pray and he gives us an example of prayer. We pray to the Father, through Jesus, in the Holy Spirit. This is what makes Christian prayer special.

To Help You Remember

1. What is prayer?

2. Describe how Jesus teaches us to pray.

3. With what kind of prayer are you most comfortable?

A Message About Prayer

Christians have always prayed short prayers, called invocations, throughout the day. Use this code to decipher this invocation. Pray it often during the day.

A	B	C	D	E	F	G	H	I	J	K	L	M	N	O	P	Q	R	S	T	U	V	W	X	Y	Z	,	.
E	T	M	Z	F	I	O	2	B	H	L	U	Y	P	K	Q	S	C	G	J	R	D	V	W	A	3	X	N

U K C Z X   B   T F U B F D F   B P   A K R N

_____ _ _____ __ ____

U K C Z X   B   2 K Q F   B P   A K R N

_____ _ ____ __ ____

U K C Z X   B   U K D F   A K R N

_____ _ ____ ____

247

Faith Vocabulary

Book of Psalms. Old Testament prayers in the form of songs and poems. Inspired by God, the Book of Psalms may be considered the words God gives us to thank him, ask for forgiveness, and request help.

Abraham, Our Father in Faith

We can learn more about prayer by returning to the Old Testament. There we can read about such great people of prayer as Moses and Miriam, Ruth and Naomi, Judith, David, and Job. Among all the people of prayer in the Old Testament, Christians look upon Abraham as our father in faith.

Scripture describes Abraham's conversation with God as a great prayer. Abraham prayed by the simple action of being present to God and walking with God in the path that God had shown him.

Even before he expressed it in words, Abraham's prayer was an act of trust in God who made promises to him. This is what God promised:

The LORD said to Abram: "Go forth from the land of your kinsfolk and from your father's house to a land that I will show you.

"I will make of you a great nation,
    and I will bless you;
I will make your name great,
    so that you will be a blessing.
I will bless those who bless you
    and curse those who
    curse you.
All the communities of the
    earth
    shall find blessing in you."

GENESIS 12:1–3

With deep faith, Abraham brought his questions and concerns honestly and directly to God. He prayed, "O Lord GOD, what good will your gifts be, if I keep on being childless?" (Genesis 15:2). Abraham took whatever was a need or concern for him and brought it to God with faith and trust. He placed everything in God's hands and placed himself in God's care.

That is why the Book of Genesis says of Abraham:

"[He] put his faith in the LORD, who credited it to him as an act of righteousness."

GENESIS 15:6

The Psalms

The psalms are also model prayers for us. Found mostly in the **Book of Psalms,** they express prayers that are very personal. Filled with emotion, they are prayers that come from the heart of people.

In the psalms we can find five basic forms of prayer:

1. *Blessing and adoration.* In prayers of blessing and adoration, we declare that God is our almighty creator. We bless God, who is the source of everything that is good. Read Psalm 95:1, 6.

2. *Petition.* In prayers of petition, we ask for God's forgiveness and help in all our needs. Read Psalm 38:22–23.

3. *Intercession.* In prayers of intercession, we pray that God will help others in times of trouble. Read Psalm 4:2.

4. *Thanksgiving.* In prayers of thanksgiving, we express our gratitude to God for all his many blessings. Read Psalm 100:4–5.

5. *Praise.* In prayers of praise, we give glory to God simply because he is God and is deserving of our praise and respect. Read Psalm 29:1–2.

Jesus and Mary and the first followers of Jesus would have prayed the psalms. Today, they continue to be a very important part of the prayer life of our Church.

To Help You Remember

1. What does Abraham teach us about prayer?

2. Describe five basic prayer forms we can find in the psalms.

3. How might you make praying the psalms something you can do each day?

Creating a Psalm Prayer

In a few verses create your own psalm, using one or more of the five basic prayer forms.

_____

_____

_____

_____

_____

_____

_____

_____

With My Family

Discuss praying together with your family. Choose a day to pray together each week. Talk about how you will get ready for prayer and some of the ways you can pray.

Growing as People of Prayer

Christians today are people of prayer, as were Abraham, Mary, and others mentioned in the Scriptures. It is within our families that we first learn to become people of prayer. The Christian family is the "domestic church." In, and with, our families, the Spirit first calls us and teaches us to pray alone and together "as Church." But how can we grow as people of prayer? There are a number of things that we can do.

Be humble. Sometimes we hesitate to pray because we feel unworthy. We need not worry. Enter into prayer just as you are. Your humble efforts, like those of the tax collector, are most welcomed by God. (Read Luke 18:9–14.)

Prepare for prayer. There are a variety of ways to get ready to pray. We can set aside a special time for our prayer. We can go to a special place, for example, to church. Or, we can sit before a holy image of Jesus or Mary in a quiet place in

our house. Most importantly, we can ask the Holy Spirit to be with us as we enter into our time of prayer. This will truly help us listen to God and speak to him honestly from our hearts.

Focus on praying. Distractions are the thoughts and ideas that get in our way while we are praying. They tend to pull us away from our prayer. They draw our attention away from God and on to other things.

What can we do about distractions in our prayer? We can let them be a reminder that we need to really try to focus our attention on God. There is something else we can do. We can simply turn our distracting thoughts and ideas over to God and pray about them, especially if the distractions express our concerns or worries.

Have courage and trust. Sometimes we are not sure if God is listening. We begin to feel discouraged. We might even begin to question the whole business of praying. Our discouragement and questions can then be brought into our prayer. We can ask God for the encouragement and grace to keep relying on him. Even when we are not clear how things will work out, we trust him.

God has promised to be with us and to bring us into his kingdom and to give us the fullness of life. In prayer, especially in moments when we feel discouraged, we return to God's promise and ask God to help us trust him more completely.

Our prayer begins with a loving faith and trust in God. Then it moves toward asking God for greater faith and trust. Our prayer is like that of the man in the Gospel who said, "I do believe, help my unbelief!" (Mark 9:24).

Prayer helps us love and trust God. It helps us become one with God. There is no deep secret to praying. We just need to really want to pray and do it—even when it is difficult.

To Help You Remember

1. Name some of the things that can get in the way of our growing as people of prayer.

2. Name some things you can do to grow as a person of prayer.

Praying Is Talking and Listening to God

Describe some of the things that make praying difficult for you. Then choose one of those things and name two ways you can deal with it.

_____

_____

_____

_____

_____

_____

_____

_____

Christians are people of prayer. Prayer can be described in many ways. It is lifting our minds and hearts to God. It is placing ourselves in God's presence, having a conversation with him. It is enjoying our friendship with God.

Invocations

Since the earliest days of the Church, Christians have prayed in many ways. To help keep in touch with God, Christians have prayed invocations. The word *invocation* means "calling on someone." Invocations are brief prayers we can say throughout the day.

One invocation that has been popular for over six hundred years is called the Jesus Prayer. The words of the prayer are simple and often are uttered with a special breathing technique.

Read the Jesus Prayer on this page. Now try praying the Jesus Prayer yourself, using the breathing actions. Memorize the prayer. Then close your eyes and silently pray it.

You now have a simple prayer to use whenever you want and wherever you are. When might you pray the Jesus Prayer?

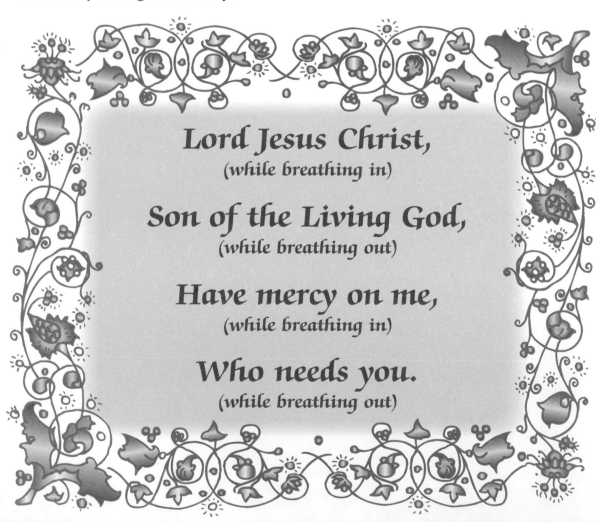

Lord Jesus Christ,
(while breathing in)

Son of the Living God,
(while breathing out)

Have mercy on me,
(while breathing in)

Who needs you.
(while breathing out)

You spend time each day enjoying the company of your family and friends. Praying is spending time with God and enjoying his company.

Times for Praying

Take the time to fill out this daily planner. When will you set aside time for praying?

7:00	
7:30	
8:00	
8:30	
9:00	
9:30	
10:00	
10:30	
11:00	
11:30	
12:00	
12:30	
1:00	
1:30	
2:00	
2:30	
3:00	
3:30	
4:00	
4:30	
5:00	

My Faith Decision

This week I will try to spend more time with God, enjoying his company and my conversations with him. I will

_____

_____ .

And now we pray.

Let us bless the Lord by whose grace we live and by whose grace we love one another. Blessed be God forever.

FROM BLESSING OF A SON OR DAUGHTER BEFORE MARRIAGE

Describe each type of prayer.

1. Prayer of blessing and adoration

   _____

2. Prayer of praise

   _____

3. Prayer of thanksgiving

   _____

4. Prayer of intercession

   _____

5. Prayer of petition

   _____

Answer the following questions.

1. Why do we describe prayer as a conversation with God?

   _____

   _____

2. How do the prayer of Abraham and the Psalms help us grow as people of prayer?

   _____

   _____

3. What can you do to overcome things that get in the way of your growing as a person of prayer?

   _____

   _____

Discuss with your family.

What is a good time for us to gather to pray together as a family?

Visit our web site at www.FaithFirst.com

Forms of Prayer

25

We Pray

My soul rests in God
alone,
from whom comes
my salvation.

PSALM 62:2

Christians are people of
prayer. In what ways does
the Church pray?

*I will call upon God. . . .
At dusk, dawn, and noon . . .
and my prayer will be heard.*
Psalm 55:17, 18

255

Pray Without Ceasing

Faith Focus

What are some practical ways to pray throughout the day?

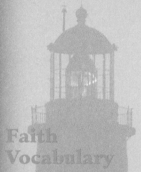

Faith Vocabulary

prayer life. The habit of giving God praise and thanksgiving at specific times of the day; making prayer part of the rhythm of our day.

Watching Olympic champions mount the platform and have a medal draped around their necks and listening to the playing and singing of the national anthem are moments of great joy and success. But how did these champions come to that moment? They took the time and made the effort to develop the gifts and abilities with which God has blessed them.

There is a gift God gives to everyone. It is the gift and ability of praying. But we need to take the time to develop that gift. We need to use it every day, not once, not twice, but often.

Our Prayer Life

Jesus is our model of prayer. He is the one who best shows us how to develop our **prayer life.** The Gospel tells us that he often went aside and spent time in conversation with his Father. Jesus especially did this at important moments in his life. With trust he presented his needs and concerns to the Father. With gratitude he blessed and thanked his Father.

Pray Always

Prayer is so important in our life as followers of Christ. Paul reminds us:

> Pray without ceasing.
> 1 THESSALONIANS 5:17

The Church today continues to live by Paul's advice. We make prayer a regular part of our life each day. We pray as the psalmist prayed, "at dusk, dawn, and noon" (Psalm 55:18).

Morning Prayer

Throughout the world the Church welcomes each new day with prayer. We join Zechariah in thanking God for the dawn of our salvation in Jesus Christ. We pray:

> "Blessed be the Lord, the God of Israel,
> for he has visited and brought redemption to his people.
> He has raised up a horn for our salvation
> within the house of David his servant,
> even as he promised through the mouth of his holy

prophets from of old:
salvation from our enemies
   and from the hand
   of all who hate us,
to show mercy to our fathers
   and to be mindful of his holy
   covenant
and of the oath he swore to
   Abraham our father,
   and to grant us that,
   rescued from the hand
   of enemies,
without fear we might
   worship him
in holiness and righteousness
   before him all our days."

LUKE 1:68–75

Evening Prayer

As the sun sets, the Church throughout the world also gathers in prayer. In the evening we join Mary in praising God for the wonders of his grace-filled ways.

"My soul proclaims the
   greatness of the Lord;
   my spirit rejoices in God my
   savior.
For he has looked upon his
   handmaid's lowliness;
   behold, from now on will all
   ages call me blessed.
The Mighty One has done great
   things for me,
   and holy is his name.
His mercy is from age to age
   to those who fear him.
He has shown might with his arm,
   dispersed the arrogant of
   mind and heart.
He has thrown down the rulers
   from their thrones
   but lifted up the lowly.

The hungry he has filled with
   good things;
   the rich he has sent away
   empty.
He has helped Israel his servant,
   remembering his mercy,
according to his promise to our
   fathers,
   to Abraham and to his
   descendants forever."

LUKE 1:46–55

You are encouraged to join with the Church. Place copies of the Canticle of Zechariah and the Canticle of Mary next to your bed. Join the Church in praying them when you wake up in the morning and retire at night.

To Help You Remember

1. What does Paul teach us about prayer?

2. Describe the purpose of morning and evening prayer.

3. When might you pray the canticles of Zechariah and Mary?

Praying Always

Make some practical suggestion on how you could "pray without ceasing."

Disbelief of Apostle Thomas by the Dutch painter Rembrandt (1609–1669).

An excellent example of adoration is found in the Gospel according to John. It is Easter Sunday night and the Risen Jesus appears to his disciples in the upper room. For some reason, the apostle Thomas is not present. When the apostles tell Thomas that Jesus has been raised from the dead, he refuses to believe them. When the Risen Jesus appears to his disciples a week later, Thomas is with them. Addressing Thomas, Jesus says:

> "Put your finger here and see my hands, and bring your hand and put it into my side, and do not be unbelieving, but believe." Thomas answered and said to him, "My Lord and my God!"   JOHN 20:27–28

Thomas's words "My Lord and my God!" are a prayer of adoration. He recognizes Jesus and acknowledges him as his saving Lord.

At Mass we too adore our Lord and God as Thomas did. Just before we receive the Eucharist, the priest, deacon, or eucharistic minister holds the bread, saying, "The body of Christ." We respond, "Amen." Next the cup of wine is held up and the minister says, "The blood of Christ." We respond, "Amen." The word *amen* means "I believe." We believe, as Thomas came to believe, that Jesus is our Lord and God, who is truly present with us in the Eucharist.

Faith Focus

What role does the prayer of adoration have in our prayer life?

Faith Vocabulary

prayer of adoration. Acknowledging God is God alone and we have been created by him.

adore. To worship or love deeply.

Each time we try to make prayer a regular part of each day, we show that God is at the center of our lives. He is the one in whom we place our faith and trust. We value our friendship with him more than anything else in our lives. When we do this, our life becomes a **prayer of adoration**.

The Prayer of Adoration

In our prayer of adoration we stand before God as his creatures. We praise God's greatness and acknowledge that he is our Creator. We worship him and admit that we depend on him for everything. When we **adore** God, we entrust ourselves to him as the Lord of our life.

Holy, Holy, Holy

At every Mass, at the end of the preface and just before the eucharistic prayer, we sing or recite the "Holy, Holy, Holy." This is another example of a prayer of adoration.

These words of adoration are taken from the Old Testament book of the prophet Isaiah. It is the song of the angels in heaven who adore and worship God. (Read Isaiah 6:3.) We join in this great act of adoration when we sing or say:

> Holy, holy, holy Lord, God of power and might,
> heaven and earth are full of your glory.
> Hosanna in the highest.
> Blessed is he who comes in the name of the Lord.
> Hosanna in the highest.

To Help You Remember

1. What does it mean to adore God?

2. Describe two examples of prayers of adoration found in the Bible.

3. In what ways throughout the day do your words and actions show you "adore" God?

Prayers of Adoration

Think about these prayer gestures we use during the celebration of the Eucharist. Describe how each is a prayer of adoration.

Standing _____

_____

_____

Kneeling _____

_____

_____

Bowing _____

_____

_____

Stained-glass window of Jesus with Martha and Mary in their home.

Faith Focus

How can we pray a prayer of meditation?

Faith Vocabulary

prayer of meditation. An expression of prayer using our imagination, mind, and desire to live our new life in Christ.

Prayer of Meditation

While Isaiah described the God we adore as one who lives in the heavens surrounded by angels, Jesus made it clear to us that God is "Abba." He is a loving Father who is part of our life each day. The **prayer of meditation** helps us connect our lives more closely with God.

In the prayer of meditation, we use our imagination, mind, and desire to live the new life in Christ that we have received in Baptism. We place ourselves in the presence of God—the Father, Son, and Holy Spirit. This helps deepen our feelings for God and our desire to live as his children.

There are different methods or ways of meditating. Here are the steps for one of them.

1. We begin by placing ourselves in the presence of God. We ask the Holy Spirit to help us and to enlighten us.

2. We prayerfully read the Bible. For example, we might read this passage from the Gospel according to Luke.

> As they continued their journey [Jesus] entered a village where a woman whose name was Martha welcomed him. She had a sister named Mary [who] sat beside the Lord at his feet listening to him speak. Martha, burdened with much serving, came to him and said, "Lord, do you not care that my sister has left me by myself to do the serving? Tell her to help me." The Lord said to her in reply, "Martha, Martha, you are anxious and worried about many things. There is need of only one thing. Mary has chosen the better part and it will not be taken from her."
>
> LUKE 10:38–42

3. We next imagine ourselves in the gospel scene. We are receiving Jesus into our home. Imagine you are Martha or Mary.

4. In our imagination we have been planning what we think we need to do for Jesus and his visit. Then we stop and think and consider what Jesus wants of us. As we listen to his words to Martha, we realize that most of all Jesus wants us to be with him.

5. We decide that we will spend time with Jesus, trying to listen to what he has to say to us. We will read his words in the Gospel. We will try to pay attention to him.

6. Before we leave our time of meditation, we offer a short prayer. "Dear Lord, I thank you for giving me your word today. I thank you for being with me. May I never lose a sense of your presence with me. Help me join Mary as a true disciple who sits at your feet and listens to every word you speak."

The goal of the prayer of meditation is to live the new life in Christ we have received in Baptism. In the prayer of meditation we spend time with Jesus. We give him all our attention and listen as he shows us how to live as his followers and children of God.

To Help You Remember

1. What is the prayer of meditation?

2. Describe the six steps in a prayer of meditation.

With My Family

Take the time and pray a prayer of meditation together.

Giving Jesus All Our Attention

Choose one of these gospel passages: Luke 14:7–11, Luke 15:1–10, or John 2:1–11. Using the six steps, pray a prayer of meditation. What might Jesus be saying to you?

_____

_____

_____

_____

_____

_____

_____

_____

Jesus is the model of prayer for Christians. As he did, we address our prayer to the Father throughout the day. Through our prayer we deepen our relationship with God and entrust our lives to him.

Hildegard of Bingen

The story of the Church is filled with people who were respected by others as people of prayer. Many turned to these people for advice and direction on how to make their lives a life of prayer.

In the twelfth century, many people turned to Hildegard of Bingen (1098–1179) to help them. She was blessed with a sense of God's closeness to her and all people. She had a great love of creation as God's great gift to us.

At the age of thirty-eight, Hildegard was elected as abbess, or leader, of a group of women who lived together in a religious community. They had joined together to live their lives according to the Rule of Saint Benedict.

The Church honors Hildegard of Bingen as a saint. We celebrate her feast day on September 17.

What can you do to make prayer a regular part of your day?

Stained-glass window of Hildegard of Bingen.

God is always inviting you to prayer. He is always by your side in everything you do.

Pray Always

Prayer can become part of everything you do. Here is a list of things that are part of our life. Describe how you can make prayer a part of each of them.

Studying _____

_____

Eating _____

_____

Playing _____

_____

Reading _____

_____

Listening to the radio or to a CD _____

_____

Watching television or a video _____

_____

My Faith Decision

This week I will try to be more aware that God is always with me. I will take the time to give my attention to God and invite him to be part of everything I do.

And now we pray.
We give thanks to you, Father, Son, and Holy Spirit, now and for ever. Amen.
FROM BLESSING OF A HOME

Describe each of these faith terms.

1. prayer life _____

_____

_____

2. prayer of adoration _____

_____

_____

3. prayer of meditation _____

_____

_____

Answer the following questions.

1. What does Paul mean when he teaches, "Pray without ceasing"?

_____

_____

_____

2. Describe each of the six steps in a prayer of meditation.

_____

_____

_____

_____

_____

_____

Discuss with your family.

How can we make praying together as a family one of the most important things we do together?

Visit our
web site at
www.FaithFirst.com

The Lord's Prayer

A Scripture Story

We already know the Lord's Prayer by heart. We pray it regularly. However, do we really know what it means? What do we pray for when we pray the Lord's Prayer?

"And I tell you, ask and you will receive; seek and you will find; knock and the door will be opened to you."

Luke 11:9

265

Bible Background

Faith Focus

What is the Lord's Prayer?

Faith Vocabulary

Lord. A title meaning "master, ruler, a person of authority." It is used in the Old Testament to name God. It is also used in the New Testament as a reference to Jesus to express our belief that Jesus is truly God.

When you were small, did you have a special little prayer book? Perhaps your family has certain prayers that you say for special celebrations. Sports clubs often begin games with prayer. The United States Congress begins its sessions with prayer. The Internet is exploding with new prayer sites every day.

The Prayer of All Christians

The most profound, the most moving, and the most central prayer of our Christian faith is the **Lord**'s Prayer. The Lord's Prayer comes to us in two different forms. A shorter form is found in the Gospel according to Luke. A longer form, which the Church uses in its liturgy, is based on the prayer in the Gospel according to Matthew. Both versions address God by name, honor God, and finally ask him to respond to our needs.

In Matthew's version the prayer follows this pattern:

1. God is addressed, or called upon: *Our Father*.

2. Three prayer verses give glory to the Father. We pray that:
   - God's name be made holy;
   - God's kingdom come;
   - God's will be done.

3. Then four petitions present our needs to God. We pray that:
- God will provide for our deepest needs;
- God will forgive our sins;
- God will help us overcome temptation;
- God will help us win the struggle over evil.

This prayer of Jesus is like a vast treasure chest of wisdom condensed into a small jewelry box. The ancient Roman writer Tertullian calls it a summary of the whole Gospel. Saint Augustine described it this way:

Run through the words of the holy prayers [in Scripture], and I do not think that you will find anything in them that is not contained and included in the Lord's Prayer.

A Portrait of the Lord's Prayer

For centuries, artists have tried to depict the feelings they have when they hear and pray the Lord's Prayer. Your artist easel awaits. Create your own depiction of what the Lord's Prayer means to you.

To Help You Remember

1. Where is the Lord's Prayer found in the Gospel?

2. Describe the parts of Matthew's version of the Lord's Prayer.

3. When might you pray the Lord's Prayer?

Reading the Word of God

With My Family

Include the praying of the Lord's Prayer in your mealtime prayers.

The Lord's Prayer

In Matthew's account of the Gospel, the Lord's Prayer is part of the Sermon on the Mount. Jesus had just finished warning his disciples about doing good deeds so that everyone could praise them. Jesus, while teaching them that they should always pray to the Father with trust, said:

"This is how you are to pray:
Our Father in heaven,
   hallowed be your name,
      your kingdom come,
   your will be done,
      on earth as in heaven.
   Give us today our daily
      bread;
   and forgive us our debts,
   as we forgive our debtors;
and do not subject us
   to the final test,
   but deliver us from
      the evil one."

MATTHEW 6:9–13

Jesus Lived His Prayer

Jesus gave us the Lord's Prayer. Jesus also prayed and lived his life trusting his Father. This trust is especially clear as he approached his death on the cross. Facing his death on the cross, he prayed:

"I am troubled now. Yet what should I say? 'Father, save me from this hour'? But it was for this purpose that I came to this hour. Father, glorify your name." JOHN 12:27–28

In a similar way, Jesus prayed this prayer to his Father in the Garden of Gethsemane that same night:

"Abba, Father, all things are possible to you. Take this cup away from me, but not what I will but what you will."

MARK 14:36

The Lord's Prayer teaches us not only how to pray, but also how to live as Jesus did. We are to live as people who place all our trust in God our Father.

To Help You Remember

1. How does Jesus teach us to pray?

2. Explain why the Lord's Prayer is a prayer of trust in God.

3. In what ways do you show that you trust God?

And Now for Today's News Headlines . . .

Today's headlines shout at us from the newspaper, television, and web screen. Who are people you know or have read about who are examples of trust in God? How do they show their trust? Create headlines about them.

Opening Up the Prayer

1. *OUR FATHER*
Through our Baptism we are joined to Jesus and become one with him and one another. The Holy Spirit is poured into our hearts, enabling us to call God our Father as Jesus did. Paul writes, "[Y]ou received a spirit of adoption, through which we cry, '*Abba*, Father!' " (Romans 8:15)

2. *WHO ART IN HEAVEN*
The word *heaven* does not so much mean a place. It points to God's majesty and glory. As members of the Church, as part of the communion of saints, we on earth even now join with the saints in heaven in praising God.

3. *HALLOWED BE THY NAME*
What do we mean when we pray that God's name be made holy? Is it not already holy? Yes, of course, it is! In this petition, we are praying that the glory and praise that truly belong to God who made us, redeemed us, and sanctified us will be acknowledged by all people.

4. *THY KINGDOM COME*
We pray that the kingdom announced by Jesus may come to completion when he comes again in glory at the end of time. We also promise to prepare a way for the coming of that kingdom.

5. *THY WILL BE DONE ON EARTH AS IT IS IN HEAVEN*
The First Letter to Timothy says that God's will is a saving will: "God our savior . . . wills everyone to be saved and to come to knowledge of the truth" (1 Timothy 2:3–4). God's will is for all people to live in communion with him forever. When we pray "thy will be done," we promise to live according to God's will and plan.

6. *GIVE US THIS DAY OUR DAILY BREAD*
As God's sons and daughters we approach God and ask for "our daily bread." We ask God to watch over not only our physical needs but our spiritual ones as well.

In the end, our daily bread is Christ himself, who said, "I am the living bread that came down from heaven; whoever eats this bread will live forever; and the bread that I will give is my flesh for the life of the world" (John 6:51).

7. *AND FORGIVE US OUR TRESPASSES AS WE FORGIVE THOSE WHO TRESPASS AGAINST US*
God is all-merciful and compassionate. We believe that God will always forgive our sins when we are sorry.

But forgiveness is a two-way street. Those who receive God's forgiveness must be willing to be as forgiving and merciful toward others as God is toward them.

8. *AND LEAD US NOT INTO TEMPTATION*
Temptation tries to convince us that there is something better than God's will. Each time we are tempted, we look toward God. We ask God for the courage to face temptation with strong faith, generous love, and confident hope.

9. *BUT DELIVER US FROM EVIL*
There are forces and influences in the world that try to lead us away from God. We know that there is a tempter whom we call Satan or the devil. He tempted Jesus with no success. Now he is trying his hand on those who follow Jesus. We know that evil can be mighty tempting. We also know that Jesus said, "I have told you this so that you might have peace in me. In the world you will have trouble, but take courage, I have conquered the world" (John 16:33). Jesus is the victor. There is no one, no power, stronger than Jesus. We pray that God's victory in Jesus Christ may be our victory as well.

To Help You Remember

1. What do the first three petitions tell us about God the Father?

2. Describe what the last six petitions tell us about ourselves.

3. Choose one of the petitions of the Lord's Prayer. How does praying it help you live your life as a child of God?

On the Road Again

Create a billboard for the Lord's Prayer. Remember, you have to compete with a lot of other messages out there. Grab people's attention with the good news of the Lord's Prayer!

Jesus taught his disciples that when they pray, they should always trust in God. To help them, he taught them to pray the Lord's Prayer.

A Rainy Night of Prayer

Allie Barstow knows all about prayer. But it was not always that way. She was like a lot of people. She was really, *really* into prayer as a young girl. But after a while . . . well, she just didn't have the time to pray.

So it came as quite a surprise for Allie to find herself huddled near a dark wet road on an icy February night, praying to God to help her get through this. "This" was a fifty-foot skid that toppled her family's car over an embankment and down a steep hill.

Her father had driven to pick her up, and now he was unconscious in the family car down that steep embankment. Allie herself had been thrown from the car. There was no sound, no movement, just pitch black darkness. Shivering in the cold, Allie kept praying the Lord's Prayer, words she used to pray so often.

How much time had passed? She could never really be certain—five minutes? A half hour? All night? She had tried

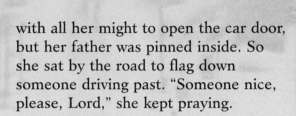

with all her might to open the car door, but her father was pinned inside. So she sat by the road to flag down someone driving past. "Someone nice, please, Lord," she kept praying.

Eventually a car's headlights picked her out of the dark. And someone nice, a local farmer and his wife, stopped to help. They quickly called 911 on their cell phone (Dad always carried the cell phone in his jacket, thought Allie). The ambulance arrived. Dad was bruised but okay.

Life went back to normal. But not exactly, for Allie Barstow remembered that in the terror of that night, she had felt strangely calm. She could handle it. "I guess God was with me, no matter what," she told friends. Prayer had helped her through. And since then, she never just says the words. When Allie Barstow prays, she talks and listens to God.

When has prayer made a difference in a day in your life?

Jesus invites you to call his Father your Father. What a wonderful privilege! Stay in touch with God the Father today. He is always with you.

Praying with the Whole Wide World!

You have been given the job of webmaster of a new web site that tells the world all about the Lord's Prayer. Design the home page. Why should people keep coming back to your site? Your design will tell it all.

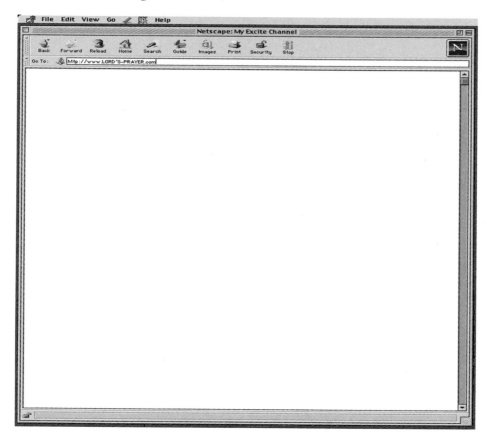

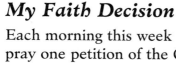

My Faith Decision

Each morning this week I will pray one petition of the Our Father. I will think about what it means and ask the Holy Spirit to help me live it.

And now we pray.
Answer when I call,
my saving God.
In my troubles,
you cleared a way;
show me favor;
hear my prayer.

PSALM 4:2

Match the terms in column A with their meanings in column B.

Column A	Column B
____ 1. Lord	a. God's majesty and glory
____ 2. hallowed	b. To make holy
____ 3. heaven	c. Father
____ 4. Abba	d. A title meaning master

Answer the following questions.

1. In the Lord's Prayer what does the phrase "who art in heaven" mean?

_____

_____

_____

_____

2. What do we promise when we pray "thy will be done"?

_____

_____

_____

_____

3. How do we give glory to the Father when we pray the Lord's Prayer?

_____

_____

_____

_____

Discuss with your family.

What can we do this week to show that we are a family of prayer?

Visit our
web site at
www.FaithFirst.com

We Celebrate
The Liturgical Seasons

The Liturgical Year/Ordinary Time

Faith Focus

How does the Church worship God throughout the year?

The Word of the Lord

These are the gospel readings for the Thirty–Second Sunday in Ordinary Time. Choose this year's reading. Read and discuss it with your family.

Year A: Matthew 25:1–13

Year B: Mark 12:38–44 or 12:41–44

Year C: Luke 20:27–38 or 20:27, 34–38

What You See

The Church uses different colors to celebrate the liturgical seasons. Green is used during Ordinary Time. Green symbolizes life and growth.

The Church's Year of Worship

2000, 2001, 2002. We celebrate our life and our history by years. The Church also celebrates its life and history on a yearly cycle. We call the Church's yearly cycle of worship the liturgical year. All the seasons and feasts of the Church's liturgical year help us remember the story of God's love for us. Celebrating the Church's year of worship enables us to take part in God's loving plan of salvation.

Seasons and Feasts

Advent, Christmas, Lent, and Easter are the four seasons of the Church's year. We remember and celebrate the announcement and fulfillment of God's plan of salvation in Jesus Christ.

The Triduum is at the center of our year of worship. Beginning on the evening of Holy Thursday and ending on Easter Sunday evening, the Triduum is our three-day celebration of the Paschal mystery.

All throughout the seasons of the year we gather on special days called feasts. Some feasts, such as the Transfiguration and the Ascension, celebrate the mysteries of our faith. Other feasts, such as Peter and Paul, Apostles; Our Lady of Guadalupe; and All Saints honor the holy men and women who are part of our faith story.

Ordinary Time

The longest part of the church year is called Ordinary Time. The word *ordinary* comes from a Latin word meaning "number." During Ordinary Time, the Sundays and weeks are named by the use of numbers; for example, the Thirty-Second Sunday in Ordinary Time.

The thirty-three or thirty-four weeks of Ordinary Time focus on the whole mystery of Christ's life. We listen to the four accounts of the Gospel over a three-year cycle: Matthew in Year A; Mark and John in Year B; and Luke in Year C.

All throughout Ordinary Time we join with the disciples. We walk along the shores of the Sea of Galilee and into Capernaum and the other towns and villages. All the time we listen, we watch, and we learn from our Teacher what it means to be his disciple.

Living the Great Commandment

On the Thirty–Second Sunday in Ordinary Time we will listen to Jesus teaching about the Great Commandment (Mark 12:28–34). In this banner create a symbol for the Great Commandment.

To Help You Remember

1. What is the liturgical year of the Church?

2. Explain how celebrating Ordinary Time helps us live as a follower of Christ.

Faith Focus

How does the Jesse tree help us celebrate Advent?

The Word of the Lord

These are the gospel readings for the First Sunday of Advent. Choose this year's reading. Read and discuss it with your family.

Year A: Matthew 24:37–44

Year B: Mark 13:33–37

Year C: Luke 21:25–28, 34–36

All families have a history and a story to tell. All the people who are part of your family history make up your family tree—your parents, brothers and sisters, grandparents, aunts, uncles, and family members who lived generations ago.

The Family Tree of Jesus

Jesus has a family tree too. We Christians use it to help us celebrate Advent. We call it the Jesse tree. The tree is named for Jesse, a shepherd from Bethlehem. He lived about one thousand years before Jesus.

Jesse was the father of David, who grew up to be the greatest king of the people of Israel. David is an ancestor of Jesus.

During Advent we remember the people—like Jesse and David—who are part of Jesus' family tree. We decorate the Jesse tree with symbols of these Old and New Testament figures. The Jesse tree is like our family tree. Each person on the Jesse tree is part of the long story of God's loving plan of salvation that is fulfilled in Jesus.

Remembering the faith stories of the people on the Jesse tree helps us remember God's great love for us—and for all people.

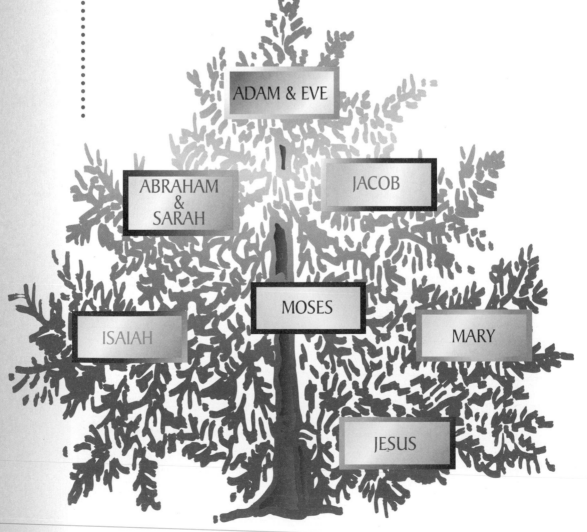

ADAM & EVE

ABRAHAM & SARAH

JACOB

MOSES

ISAIAH

MARY

JESUS

Remembering
the Story of Salvation

Make your own Jesse tree. You can use a small evergreen tree or just some branches. Make a symbol for each of these figures. Add others of your own. Put the symbols on your Jesse tree.

When **Adam** and **Eve** refused to obey,
God promised a savior would come some day.

Noah is a man to note;
while others laughed he built a boat.

Abraham and **Sarah** obeyed God's call.
Their faith is an example for one and for all.

When **Isaac** was born, Sarah was old.
Her laughter rang out, so we are told.

Isaac's son, **Jacob,** was rich and able;
soon twelve healthy sons sat at his table.

Joseph saved his family from starvation.
In Egypt they grew into a very strong nation.

Moses, leader and man of God,
led Israel through the Red Sea dryshod.

David, the Lord's shepherd and king,
could rule, protect, play, and sing.

Isaiah was one who spoke for his Lord.
The faithful listened to every word.

John the Baptizer's announcement was clear.
"Prepare the way! The Lord draws near!"

On **Mary** God's blessings were abundantly poured.
Yes was her response to the angel of the Lord.

Joseph cared for Mary as he promised he would,
Joseph the mild, the patient, the good.

Angels came and shepherds adored,
Jesus is born, our Savior and Lord!

To Help You Remember

1. What is a Jesse tree?

2. How does using a Jesse tree help us celebrate Advent?

3. What can you do to celebrate Advent?

Faith Focus

What do we prepare for during Advent?

The Word of the Lord

These are the gospel readings for the Second Sunday of Advent. Choose this year's reading. Read and discuss it with your family.

Year A: Matthew 3:1–12

Year B: Mark 1:1–8

Year C: Luke 3:1–6

As we prepare for something wonderful in our life, we experience many different feelings. We feel excitement and anticipation. We feel happiness and joy. We can hardly wait for the wonderful time that is to come!

The Lord's Coming

During Advent we prepare for our celebration of the birth of Jesus. We remember that the Son of God took on flesh and lived among us. Our faith tells us that this coming of the Son of God among us is a sign that he is with us each moment of every day.

During Advent we make room for the Lord in our lives and hearts. We pray with Mary and Joseph as they prepare to welcome Jesus into their family.

On Christmas Eve, the last day of Advent, we listen to the Scripture and God speaks to us about that great day, the birth of Jesus the King and Savior promised to David. We pray:

Come, Lord Jesus,
do not delay.
FROM OPENING PRAYER
MASS IN THE MORNING
DECEMBER 24

When we faithfully keep the Advent season, we are ready to welcome Jesus on Christmas Day. Peace rules our hearts and our homes. Peace rules the earth. God's Promised One has come.

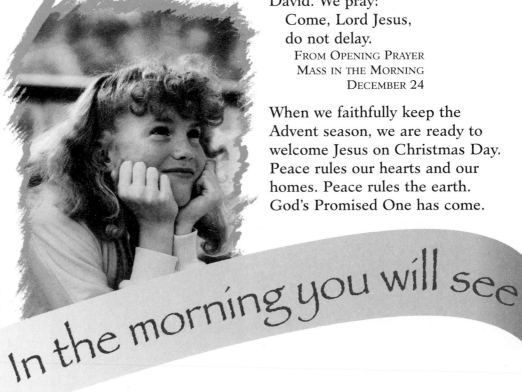

In the morning you will see

The Lord Is Near

"Rejoice in the Lord always. I shall say it again: rejoice! Your kindness should be known to all. The Lord is near" (Philippians 4:4–5).

Joy is a gift of a loving person. Joy is yours to keep and yours to spread. Tell how your presence and actions spread joy during Advent.

_____

_____

_____

_____

_____

_____

_____

_____

To Help You Remember

1. What do we prepare for during Advent?

2. How can you make room in your life and heart for Christ during Advent?

the glory of the Lord.

Faith Focus

How does celebrating Advent strengthen our faith in Jesus' presence with us?

The Word of the Lord

These are the gospel readings for the Third Sunday of Advent. Choose this year's reading. Read and discuss it with your family.

Year A: Matthew 11:2–11

Year B: John 1:6–8, 19–28

Year C: Luke 3:10–18

Day of the Lord

With joy we welcome new people into our lives. We may prepare for them by cooking special foods and sharing a meal with them. Advent is the time the Church helps us get ready to welcome Jesus. We pray:

Father of our Lord Jesus
    Christ,
ever faithful to your promises
and ever close to your Church:
the earth rejoices in hope of
    the Savior's coming
and looks forward with longing
to his return at the end
    of time.

FROM ALTERNATIVE OPENING PRAYER
THIRD SUNDAY OF ADVENT

Advent reminds us of three things:

- The Lord comes in history at Christmas.
- The Lord comes in mystery each day.
- The Lord comes in majesty at the end of time.

The prophets of the Old Testament often used the phrase *day of the Lord* to describe the Lord's coming. Through the prophets, God encouraged the people of Israel to seek out and welcome his Promised One.

Through the prophet Isaiah, God described a day when the Messiah, the Promised One, would come (Isaiah 11:6–9). Then even enemies would come and live together in peace.

All throughout Advent the Church recalls Israel's waiting for the coming of the Lord. Our hearts are filled with the hope of the prophet Zephaniah:

Shout for joy, O daughter Zion!
    sing joyfully, O Israel!
The LORD, your God, is in
    your midst,
    a mighty savior;
He will rejoice over you with
    gladness,
    and renew you in his love.

ZEPHANIAH 3:14, 17

We believe that Jesus is our Lord and the promised Messiah. We remember his birth at Christmas. We also look forward to the time when he will come again in glory.

During Advent we seek to grow more loving day by day. We pray that we will be ready when the Lord comes to welcome us into the kingdom of heaven.

On the Day of the Lord . . .

This rebus will give you an image of the kingdom of peace. Replace each picture with a word. Then look up Isaiah 11:6–9 to see what he wrote.

The shall be the guest of the ,

and the shall lie down with the ;

The calf and the young shall browse together,

with a little to guide them.

The and the shall be neighbors;

together their young shall rest;

the shall eat hay like the .

The shall play by the 's den, . . .

There shall be no harm or ruin on all my holy 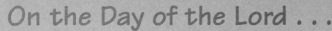;

for the shall be filled with knowledge of the LORD.

Based on Isaiah 11:6-9

To Help You Remember

1. What three things does Advent celebrate?

2. How can you be a sign to others of the kingdom of peace described by Isaiah?

Fourth Week of Advent

What are the gospel stories of the Annunciation and the Visitation?

The Word of the Lord

These are the gospel readings for the Fourth Sunday of Advent. Choose this year's reading. Read and discuss it with your family.

Year A: Matthew 1:18–24

Year B: Luke 1:26–38

Year C: Luke 1:39–45

Stained–glass window depicting the Annunciation.

Stained–glass window depicting the Visitation.

We like to hear stories about our birth: who visited us just after we were born; why our parents gave us our name. We also like to hear stories about when we were infants and toddlers: our first giggle, our first words, our first steps. Our parents know all these stories, and they share them with us.

Stories About Jesus' Birth

The gospel accounts of Luke and Matthew tell us the stories about Jesus' birth and infancy. Both Luke and Matthew tell us the story of the angel Gabriel's announcement of the birth of Jesus. In Luke, we read the story of the angel's announcement to Mary.

She said yes to God and agreed to become the mother of Jesus. We call this announcement to Mary the Annunciation.

In Matthew we read the story of the announcement to Joseph. An angel helped him understand that Mary's child would be the savior promised by God.

Many years before, through the prophet Isaiah, God had announced that "the virgin shall be with child, and bear a son" (Isaiah 7:14). The angel helped Joseph understand that this virgin was Mary.

When the angel asked Joseph to take care of Mary, he agreed and immediately he took her into his home.

During Advent Christians listen to these stories and remember the events. These events help us celebrate Advent.

Luke's account of the Gospel also tells us the story of Zechariah and Elizabeth. For a long time they had prayed for a child. God heard their prayer, and Elizabeth gave birth to a son, who they named John.

Zechariah praised God for their son and announced John's future work: "And you, child, will be called prophet of the Most High, for you will go before the Lord to prepare his ways"(Luke 1:76).

After Mary learned about Zechariah and Elizabeth's good news, she went to visit them. We call this story the Visitation. When Mary visited her cousin, Elizabeth said, "Most blessed are you among women" (Luke 1:42).

To Help You Remember

1. How did God prepare Mary and Joseph for the birth of Jesus?

2. How are you preparing for our celebration of the birth of Jesus?

Praying the Story of Mary

The story of the Annunciation also became a prayer called the Angelus. This prayer is customarily said three times a day: morning, noon, and night. Take the time to pray it now.

Leader: The angel spoke God's message to Mary,

All: and she conceived of the Holy Spirit.
Hail, Mary . . .

Leader: "I am the lowly servant of the Lord:

All: let it be done to me according to your word."
Hail, Mary . . .

Leader: And the Word became flesh

All: and lived among us.
Hail, Mary . . .

Leader: Pray for us, holy Mother of God,

All: that we may become worthy of the promises of Christ.

Leader: Let us pray.
Lord,
fill our hearts with your grace:
once, through the message of an angel
you revealed to us the incarnation of your Son;
now, through his suffering and death
lead us to the glory of his resurrection.
We ask this through Christ our Lord.

All: Amen.

The First Week of Christmas

Shepherds First

Sometimes the people in our lives surprise us. They do something we do not expect. When that happens, we learn a new thing about them. What happened on the night Jesus was born tells us something new about him.

Luke's account of the Gospel includes the announcement of the birth of Jesus to the shepherds. They were the first to receive the good news of Jesus' birth. As the shepherds watched their sheep, an angel appeared to them and said:

> "[T]oday in the city of David a savior has been born for you who is Messiah and Lord."　Luke 2:11

The shepherds hurried to Bethlehem. There they found Jesus and Mary and Joseph as the angel said they would.

Throughout the history of Israel, the writers of the Sacred Scriptures used the image of shepherds to speak about God. For the Israelites God was a shepherd who watched over them, his sheep. They often prayed:

> "The Lord is my shepherd."　Psalm 23:1

However, at the time of Jesus' birth many people thought that shepherds were of little worth. Their hard, dangerous work kept them in the fields day and night. This meant that they were unable to observe religious practices. Because of this, religious leaders thought shepherds were unfaithful, unimportant people.

But it was to shepherds, Luke tells us, that God announced the birth of the Savior. Jesus is the Messiah and Lord of all.

The Lord Is Our Shepherd

For each letter of the word *shepherds*, write a word or phrase that tells us about who Jesus is. Then use your words and phrases and write a paragraph telling others about Jesus.

To Help You Remember

1. What did the angel tell the shepherds?

2. What can you do to share the good news of Jesus' birth with others?

The Second Week of Christmas

Faith Focus

How does the Church honor Mary during the Christmas season?

The Word of the Lord

These are the readings for the Solemnity of Mary, the Mother of God. Read and discuss them with your family.

First Reading:
Numbers 6:22–27

Second Reading:
Galatians 4:4–7

Gospel:
Luke 2:16–21

Each year on Mother's Day we honor our mother. We thank her for taking us to the soccer game. We thank her for cooking our meals and for working to clothe us. We thank her for her love each day of the year. What are some other special times when you honor your mother?

Mary, Mother of God

The Church honors Mary, the Mother of God, many times during the year. During the Christmas season we think about Mary in a special way.

While the celebration of the birth of Jesus is at the heart of our Christmas season, we also celebrate the feast of the Holy Family between Christmas and January 1. At our celebration of Mass on that day, we pray that through Mary's prayers and the prayers of her husband, Joseph, our families may live in peace and love.

The Church also sets aside the first day of the new year, January 1, as the Solemnity of Mary, the Mother of God. On this holy day and holiday, we gather to celebrate Mass. We ask God to bless our new year. We ask that Mary's prayer and her motherly love bring us joy forever.

By remembering Mary as the Mother of God and our mother too, we begin the year with blessings. Mary reminds us of what the whole Church desires to do. We all want to say yes to God as she did. We all want to do God's will all our life, just as Mary did.

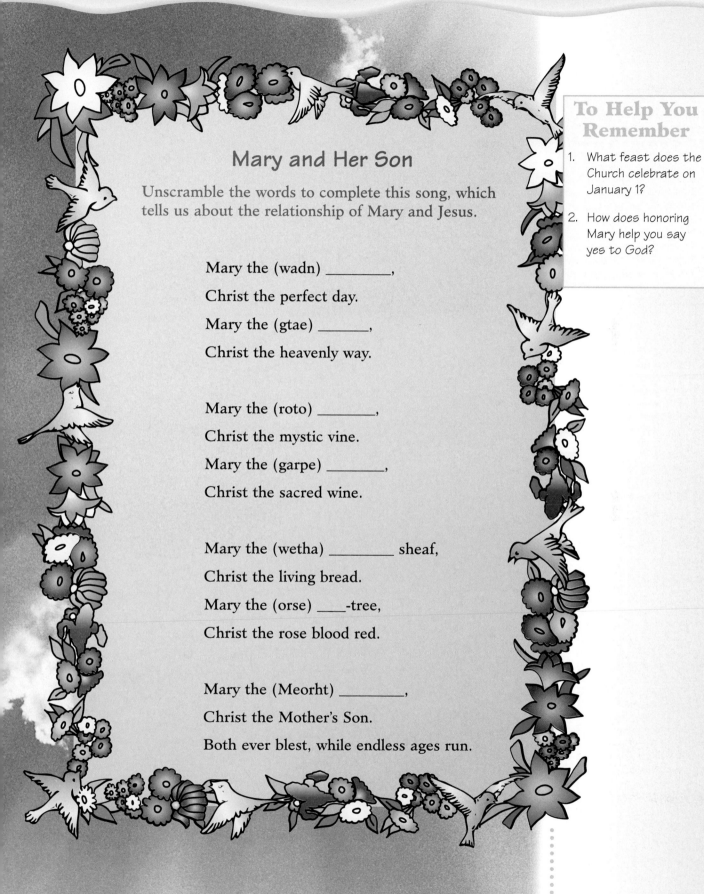

Mary and Her Son

Unscramble the words to complete this song, which tells us about the relationship of Mary and Jesus.

Mary the (wadn) _____,

Christ the perfect day.

Mary the (gtae) _____,

Christ the heavenly way.

Mary the (roto) _____,

Christ the mystic vine.

Mary the (garpe) _____,

Christ the sacred wine.

Mary the (wetha) _____ sheaf,

Christ the living bread.

Mary the (orse) ____-tree,

Christ the rose blood red.

Mary the (Meorht) _____,

Christ the Mother's Son.

Both ever blest, while endless ages run.

To Help You Remember

1. What feast does the Church celebrate on January 1?

2. How does honoring Mary help you say yes to God?

The First Week of Lent

Faith Focus

What are we called to do during Lent?

The Word of the Lord

Choose this year's gospel reading for the First Sunday of Lent. Read and discuss it with your family.

Year A: Matthew 4:1–11

Year B: Mark 1:12–15

Year C: Luke 4:1–13

What You See

In our churches we see signs that Lent is a season of discipline. The color of Lent is purple, the color of penitence. No flowers or brightly colored decorations greet us. We sing no joyous Alleluia and Gloria.

Lent

For many of us, the winter landscape seems bare. Leaves fall from trees, flowers die, and grass turns brown. But we trust that after winter, spring will come and bring new life. Each year during Lent we renew the new life of Christ we received in Baptism.

Lent begins on Ash Wednesday. On Ash Wednesday the Church gathers to begin our Lenten journey. As ashes are placed on our head, we hear the words:

> Turn away from sin and be faithful to the Gospel.

During Lent the Church calls us to enter more fully into Jesus' death and resurrection. We make sacrifices to do this. We may decide to share more of our time and talents with others. We may give up something that we enjoy. We want habits of goodness to live in us. We support one another in our decisions during Lent. Together we look forward to celebrating the joy of Easter.

Take Up Your Cross

Introduction

LEADER: During Lent we walk with Jesus. We hope to share in his resurrection at Easter.

The Word of God

READER: (Mark 10:35–45)

LEADER: Jesus looked ahead at the cross he would bear.
Are you willing to take up your small cross this Lent?

ALL: We are.

Lenten Commitment

LEADER: Let us pause and decide on one thing we know we need to do to be more like Jesus. [Pause.]

As I call your name, please come forward.

_____, will you strive to take up your Lenten cross and follow Jesus?

STUDENT: I will.

Closing Prayer

LEADER: May the cross of Christ remind us to open our mind and heart to God.

ALL: Amen!

LEADER: May we all walk with Jesus and enter into the joy of Easter.

ALL: Amen!

LEADER: May we pray for one another. May we support one another as we take up our cross as a sign of our love of Jesus, who carried his cross because of his love for us.

ALL: Amen!

To Help You Remember

1. What words are used when we are signed with ashes on Ash Wednesday?

2. What will you do during Lent to grow in your love for God and others?

Faith Focus

How did God show his compassion through Jesus?

The Word of the Lord

Choose this year's gospel reading for the Second Sunday of Lent. Read and discuss it with your family.

Year A: Matthew 17:1–9

Year B: Mark 9:2–10

Year C: Luke 9:28–36

What You Hear

During Lent only a psalm verse is used before the gospel reading. The Alleluia that is sung in every season outside of Lent is not said or sung.

When something sad or bad happens to someone we love, we feel compassion for that person. The word *compassion* means "to suffer with" another person. Can you remember a time you felt the suffering of another person?

The Compassion of God

The story of Jesus is the story of a man of compassion. When we see the compassion of Jesus, we see God's compassion for us. At the beginning of his public ministry, Jesus urged his followers to be filled with compassion, just as their heavenly Father was filled with compassion (Luke 6:36). All through his life, Jesus suffered with the suffering people who came to him for healing and forgiveness.

Toward the end of his life, Jesus looked over the city of Jerusalem. Deeply saddened that so many people turned away from God, he wept and prayed:

"Jerusalem, . . . how many times I yearned to gather your children together, as a hen gathers her young under her wings, but you were unwilling!"

MATTHEW 23:37

During the season of Lent the Church invites us to imitate the compassion of God. He asks us to reach out to those who need our help. Find out what your parish is doing during Lent to help others. Join with other parishioners so others can know the compassion of God by the way you treat them.

To Help You Remember

1. What does the word compassion mean?

2. How can you show compassion to others?

The Lord Is Compassionate

LEADER: Bless the Lord, O my soul.

ALL: Bless the Lord, O my soul.

BOYS: Bless the Lord, O my soul; bless the Lord, all my being.

GIRLS: Bless the Lord, O my soul; never forget the Lord's greatness.

BOYS: The Lord pardons our offenses and heals our ills.

GIRLS: The Lord redeems us from death and crowns us with goodness and compassion.

BOYS: The Lord fills us with good and renews our strength like the eagle's.

GIRLS: The Lord upholds the poor; the Lord guards the oppressed.

BOYS: Merciful and gracious is the Lord, slow to anger, quick to bless.

GIRLS: The Lord does not treat us with anger; the Lord treats us with mercy and compassion.

BOYS: As high as the heavens are above the earth, so is God abundant in mercy.

GIRLS: Just as parents are compassionate toward their children, so the Lord is compassionate toward those who show reverence to him.

BOYS: The compassion of the Lord lasts forever.

LEADER: May the Lord have compassion on us.

ALL: Bless the Lord, O my soul. Amen.

The Third Week of Lent

Faith Focus

What does praying make us more aware of?

The Word of the Lord

Choose this year's gospel reading for the Third Sunday of Lent. Read and discuss it with your family.

Year A: John 4:5–42 or John 4:5–15, 19–26, 39, 40–44

Year B: John 2:13–25

Year C: Luke 13:1–9

We like to spend time with our friends, talking and playing and laughing together. But most of us like to spend time alone too. We enjoy a quiet moment to think our own thoughts.

God Is Near

One friend who is with us all the time is God. Faith tells us that God is always near. Prayer helps us become more aware of how close God is to us. Sometimes we pray with others; sometimes we pray alone in the quiet of our heart.

When we pray together, we are sometimes silent together. In fact, our prayer together includes and depends on moments of silence. In silence, we are better able to pay close attention to God. The psalmist tells us:

> Be still before the Lord; wait for God.
>
> PSALM 37:7

During Lent we sharpen our awareness of how Jesus taught us to pray. Jesus told us to pray quietly without drawing attention to ourselves. He taught us that prayer should be a normal part of our life. He taught us to pray and to trust that God is near and listens to our prayer.

Lent is a good time to resolve to pray frequently. In prayer you draw near to God, who is always near to you.

Be Still and Wait for God

Pray this prayer together. Then choose one of the petitions and make a bookmark as a reminder to pray always.

LEADER: Let us come together and worship the Lord, our God, who is always near.

ALL: Be still before the Lord; wait for God.

LEADER: Let us pray for peace in the world.

ALL: Be still before the Lord; wait for God.

LEADER: Let us pray for those who are doing good works during Lent.

ALL: Be still before the Lord; wait for God.

LEADER: Let us pray to continue our own prayers and good works during Lent.

ALL: Be still before the Lord; wait for God.

LEADER: Lord, hear our prayer that we may be ready to celebrate Easter. We ask this in Jesus' name. Amen.

To Help You Remember

1. Why do we pray together as God's people?

2. When can you pray alone each day? Pick a time and do it often during Lent.

Faith Focus

Why do we give things up during Lent?

The Word of the Lord

Choose this year's gospel reading for the Fourth Sunday of Lent. Read and discuss it with your family.

Year A: John 9:1–41 or John 9:1, 6–9, 13–17, 34–38

Year B: John 3:14–21

Year C: Luke 15:1–3, 11–32

Sometimes we enjoy giving our time to help others. But giving time to others is not always easy. Sometimes we enjoy giving up something that matters to us when someone else needs it. But that is not always easy either.

Giving and Giving Up

During Lent the Church invites us to give to others. To give a little more is called almsgiving. Long ago an alms was an amount of money. Almsgiving today includes sharing our time, talents, and goods, as well as our money, with others.

Fasting is another way of doing penance or giving something up for a greater good. When we fast, we voluntarily give up food for a certain amount of time. Following the example of Christ, who fasted often, this practice has long been a part of Catholic tradition. Lent, and each Friday of the year, in honor of Jesus' death, are special times of fasting in the Church. On Ash Wednesday and Good Friday, Catholics, between the ages of 18 and 59, fast by eating only one full meal a day. Fasting can help us make up for our sins and deepen our relationship with God, and others. Some people fast in order to identify more closely with the poor and hungry of the world.

But, we can think of fasting in a bigger way. Fasting can include giving up bad habits, such as: eating and drinking unhealthy foods, or giving up our greedy desires.

In Jesus' time, Jerusalem was a city surrounded by a wall. The people there called one of its narrow gates the "Eye of a Needle." So when a rich man asked Jesus what he had to do to get to heaven, Jesus told a parable about a camel passing through the eye of a needle. The camel carried so much baggage on its back that it could not get through the narrow gateway.

In this story Jesus reminds us that things we have can sometimes get in our way on our journey to God. Jesus told the man to give away what he had and follow Jesus. But the man couldn't do it. He went away sad. Remembering this story during Lent helps us remember to share our possessions with others. This is one way we can live as Jesus wants us to live.

To Help You Remember

1. What did Jesus tell the rich man?

2. Choose a possession that would be hard for you to give away. Then share it with someone.

Living God's Message

Write about someone you know who gives possessions or time to help people.

_____

_____

_____

_____

_____

_____

Faith Focus

What does Jesus teach us about repentance?

The Word of the Lord

Choose this year's gospel reading for the Fifth Sunday of Lent. Read and discuss it with your family.

Year A: John 11:1–45 or John 11:3–7, 17, 20–27, 33–45

Year B: John 12:20–33

Year C: John 8:1–11

Think of a time you have hurt someone you really care about. How did you feel? What did you want to do? We just want to be forgiven. We wish we had never hurt our friend. We just want things to be fixed. We want to change.

Turn and Live

Jesus told us over and over again that God always forgives us. He always wants things to be just right between himself and us.

What we need to do is to trust God and repent. We need to turn *from* unloving and hurtful words, actions, and attitudes. We need to turn *to* loving words, actions, and attitudes that bring harmony and life.

In the parable of the Good Shepherd, Jesus told of a shepherd who searched for a single lost sheep. The shepherds of Israel often faced great danger from howling hyenas, baying wolves, sly jackals, and sharp-toothed bears. When a sheep wandered away, the shepherd went out to battle these wild animals and rescue the one who had strayed.

In his parable Jesus said that as the good shepherd in the parable, he would risk his life for his sheep. He is our Good Shepherd, and we are his sheep.

We stray when we sin. Jesus will come after us. He will come in search of us to forgive us and bring us home.

During Lent we celebrate the sacrament of Reconciliation. We recognize and admit our hurtful actions. We confess our sins.

These special celebrations are the welcoming arms of Jesus today. The sacrament of Reconciliation is the Church's way of helping us choose life with God and with one another in harmony and community.

A Litany of Repentance

LEADER: Lord, you announced the good news of God's love for us.

ALL: Lord, have mercy.

LEADER: You announced the coming of the kingdom of God.

ALL: Lord, have mercy.

LEADER: You preached a message of repentance.

ALL: Lord, have mercy.

LEADER: You forgave and healed the sinful man who could not walk.

ALL: Lord, have mercy.

LEADER: You invited the tax collectors Levi and Zacchaeus and the good thief into the kingdom.

ALL: Lord, have mercy.

LEADER: You forgave the woman who sinned.

ALL: Lord, have mercy.

LEADER: You will surely forgive us our sins, especially . . . [Pause.] Help us forgive others as abundantly as you forgive us.

ALL: Lord, have mercy.

To Help You Remember

1. How did Jesus use the parable of the Good Shepherd to explain the sacrament of Reconciliation?

2. During Lent how does the Church help you choose life with God?

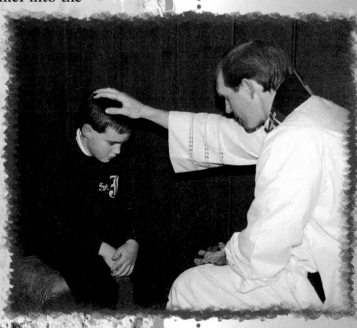

299

Palm Sunday of the Lord's Passion

Faith Focus

Why do we celebrate Palm Sunday of the Lord's Passion?

The Word of the Lord

Choose this year's gospel reading for Palm Sunday of the Lord's Passion. Read and discuss it with your family.

Year A: Matthew 26:14–27, 66 or 27:11–54

Year B: Mark 14:1–15, 47 or 15:1–39

Year C: Luke 22:14–23, 56 or 23:1–49

Holy Week

When a well-known person comes to your school or town, you welcome them with a marching band and banners and balloons. When Jesus entered the city of Jerusalem, the people gave him a special welcome.

On that day, the people of Jerusalem welcomed Jesus as a messiah. He did not ride on a mighty horse or in a gilded chariot as a great soldier or a conquering hero. Jesus entered Jerusalem riding a donkey. But as he entered the people cheered as they would a great king:

"Hosanna to the Son of David; blessed is he who comes in the name of the Lord; hosanna in the highest."

MATTHEW 21:9

The people prayed *Hosanna*, which means "Lord, grant salvation."

The people spread cloaks on the road to make the path smooth and less dusty for Jesus. They waved branches taken from palm trees. This welcome of Jesus, as the Messiah riding on a donkey, reminds us that Jesus is the king of everyone, even the lowly. Jesus is a king filled with compassion and care.

The celebration of Palm Sunday begins Holy Week. We begin our celebration with a procession. Everyone walks into Church carrying palm branches. This recalls the day Jesus rode into Jerusalem.

To Help You Remember

1. How did the people welcome Jesus when he came into Jerusalem?

2. Explain how your parish celebrates Palm Sunday of the Lord's Passion.

Hosanna! A Meditation

Sit quietly.

Close your eyes and breathe slowly.

Remember the story of Jesus' entry into Jerusalem.

Compare the meaning of this story to your own life and share your thoughts with Jesus.

After a few quiet moments, write down any key words or phrases that will help you remember this prayer experience.

A time of hope, love, faith in Jesus God + saints, a time of Hosanna. Where people help people

Triduum / Holy Thursday

Faith Focus

What do we remember as the Church celebrates Holy Thursday?

The Word of the Lord

Choose one of the Scripture readings for Holy Thursday. Read and discuss it with your family.

Reading I: Exodus 12:1–8, 11–14

Reading II: 1 Corinthians 11:23–26

Gospel: John 13:1–15

The Last Supper by 20th century Brazilian painter Mimida Roveda.

Do you remember eating a special meal with your family or your friends? What made it special to you? Did you eat special food? Did someone say something that made you feel good about yourself? The Church remembers a special meal that Jesus ate with his disciples.

Do This in Memory of Me

On the evening of Holy Thursday, we remember the last time Jesus gathered the disciples and shared a meal with them. This meal celebrated the Passover. On this special day, the Jewish people celebrate their passage from slavery in Egypt to freedom. They remember their covenant with God.

All his life Jesus celebrated this greatest of Jewish feasts with his family and friends. Now he shared the foods of the Passover for the last time. But at this Last Supper, Jesus did something special. Jesus changed the bread and wine he shared with his disciples into his own Body and Blood. He took the bread and broke it and said,

> "This is my body, which will be given for you."
>
> LUKE 22:19

After the meal, he passed the cup of wine for them to drink. He said,

> "This cup is the new covenant in my blood, which will be shed for you."
>
> LUKE 22:20

Jesus then commanded his disciples to share this meal with one another. He said,

> "Do this in memory of me."
>
> LUKE 22:19

Today, at the celebration of the Eucharist, the Church continues to do what Jesus asked his disciples to do. On Holy Thursday we especially remember his last Passover. We call our celebration on that day the Mass of the Lord's Supper.

The Lord's Supper

Create an announcement inviting the people of your parish to join in celebrating the Mass of the Lord's Supper.

All are invited to join the Lord's supper. It's one that's very special. It will be his last. So come and bless this day with him. All who wish to come can come. Please be there in memory of him

Thank you!

Triduum / Good Friday

Faith Focus

How does the Church remember the death of Jesus?

The Word of the Lord

Choose one of the Scripture readings for Good Friday. Read and discuss it with your family.

Reading I: Isaiah 52:13–53:12

Reading II: Hebrews 4:14–16, 5:7–9

Gospel: John 18:1–19, 42

At some time in your life, someone you love will die. This may have already happened to you. You know that when this happens, everyone in your house is sad. People tell stories about the one who has died. The Church does this too as it remembers the death of Jesus.

Good Friday

On Good Friday our churches have no decorations. The tabernacle is empty; its door is open. There is no altar cloth covering the altar table. The Church gathers to reflect on the passion and death of Jesus.

Our liturgy on Good Friday is called the celebration of the Lord's Passion. It is made up of three parts:

- The first part is the Liturgy of the Word. The gospel reading is a proclamation of the passion and death of Jesus according to John. After the gospel proclamation, the Church invites us to pray for the needs of the world.

- The second part of the celebration of the Lord's Passion is the Veneration of the Cross. In this part of the liturgy, we show reverence and respect for the cross because Jesus died for us on a cross. We might do this by walking in procession; bowing before the cross, and kissing it.

- The third part of the celebration of the Lord's Passion is Holy Communion. The Church invites us to receive the Body and Blood of Christ, which was consecrated at Mass on Holy Thursday.

The celebration of the Lord's Passion ends as it began. The altar cloth is removed from the altar and the tabernacle is empty. In deep silence we leave to begin the long sabbath rest until the celebration of the Easter Vigil.

Each day you do many things to show your love for God and others as Jesus did. You make sacrifices. You give your time. You share your gifts. You take up your cross and follow Jesus as he asked you to do.

What I didn't do to the person

Helped clean the house a little little

My mom didn't have to do so much when her back was hurting

helped someone did with good work

Jesus Asks, You Respond

On one of the beams of this cross, describe something you did for someone. On the other cross beam, describe how it helped the person.

Faith Focus

Why is the Easter season a time of rejoicing?

The Word of the Lord

Choose the gospel readings for Easter Sunday this year. Read and discuss them with your family.

Year A: John 20:1–9 or
Matthew 28:1–10 or
Luke 24:13–35

Year B: John 20:1–9 or
Matthew 16:1–7 or
Luke 24:13–35

Year C: John 20:1–9 or
Luke 24:1–12 or
Luke 24:13–35

Alleluia

On our best days, we feel great joy just to be alive. We can do many wonderful things. Easter is a wonderful day in the Church—a day when we rejoice because God has raised Jesus to new life.

Saint Augustine reminds us that we are Easter people and Alleluia is our song. *Alleluia* is a Hebrew word that means "Praise the Lord." At the Easter Vigil the presider solemnly intones the Alleluia, which we have not heard all during Lent. The Church sings, "Alleluia!" repeatedly during the Easter season. We continuously thank and praise God for the new life of Easter. We praise God because we have passed from death to life through our baptism.

Throughout Lent we focused on turning away from sin to become followers of Jesus. During the Easter season we rejoice in our new life in Christ. We sing Alleluia and proclaim, "This is the day the LORD has made, let us rejoice and be glad in it."

To Help You Remember

1. What do we celebrate during Easter?

2. How can Christians be Easter people all year long?

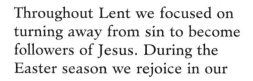

Celebrating Easter

Write a cinquain to celebrate Easter.

Title	**Easter**
Write two words that describe the title.	_____ _____
Write three action words that describe the title.	_____ _____ _____
Write four words that tell a feeling about the title.	_____ _____ _____ _____
Write another word for the title.	_____

The Second Week of Easter

Faith Focus

How does the story of Thomas remind us of our gift of faith?

The Word of the Lord

This is the gospel reading for the Second Sunday of Easter. Read and discuss it with your family.

John 20:19–31

When someone tells us about an event they have witnessed, we believe them. We believe them because they were there.

Thomas' Profession of Faith

When Jesus first appeared to the disciples, Thomas was not with them. The disciples told Thomas that Jesus appeared to them, but Thomas refused to believe them.

He said he would believe only when he saw the Risen Jesus himself—when he could see Jesus' wounds. This refusal of Thomas to believe the other disciples has become so famous that someone who demands evidence before they believe others is now called a "doubting Thomas."

John's account of the Gospel tells us that a week later the Risen Jesus again appeared to his disciples. This time Thomas was with them. Jesus showed Thomas his wounds and said to him:

"[D]o not be unbelieving, but believe." JOHN 20:27

Thomas answered:

"My Lord and my God!" JOHN 20:28

He then became a strong believer in Jesus, the Risen Lord.

We believe that Jesus was raised from the dead and lives in a new way. This is a gift of faith.

To Help You Remember

1. What was Thomas's answer when Jesus asked him to believe?

2. How can you show that you believe in the Risen Jesus?

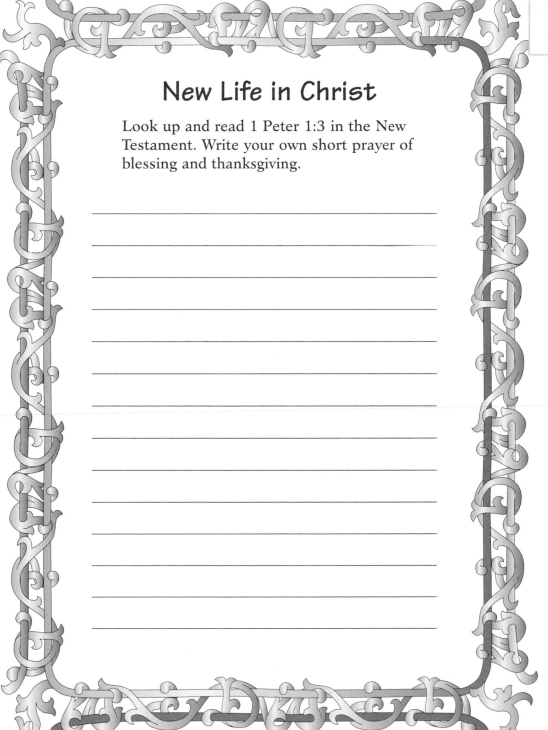

New Life in Christ

Look up and read 1 Peter 1:3 in the New Testament. Write your own short prayer of blessing and thanksgiving.

_____

_____

_____

_____

_____

_____

_____

_____

_____

_____

_____

_____

_____

The Third Week of Easter

Called and Sent

At home, most of us have chores to do. Our tasks help all our family members and create happiness and harmony within our family. The Gospel tells us that Jesus asks the members of the church family to serve one another:

> "[A]s I have done for you, you should also do."
> JOHN 13:15

The Gospel clearly tells us that Jesus told the apostles that they were to serve others and not want to be served. This was a new type of leadership. It was the way Jesus taught them to live through his own life. They were to lead as he led as a good shepherd.

Today bishops are ordained to serve the Church as Christ served others. They are called to serve as Peter and the other apostles did. All the baptized are also called to live a life in service of others. This service is lived out daily in our homes, in our schools, and in our communities. Each day is filled with opportunities to serve others as Jesus asked us to do.

Faith Focus

How do members of the Church serve one another?

The Word of the Lord

Choose the gospel reading for the Third Sunday of Easter this year. Read and discuss it with your family.

Year A: Luke 24:13–35

Year B: Luke 24:35–48

Year C: John 21:1–19 or 21:1–14

To Help You Remember

1. How did Peter serve the Church?

2. Who are some of the people in your church who share the work of your parish?

Live to Serve

Look at the photos on these pages. Think about how you might live Jesus' command to serve others. Write down some of your ideas. Then choose one and do it.

_____

_____

_____

_____

_____

_____

_____

_____

The Fourth Week of Easter

The Word of the Lord

Choose this year's gospel reading for the Fourth Sunday of Easter. Read and discuss it with your family.

Year A: John 10:1–10

Year B: John 10:11–18

Year C: John 10:27–30

Water tastes so good on a hot day when we have been outside playing hard. It makes us feel new again.

Water Brings Us Life

At the Easter Vigil, the presider blesses water. The prayers of this blessing remind us of waters that brought life to God's people throughout their history. We celebrate that life when we bless ourselves with holy water.

In the beginning, God created the vast seas and the rains that nourish the earth and all its creatures. God led the Hebrews to freedom through the waters of the Red Sea. God brought refreshing waters as his people wandered in the dry, stony desert.

The prophet Ezekiel spoke of water when he wrote of a new covenant between the people and God:

"I will sprinkle clean
     water upon you . . .
I will cleanse you.
I will give you a
     new heart and
     place a new spirit
     within you. . . .
[Y]ou shall be my
     people, and I will
     be your God."

EZEKIEL 36: 25–26, 28

The blessing of water at the Easter Vigil also recalls Jesus' baptism in the Jordan River. Water reminds us of our baptism in the death and resurrection of Jesus. It reminds us of how we are made new again through the death and resurrection of Jesus.

To Help You Remember

1. What does the blessing of water at the Easter Vigil recall?

2. How can water remind you of your baptism?

Water and New Life

Write chapter titles for a book. The titles should remind us of the times that water brought life to God's people.

The Fifth Week of Easter

Faith Focus

How can we learn from the early Church to be true followers of Jesus?

The Word of the Lord

Choose this year's gospel reading for the Fifth Sunday of Easter. Read and discuss it with your family.

Year A: John 14:1–12

Year B: John 15:1–8

Year C: John 13:31–35

When we see someone in need, we can talk about what we have seen. Or we can do something for the person in need. The Church calls us to put our words into action.

Love One Another

During the Sundays of Easter, the first reading of the Liturgy of the Word is always from the Acts of the Apostles. These readings tell us how the early Christians put their faith and words into action.

The early Church remembered that on the night before he died, Jesus gave his disciples a new commandment. He said:

> "[L]ove one another. As I have loved you, so you also should love one another. This is how all will know that you are my disciples, if you have love for one another." JOHN 13:34–35

The First Letter of John in the New Testament reminded the early Christians that their love for God must show in their love for one another. If we refuse to love a person we can see, how can we say that we love God, whom we cannot see?

The first followers of Jesus showed this love in many ways. They took care of those who were most in need. They forgave one another.

They welcomed travelers. They gave them food, clothing, and a warm place to live. They prayed for one another. They brought the healing presence of Christ to those who were sick and troubled.

These welcoming and loving followers of Jesus attracted others who wanted to live in this new way. This is still true today. True followers do not simply talk about the good news of Jesus' resurrection. They show their love for one another.

Bless this House

To Help You Remember

1. How did the early followers of Jesus show their love for others?

2. How can you be welcoming and show your love today?

This blessing is found on the door of St. Stephen's Church in London.

O God, make the door of this house wide enough to receive all who need human love and fellowship, narrow enough to shut out all envy, pride, and strife.

Make its threshold smooth enough to be no stumbling block to children, nor to straying feet, but rugged and strong enough to turn back the tempter's power.

God, make the door of this house the gateway to your eternal kingdom.

House Blessing

Write a blessing that you would put on the door of your own house.

_____

_____

_____

_____

_____

_____

_____

_____

_____

The Sixth Week of Easter

Faith Focus

How would the apostles be a witness to Jesus?

The Word of the Lord

Choose this year's gospel reading for the Sixth Sunday of Easter. Read and discuss it with your family.

Year A: John 14:15–21

Year B: John 15:9–17

Year C: John 14:23–29

Ascension of Christ by unknown German painter.

Waiting can be hard. But when someone we love promises to give us something, we trust that the waiting will lead to good things. Jesus' apostles waited for the gift Jesus promised to send them.

Promise of the Spirit

After his resurrection, Jesus appeared to many of his followers. He told them that he would send them the Holy Spirit.

One day, Jesus led the apostles to Bethany outside Jerusalem. He reminded them that he had fulfilled all that was written in the Scriptures: He suffered, died, and was raised to new life.

Jesus reminded the apostles that they had witnessed all that he had done. He told them that they would be his witnesses throughout Judea and Samaria and to the very ends of the earth. They were to tell others about him.

Then Jesus asked them to wait for the coming of the promised Spirit. He then blessed the apostles and returned to his Father in heaven.

Witnessing Today

Read each modern-day saying and look up the matching Scripture passage that tells you how Jesus wants you to be a witness to his life today. Then choose one and make up an ad featuring Jesus' words.

Shop 'til you drop.
Matthew 6:19–21

You can have it all!
Luke 9:57–62

Don't get mad. Get even.
Matthew 5:38–41

Might makes right.
Luke 9:46–48

To Help You Remember

1. What promise did Jesus make to the apostles?

2. How can you witness to the message of Jesus?

The Seventh Week of Easter

Good News!

Christ is risen to new life! Alleluia! During the seven weeks in the Easter season, we praise God with greater joy than ever before. We celebrate new life with the Risen Jesus.

The gospel readings for the seven Sundays of Easter tell us of the appearances Jesus made after his resurrection.

In John's account of the Gospel, we read that Mary Magdalene saw Jesus and proclaimed the good news to the disciples:

"I have seen the Lord."
JOHN 20:18

In Luke's account of the Gospel, we read that two disciples recognized their Risen Lord in the breaking of bread.

Jesus' resurrection is good news for us too. We share in the new life of Jesus' resurrection.

Jesus is our Lord and Savior. Each time we gather for Eucharist we celebrate our faith. We profess our faith in Jesus, our Risen Lord and God.

Faith Focus

What is proclaimed in the gospel readings during the Easter season?

The Word of the Lord

Choose this year's gospel reading for the Seventh Sunday of Easter. Read and discuss it with your family.

Year A: John 17:1–11

Year B: John 17:11–19

Year C: John 17:20–26

Easter

To Help You Remember

1. How did the first witnesses to Jesus know the Risen Lord?

2. What helps you know Jesus?

Alleluia. He Is Risen

Share your Easter Joy.

All: Alleluia. Alleluia. Alleluia.

First Reader: Give thanks to the Lord, for he is good,
for his mercy endures forever.
Let the house of Israel say,
"His mercy endures forever."

All: Alleluia. Alleluia. Alleluia.

Second Reader: The right hand of the Lord has struck
with power;
the right hand of the Lord is exalted.
I shall not die, but live,
and declare the works of the Lord.

All: Alleluia. Alleluia. Alleluia.

Third Reader: The stone which the builders rejected
has become the cornerstone.
By the Lord has this been done;
it is wonderful in our eyes.

All: Alleluia. Alleluia. Alleluia.

Pentecost

Faith Focus

How did the gift of the Holy Spirit on Pentecost strengthen the disciples?

The Word of the Lord

Choose the gospel reading for Pentecost this year. Read and discuss it with your family.

Year A: John 20:19–23

Year B: John 20:19–23 or John 15:26–27, 16:12–15

Year C: John 20:19–23 or John 14:15–16, 23–26

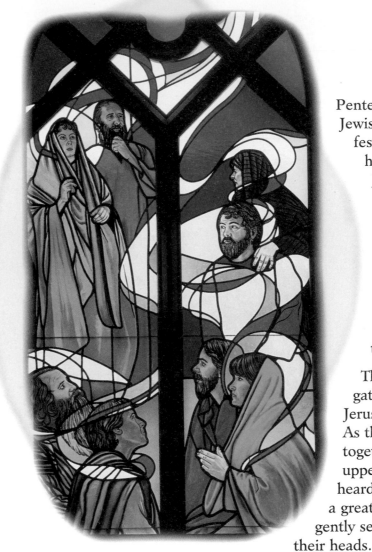

Pentecost is a Jewish harvest festival. On this holy day the Jewish people offer the first fruits of the new harvest to God. At the time of Jesus, Jews traveled to Jerusalem for this great feast.

The disciples gathered in Jerusalem too. As they prayed together in an upper room, they heard the noise of a great wind. Flames gently settled over their heads.

Can you think of a day when you felt as if you could do anything you set your mind to? What had happened to make you feel that way? Did someone say something to you or give you a gift?

The Holy Spirit

The disciples knew a day like that. They received a great gift that made them strong in their belief in the Risen Lord. That day was Pentecost.

They were filled with the Holy Spirit. They felt new and strong. They went out and boldly proclaimed the Risen Lord. As they spoke, all the people in the crowd heard the message in their own language. People who could not understand one another before suddenly did! People who were separated drew together. The Holy Spirit came upon the disciples as Jesus promised. The Church was born. The work of the Church, filled with the Spirit, had begun.

Peter stood up in front of a huge crowd and spoke strongly and courageously of Jesus' life, death, and resurrection. His proclamation ended with the following words:

"Therefore let the whole house of Israel know for certain that God has made him both Lord and Messiah, this Jesus whom you crucified."

ACTS OF THE APOSTLES 2:36

The people asked Peter and the others, "What are we to do, my brothers?" Peter told them to repent, be baptized, and receive the Holy Spirit. From that day forward, they grew into a great people committed to new life in the Risen Lord.

To Help You Remember

1. What did Peter proclaim to the people on Pentecost?

2. How do you proclaim the message of Jesus' resurrection in your life?

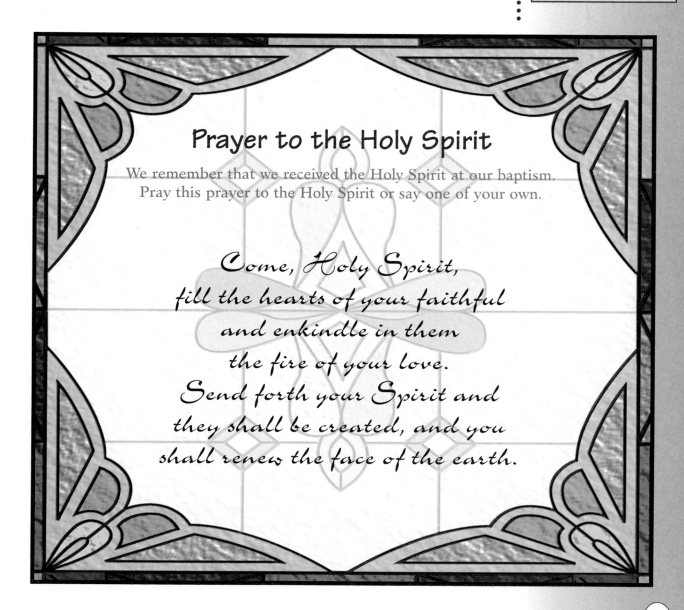

Prayer to the Holy Spirit

We remember that we received the Holy Spirit at our baptism.
Pray this prayer to the Holy Spirit or say one of your own.

Come, Holy Spirit,
fill the hearts of your faithful
and enkindle in them
the fire of your love.
Send forth your Spirit and
they shall be created, and you
shall renew the face of the earth.

Catholic Prayers and Practices

Sign of the Cross

In the name of the Father,
and of the Son,
and of the Holy Spirit. Amen.

Glory Prayer

Glory to the Father,
    and to the Son,
    and to the Holy Spirit:
as it was in the beginning, is now,
    and will be for ever. Amen.

Prayer to the Holy Spirit

Come, Holy Spirit, fill the hearts
    of your faithful.
And kindle in them the
    fire of your love.
Send forth your Spirit and
    they shall be created.
And you will renew the
    face of the earth.

Lord's Prayer

Our Father, who art in heaven,
hallowed be thy name;
Thy kingdom come;
Thy will be done on earth
    as it is in heaven.
Give us this day our daily bread;
and forgive us our trespasses
as we forgive those who trespass
    against us;
and lead us not into temptation,
but deliver us from evil.
Amen.

Hail Mary

Hail Mary, full of grace,
the Lord is with you!
Blessed are you among women,
and blessed is the fruit
    of your womb, Jesus.
Holy Mary, Mother of God,
pray for us sinners,
now and at the hour of our death.
Amen.

Act of Contrition

My God,
I am sorry for my sins
    with all my heart.
In choosing to do wrong
and failing to do good,
I have sinned against you
whom I should love above all things.
I firmly intend, with your help,
to do penance,
to sin no more,
and to avoid whatever leads me to sin.
Our Savior Jesus Christ
suffered and died for us.
In his name, my God, have mercy.

Apostles' Creed

I believe in God,
the Father almighty,
creator of heaven and earth.

I believe in Jesus Christ,
his only Son, our Lord.
He was conceived by the power
of the Holy Spirit
and born of the Virgin Mary.
He suffered under Pontius Pilate,
was crucified, died, and was buried.
He descended to the dead.
On the third day he rose again.

He ascended into heaven,
and is seated at the right hand
of the Father.
He will come again to judge
the living and the dead.

I believe in the Holy Spirit,
the holy catholic Church,
the communion of saints,
the forgiveness of sins,
the resurrection of the body,
and the life everlasting. Amen.

Nicene Creed

We believe in one God,
the Father, the Almighty,
maker of heaven and earth,
of all that is, seen and unseen.

We believe in one Lord, Jesus Christ,
the only Son of God,
eternally begotten of the Father,
God from God, Light from Light,
true God from true God,
begotten, not made, one in Being
with the Father.
Through him all things were made.
For us men and for our salvation
he came down from heaven:

by the power of the Holy Spirit
he was born of the Virgin Mary, and
became man.

For our sake he was crucified under
Pontius Pilate;
he suffered, died, and was buried.

On the third day he rose again
in fulfillment of the Scriptures;
he ascended into heaven
and is seated at the right hand
of the Father.
He will come again in glory to judge
the living and the dead,
and his kingdom will have no end.

We believe in the Holy Spirit, the Lord,
the giver of life,
who proceeds from the Father
and the Son.
With the Father and the Son he is
worshiped and glorified.
He has spoken through the Prophets.
We believe in one holy catholic and
apostolic Church.
We acknowledge one baptism for the
forgiveness of sins.
We look for the resurrection of the dead,
and the life of the world to come.
Amen.

Catholic Prayers and Practices

Rosary

Catholics pray the rosary to honor Mary and remember the important events in the life of Jesus and Mary. There are fifteen mysteries of the rosary. The word *mystery* means "the wonderful things God has done for us."

We begin praying the rosary by praying the Apostles' Creed, the Lord's Prayer, and three Hail Marys. Each mystery of the rosary is prayed by praying the Lord's Prayer once, the Hail Mary ten times, and the Glory Prayer once. When we have finished the last mystery, we pray the Hail, Holy Queen.

Joyful Mysteries

1. The Annunciation
2. The Visitation
3. The Nativity
4. The Presentation
5. The Finding of Jesus in the Temple

Sorrowful Mysteries

6. The Agony in the Garden
7. The Scourging at the Pillar
8. The Crowning with Thorns
9. The Carrying of the Cross
10. The Crucifixion

Glorious Mysteries

11. The Resurrection
12. The Ascension
13. The Coming of the Holy Spirit
14. The Assumption of Mary
15. The Coronation of Mary

Hail, Holy Queen

Hail, holy Queen, mother of mercy,
hail, our life, our sweetness,
 and our hope.
To you we cry, the children of Eve;
to you we send up our sighs,
mourning and weeping
 in this land of exile.
Turn, then, most gracious advocate,
your eyes of mercy toward us;
lead us home at last
and show us the blessed fruit
 of your womb, Jesus:
O clement, O loving, O sweet
 Virgin Mary.

A Vocation Prayer

God, I know you will call me
for special work in my life.
Help me follow Jesus each day
and be ready to answer your call.

The Divine Praises

Blessed be God.
Blessed be his holy name.
Blessed be Jesus Christ, true God and true
man.
Blessed be the name of Jesus.
Blessed be his most sacred heart.
Blessed be his most precious blood.
Blessed be Jesus in the most holy sacrament
of the altar.
Blessed be the Holy Spirit, the Paraclete.
Blessed be the great mother of God, Mary
most holy.
Blessed be her holy and immaculate
conception.
Blessed be her glorious assumption.
Blessed be the name of Mary, virgin and
mother.
Blessed be Saint Joseph, her most chaste
spouse.
Blessed be God in his angels and in his saints.

Grace before Meals

Bless us, O Lord,
   and these your gifts
which we are about to receive
   from your goodness.
Through Christ our Lord.
Amen.

Grace after Meals

We give you thanks for all your gifts,
   almighty God,
living and reigning now and for ever.
Amen.

The Great Commandment

"You shall love the Lord,
your God, with all your
heart, with all your soul,
and with all your mind. . . .
You shall love your neighbor as yourself."

MATTHEW 22:37, 39

The Ten Commandments

1. I am the LORD your God: you shall not
   have strange gods before me.
2. You shall not take the name of the LORD
   your God in vain.
3. Remember to keep holy the
   LORD's Day.
4. Honor your father and your mother.
5. You shall not kill.
6. You shall not commit adultery.
7. You shall not steal.
8. You shall not bear false witness against
   your neighbor.
9. You shall not covet your neighbor's wife.
10. You shall not covet your neighbor's goods.

The Seven Sacraments

Sacraments of Initiation
   Baptism
   Confirmation
   Eucharist

Sacraments of Healing
   Reconciliation
   Anointing of the Sick

**Sacraments at the Service
of Communion**
   Holy Orders
   Matrimony

The Beatitudes

"Blessed are the poor in spirit,
   for theirs is the kingdom of heaven.
Blessed are they who mourn,
   for they will be comforted.
Blessed are the meek,
   for they will inherit the land.
Blessed are they who hunger
      and thirst for righteousness,
   for they will be satisfied.
Blessed are the merciful,
   for they will be shown mercy.
Blessed are the clean of heart,
   for they will see God.
Blessed are the peacemakers,
   for they will be called children of God.
Blessed are they who are persecuted for the
      sake of righteousness,
   for theirs is the kingdom of heaven.
Blessed are you when they insult
      you and persecute you and utter every
      kind of evil against you [falsely]
      because of me.
   Rejoice and be glad, for your reward
      will be great in heaven." MATTHEW 5:3–12

Corporal Works of Mercy

Feed people who are hungry.
Give drink to people who are thirsty.
Clothe people who need clothes.
Visit prisoners.
Shelter people who are homeless.
Visit people who are sick.
Bury people who have died.

Spiritual Works of Mercy

Help people who sin.
Teach people who are ignorant.
Give advice to people who have doubts.
Comfort people who suffer.
Be patient with other people.
Forgive people who hurt you.
Pray for people who are alive and for those
   who have died.

Precepts of the Church

1. Participate in Mass on Sundays and holy days of obligation.
2. Confess sins at least once a year.
3. Receive Holy Communion at least during the Easter season.
4. Keep holy Sunday and the holy days of obligation.
5. Observe the prescribed days of fasting and abstinence.
6. Provide for the material needs of the Church, according to one's abilities.

Gifts of the Holy Spirit

Wisdom
Understanding
Right judgment (Counsel)
Courage (Fortitude)
Knowledge
Reverence (Piety)
Wonder and awe (Fear of the Lord)

Stations of the Cross

1. Jesus is condemned to death.
2. Jesus accepts his cross.
3. Jesus falls the first time.
4. Jesus meets his mother.
5. Simon helps Jesus carry the cross.
6. Veronica wipes the face of Jesus.
7. Jesus falls the second time.
8. Jesus meets the women.
9. Jesus falls the third time.
10. Jesus is stripped of his clothes.
11. Jesus is nailed to the cross.
12. Jesus dies on the cross.
13. Jesus is taken down from the cross.
14. Jesus is buried in the tomb.
15. Jesus is raised from the dead.

Moral Virtues

Prudence
Justice
Fortitude
Temperance

Celebrating Reconciliation

Individual Rite of Reconciliation

Greeting

Scripture Reading

Confession of Sins

Act of Contrition

Absolution

Closing Prayer

Communal Rite of Reconciliation

Greeting

Scripture Reading

Homily

Examination of Conscience with Litany of
Contrition and the Lord's Prayer

Individual Confession and Absolution

Closing Prayer

Celebrating Mass

Introductory Rites

Gathering
Entrance Procession and Hymn
Greeting
Penitential Rite
Gloria
Opening Prayer

Liturgy of the Word

First Reading
(Usually from the Old Testament)
Responsorial Psalm
Second Reading
(Usually from New Testament Letters)
Gospel Acclamation
Gospel
Homily
Creed (Profession of Faith)
General Intercessions

Liturgy of the Eucharist

Preparation of the Altar and Gifts
Prayer Over the Gifts
Eucharistic Prayer
Communion Rite
Lord's Prayer
Sign of Peace
Breaking of Bread
Communion
Prayer After Communion

Concluding Rite

Greeting
Blessing
Dismissal

The Books of the Bible

The Old Testament

Law (Torah) or Pentateuch

Genesis	(Gn)
Exodus	(Ex)
Leviticus	(Lv)
Numbers	(Nm)
Deuteronomy	(Dt)

Historical Books

Joshua	(Jos)
Judges	(Jgs)
Ruth	(Ru)
First Book of Samuel	(1 Sm)
Second Book of Samuel	(2 Sm)
First Book of Kings	(1 Kgs)
Second Book of Kings	(2 Kgs)
First Book of Chronicles	(1 Chr)
Second Book of Chronicles	(2 Chr)
Ezra	(Ezr)
Nehemiah	(Neh)
Tobit	(Tb)
Judith	(Jdt)
Esther	(Est)
First Book of Maccabees	(1 Mc)
Second Book of Maccabees	(2 Mc)

The Poetry and Wisdom Books

Job	(Jb)
Psalms	(Ps)
Proverbs	(Prv)
Ecclesiastes	(Eccl)
Song of Songs	(Sg)
Wisdom	(Wis)
Sirach/Ecclesiasticus	(Sir)

Prophets

Isaiah	(Is)
Jeremiah	(Jer)
Lamentations	(Lam)
Baruch	(Bar)
Ezekiel	(Ez)
Daniel	(Dn)
Hosea	(Hos)
Joel	(Jl)
Amos	(Am)
Obadiah	(Ob)
Jonah	(Jon)
Micah	(Mi)
Naham	(Na)
Habakkuk	(Hb)
Zephaniah	(Zep)
Haggai	(Hg)
Zechariah	(Zec)
Malachi	(Mal)

The New Testament

The Gospels

Matthew	(Mt)
Mark	(Mk)
Luke	(Lk)
John	(Jn)

Early Church

Acts of the Apostles	(Acts)

Letters of Paul and Other Letters

Romans	(Rom)
First Letter to the Corinthians	(1 Cor)
Second Letter to the Corinthians	(2 Cor)
Galatians	(Gal)
Ephesians	(Eph)
Philippians	(Phil)
Colossians	(Col)
First Letter to the Thessalonians	(1 Thes)
Second Letter to the Thessalonians	(2 Thes)
First Letter to Timothy	(1 Tm)
Second Letter to Timothy	(2 Tm)
Titus	(Ti)
Philemon	(Phlm)
Hebrews	(Heb)
James	(Jas)
First Letter of Peter	(1 Pt)
Second Letter of Peter	(2 Pt)
First Letter of John	(1 Jn)
Second Letter of John	(2 Jn)
Third Letter of John	(3 Jn)
Jude	(Jude)

Revelation

Revelation	(Rv)

A-B

absolution
The formal forgiveness of sin given by the priest during the sacrament of Reconciliation. (page 174)

adore
To worship or love deeply. (page 258)

Annunciation
The announcement made to the Virgin Mary by the archangel Gabriel that she was chosen by God to become the mother of Jesus by the power of the Holy Spirit. (page 90)

Baptism
The sacrament in which we are joined to Jesus Christ, become members of the Church, and are reborn as God's children. In Baptism we receive the gift of the Holy Spirit, and original sin and our personal sins are forgiven. (page 132)

Bible
God's own word to us; the collection of forty-six books in the Old Testament and twenty-seven books in the New Testament. (page 20)

Book of Psalms
Old Testament prayers in the form of songs and poems. Inspired by God, the Book of Psalms may be considered the words God gives us to thank him, ask for forgiveness, and request help. (page 248)

C

capital sins
Seven sins named by the Church that are the sources of other sins. They are pride, greed, envy, lust, gluttony, and laziness. (page 208)

Church
The Body of Christ; people God the Father has called together in Jesus Christ through the power of the Holy Spirit. (page 70)

communion
From two Latin words meaning "sharing with." The sharing of Christians in the life of Christ. (page 182)

compassion
Sharing in the sufferings of others and often expressed by giving some form of aid or comfort. (page 104)

Confirmation
The sacrament that completes Baptism; the sacrament in which we celebrate the special gift of the Holy Spirit. (page 134)

conscience
The gift of God that is part of every person that helps us judge what is right and what is wrong. (page 204)

consecrate
To set apart someone or something as sacred, often dedicated for some specific holy purpose. (page 182)

covenant
The faithful, loving commitment God made with the People of God and was renewed in Christ, the New Covenant. (page 30)

creation
God bringing the world and humanity into existence from nothing. (page 42)

creed
A summary of the principal beliefs of the Church that are often proclaimed as a profession of faith. Creeds are also called symbols of our faith. (page 14)

D-E

Ephesians
The people who lived in the city of Ephesus, which today is in the nation of Turkey. (page 62)

Epiphany
An appearance or manifestation of God. The feast of the Epiphany commemorates the magi's visit to Jesus and the first manifestation of Jesus as Savior of all people. (page 116)

epistle
A longer, more formal type of letter. (page 60)

eternal
Having no end; timeless; everlasting. (page 42)

Eucharist
The sacrament in which we share in the Paschal mystery of Christ and receive the Body and Blood of Christ, who is truly and really present under the appearance of bread and wine. The word *eucharist* is from a Greek word meaning "thanksgiving" or "to show gratitude." (page 156)

Glossary

evangelist
A word meaning "announcer of the good news"; Matthew, Mark, Luke, and John, writers of the accounts of the Gospel in the New Testament. (page 100)

Exile
The time in the history of God's people when they were forced to leave their homeland and live in the country of their conquerors. (page 32)

F-G

faith
The gift of God's invitation to us to believe and trust in him; it is also the power God gives us to respond to his invitation. (page 12, 214)

gifts of the Holy Spirit
In the sacrament of Confirmation the bishop prays that those to be confirmed be given these gifts. They are: wisdom, understanding, right judgment, courage, knowledge, reverence, and wonder and awe. (page 134)

Gospel
An old English word that means "good news." The Gospel according to Matthew, Mark, Luke and John are the four written accounts of the Gospel in the Bible. (page 100)

H-K

holiness
The characteristic of a person who is in the right relationship with God. Holiness refers to God's presence in us and our fidelity to this abiding God. (page 194)

Holy Orders
The sacrament of the Church in which a baptized man is consecrated to serve the Church as a bishop, a priest, or a deacon. (page 184)

Holy Trinity
The one God, who is three Persons—God the Father, God the Son, God the Holy Spirit. (page 40)

hope
Trust in God and in his promises above everyone and everything else. (page 24)

idol
Something that takes the place of God in our life. It is something that takes over our life. (page 218)

Incarnation
A word meaning "take on flesh"; it is the term the Church uses to name our belief that the Son of God "took on flesh," or became man. Jesus is true God and true man. (page 52)

kingdom of God
All people and creation living in communion with God. The kingdom will be fully realized when Christ comes again in glory at the end of time. Then all people will live justly, peacefully, and lovingly with God and each other. (page 84, 102)

L

Leviticus
The third book of the Pentateuch. It centers on the call to holiness and the laws and rituals of worship used by the Israelites. (page 122)

liturgical year
The cycle of seasons and feasts that makes up the Church's year of worship. (page 116)

liturgy
The Church's work of worshiping God. (page 112)

Lord
A title meaning "master, ruler, a person of authority." It is used in the Old Testament to name God. It is also used in the New Testament as a reference to Jesus to express our belief that Jesus is truly God. (page 266)

M

manna
A breadlike substance from a shrub. (page 152)

marks of the Church
Essential features of the Church and her mission. The marks of the Church are one, holy, catholic, and apostolic. (page 72)

Matrimony
The sacrament of the Church that unites a baptized man and a baptized woman in a lifelong bond of faithful love as a sign of Christ's love for the Church. (page 186)

moral decisions
The things we choose to say and do, or not to say and do, to live as children of God and followers of Jesus Christ. (page 204)

morality

A means of evaluating whether our actions are good or evil; a way of judging whether our actions lead us to God or away from God. (page 204)

mortal sin

A serious failure in our love and respect for God, our neighbor, creation, and ourselves. (page 208)

mystery

Unknown or unknowable. God is, and his loving plan for us is, a mystery. We only know who God is and what his plan for us is because he revealed it, or made it known to us. (page 40)

N-O

natural law

The original moral sense that is part of our very being and enables us, by human reason, to know good and evil. (page 216)

original sin

The sin Adam and Eve committed by turning away from God and freely choosing to do what they knew God did not want them to do. (page 44)

P-Q

parables

Stories Jesus used to teach us. A parable compares one thing to another to help listeners or readers understand the main point of the story. (page 162)

Paschal mystery

The Passover events of Jesus' death, resurrection, and ascension. (page 54, 114)

Passover

The feast of the Israelites that celebrated their passage from slavery in Egypt to freedom. (page 124)

Pentecost

The feast on which the Church remembers and celebrates the coming of the Holy Spirit upon the apostles and the opening of the Church to all peoples. On that day over three thousand people were baptized. (page 70)

prayer

Talking and listening to God. (page 246)

prayer life

The habit of giving God praise and thanksgiving at specific times of the day; making prayer part of the rhythm of our day. (page 256)

prayer of adoration

Acknowledging God is God alone and we have been created by him. (page 258)

prayer of meditation

An expression of prayer using our imagination, mind, and desire to live our new life in Christ. (page 260)

precept

A rule or principle that imposes a particular standard of conduct. (page 216)

prefigure

To suggest, indicate, or point to. (page 152)

prophet

A man or woman who speaks for God, who utters divinely inspired words. (page 24)

proverb

A short, concise saying stating a well-accepted truth of fact. Example: Haste makes waste. (page 236)

prudence

A virtue that helps us know what is truly good for us and how to choose the right way of achieving that good. It is one of the four moral virtues; the others are justice, fortitude, and temperance. (page 34)

R-S

redemption

The saving activity of God through Christ delivering humanity from sin. We call Jesus our Redeemer. (page 14)

reparation

The process of righting a wrong; making amends; doing something or paying something to make up for damages we have caused. (page 228)

respect

The feeling of esteem and the willingness to demonstrate it by acts of consideration and courtesy. (page 224)

revelation

God making himself known to us. (page 40)

sabbath

In Hebrew the word means "to cease or desist from labor, to rest." For the Israelites the day of rest was a day dedicated to God. (page 124)

Glossary

sacraments

The seven main liturgical actions of the Church, given to us by Jesus Christ, that make his saving work present to us and allow us to share in the life of God. (page 112)

salvation

Humanity's deliverance from the power of sin and death through Jesus Christ who "died for our sins in accordance with the Scriptures." (page 50)

sexuality

The gift of being male or female—a boy or a girl, a man or a woman. (page 226)

sin

Freely choosing to say or do what we know is against God's law. Sin sets itself against God's love for us and turns our hearts away from it. (page 44, 172)

soul

Our innermost being; that which bears the imprint of God's image. (page 42)

T-V

temptation

A strong feeling to do or say something that is wrong or not to do something good we know and can do. (page 44)

theological virtues

Strengths or habits given to us by God to help us attain holiness. (page 196)

trust

To have confidence in someone because of the person's character, strength, ability, or truth; to depend with confidence on someone. (page 12)

unleavened bread

Bread made without yeast. (page 126)

venial sin

A sin that is less serious than a mortal sin. It weakens our love for God and for one another. (page 208)

vow

A solemn promise binding a person to a particular act, service, or condition. (page 82)

W-Z

wisdom

The knowledge of how to do things according to God's plan of creation and salvation. Wisdom helps us see the world through the eyes of faith. We are helped to see the world as God sees it. (page 234)

Yahweh

A name meaning "I am who am"; the name God used for himself. (page 22)

Index

Cover: Carol-Anne Wilson

PHOTO CREDITS:

Abbreviated as follows: (bkgd) background; (t) top; (b) bottom; (l) left; (r) right; (c) center.

Chapter 1: Page 7 (t,l), © Arnold Mulcahy/Liaison International; 7 (t,r), © Alan Kearney/FPG International; 7 (b), © Bassignac/Gamma, © Pool Jean-Paul II à Paris/Gamma Press Images; 9, © John Warden/Tony Stone Images; 10, © MCMXCVI DiMaggio/Kalish/The Stock Market; 11, © Bill Wittman; 12, © SuperStock, Inc.; 13 (all), © 2000 The Crosiers/Gene Plaisted, OSC; 14 (bkgd), © Corbis/Digital Stock; 16, © DeVille/Gamma, © Pool Jean-Paul/Gamma.

Chapter 2: Page 19, © 2000 The Crosiers/Gene Plaisted, OSC; 20, © Bruce Zuckerman/Photo Edit; 22, © Leslie Xuereb/SuperStock; 24 (all), © 2000 The Crosiers/Gene Plaisted, OSC; 26 (t), © 2000 The Crosiers/Gene Plaisted, OSC; 26 (b), © James L. Shaffer.

Chapter 3: Page 29, © Silvio Fiore/SuperStock; 30 (t,l), © Tommy Dodson/Unicorn Stock Photos; 30 (t,r & c,b) © 2000 The Crosiers/Gene Plaisted, OSC; 31, © Arena Chapel, Cappella Degli Scrovegni, Padua, Italy/SuperStock; 34, © Bibliotheque Nazarine, Paris, France/Explorer, Paris/SuperStock, Inc.; 36 (all), © 2000 The Crosiers/Gene Plaisted, OSC.

Chapter 4: Page 39, © Alan Kearney/FPG International; 40, © 2000 The Crosiers/Gene Plaisted, OSC; 42 (all), © Corbis Images; 44 (all), © Photo Disc, Inc.; 45, © Photo Disc, Inc.; 46 (t), © Church of Sant Apollinare in Classe; Ravenna, Italy/Canali Photo Bank, Milan/SuperStock; 46 (b), © Church of Sant Apollinare Nuvo, Ravenna, Italy/Canali Photo Bank, Milan/SuperStock.

Chapter 5: Page 49, © Arnold Mulcahy/Liaison International; 50 (all), 51, © 2000 The Crosiers/Gene Plaisted, OSC; 52, © William Greenblatt/Liaison Agency; 54, © Donald Nausbaum/Tony Stone Images; 56, © Robert Caputo/Aurora/PNI.

Chapter 6: Page 59, © SuperStock, Inc.; 60, © Alan Jacobs Gallery, London/Bridgeman Art Library, London/SuperStock; 64 (t), © Don Smetzer/Tony Stone Images; 64 (b), © Phyllis Picardi/Stock South/PNI; 66, © Hunter Freeman/Tony Stone Images.

Chapter 7: Page 69, © Bassignac/Gamma/ © Pool Jean-Paul II à Paris/Gamma; 70, © Yoav Levy/Photo Take/PNI; 70 (bkgd), © Corbis/Digital Stock; 72, © Bruno Barbey/Magnum/PNI; 74 (t,r), © SuperStock, Inc. 74 (t,l), © Rob Lang/FPG International; 74 (b), © Rob Gage/FPG Internationala; 74 (bkgd), Corbis/Digital Stock; 76, © Reuters/Arturo Mari/Archive Photos.

Chapter 8: Page 79, © 2000 The Crosiers/Gene Plaisted, OSC; 80, © James L. Shaffer; 82, © Bill Wittman; 82, 83, (b) © Myrleen Ferguson/Photo Edit; 83, © The Stock Market; 84 (t), © Bill Wittman; 84 (b), © David Young-Wolff/Photo Edit; 85, © David Young-Wolff/Photo Edit/PNI; 86 (all), © 2000 The Crosiers/Gene Plaisted, OSC.

Chapter 9: Page 89, © SuperStock, Inc.; 90, © Newberry Library, Chicago/SuperStock; 94, © Donald F. Wristen/RCL; 96 (t,l & t,r), SuperStock, Inc.; 96 (r), © Stephen Simpson/FPG International.

Chapter 10: Page 99, © SuperStock, Inc.; 100-101 (all), © 1996 The Order of St. Benedict, Inc.; 104 (t), © Bob Daemmrich/Stock, Boston/PNI; 104 (c), © David Young-Wolff/Photo Edit/PNI; 104 (b), © SuperStock, Inc.; 106 (t), © Ellis Herwig/Stock, Boston/PNI; 106 (b), © David Young-Wolff/Photo Edit/PNI.

Chapter 11: Page 109 (t,l & t,r), © 2000 The Crosiers/Gene Plaisted, OSC; 109 (b), © SuperStock, Inc.; 111, 112, © 2000 The Crosiers/Gene Plaisted, OSC; 114 (all), © Joanna B. Pinneo/Aurora/PNI; 116, © Bill Wittman; 118 (t), © Donald F. Wristen/RCL; 118 (c), © James L. Shaffer; 118 (b), © Sam Martinez/RCL; 118 (bkgd), © 1999 "D.I."/Picture Perfect.

Chapter 12: Page 121, © 2000 The Crosiers/Gene Plaisted, OSC; 122 (t), © SuperStock, Inc.; 122 (b), © Zev Radovan/Biblical Archaeology Society; 126, © Richard Nowitz/FPG International; 128 (t), (Donald F. Wristen/RCL; 128 (c), © 2000 The Crosiers/Gene Plaisted, OSC; 128 (b), © James L. Shaffer.

Chapter 13: Page 131, © 2000 The Crosiers/Gene Plaisted, OSC; 132, © Sam Martinez/RCL; 134 (all), © 2000 The Crosiers/Gene Plaisted, OSC; 136, (t,r & b), © Myrleen Ferguson/Photo Edit; 136 (t,r), © Gary Wagner/Stock, Boston/PNI; 138 (t), © 2000 The Crosiers/Gene Plaisted, OSC; 138 (b), © Comstock,

Inc.

Chapter 14: Page 141, © 2000 The Crosiers/Gene Plaisted, OSC; 142 (t), © Raymond Schoder, courtesy of Loyola University, Chicago; 142 (b,l), © Erich Lessing/Art Resource, NY; 142 (b,r), © Mark Link; 146 (t), © James L. Shaffer; 146 (b,l), © Bill Wittman; 146 (b,r), © Michael Newman/Photo Edit; 147, © James L. Shaffer; 148 (all), © 2000 The Crosiers/Gene Plaisted, OSC.

Chapter 15: Page 151, © SuperStock, Inc.; 152 (t), © 2000 The Crosiers/Gene Plaisted, OSC; 152 (b), © James L. Shaffer; 154 (all), © 2000 The Crosiers/Gene Plaisted, OSC; 156 (t), © Sam Martinez/RCL; 156 (b), © 2000 The Crosiers/Gene Plaisted, OSC; 158 (t,l), © JB Boykin/The Picture Cube; 158 (t,r), © Matt Ristow/RCL; 158 (b), © Ann Purcell; Carl Purcell/Words & Pictures/PNI.

Chapter 16: Page 161, © 2000 The Crosiers/Gene Plaisted, OSC; 162, 163, © Planet Art; 163 (t), © (Garo Nalbandian/Biblical Archaeology Society; 163 (b), © Nahman Avigad/Biblical Archaeology Society; 166 (t,l), © 2000 The Crosiers/Gene Plaisted, OSC; 166 (t,r), © Bob Daemmrich/Stock, Boston/PNI; 166 (b), © Spoencer Grant/Photo Edit; 168 (all), © Barbara Stephenson/Catholic Campaign for Human Development.

Chapter 17: Page 171, © David Joel/Tony Stone Images; 172, © Bill Wittman; 174, © David Falconer/Words & Pictures/PNI; 175, © James L. Shaffer; 176 (t,l), © Bill Wittman; 176 (t,r), © 2000 The Crosiers/Gene Plaisted, OSC; 177 (t), © SuperStock, Inc.; 178 (c & b), © Joe Polillio/Tony Stone Images.

Chapter 18: Page 181, © James L. Shaffer; 182 (t), © Terry Farmer/Tony Stone Images; 182 (b), © 2000 The Crosiers/Gene Plaisted, OSC; 182 (bkgd), © 1997 Photo Disc, Inc.; 184, © 2000 The Crosiers/Gene Plaisted, OSC; 185, © James L. Shaffer; 186 (t), © Comstock Klips; 186 (b), © Dick Luria/FPG International; 188 (t), courtesy of Monastery of St. Clare, Brenhem, Tx.; 188 (b,l), © Mike Yamashita/Woodfin Camp/PNI; 188 (b,r), © Daniel Beltra/Gamma.

Chapter 19: Page 191 (t,l), © 2000 The Crosiers/Gene Plaisted, OSC; 191 (t,r), © Mark Gamba/The Stock Market; 191 (b), © Corbis/Digital Stock; 193, © Mark Gamba/The Stock Market; 194 (all), © Bill Wittman; 196 (t & b), © Myrleen Ferguson/Photo Edit/PNI; 196 (c), © Sue Ann Miller/Black Star/PNI; 200 (t), © Jewish Museum, New York/SuperStock, Inc.; 2000 (b), © Stephen McBrady/Photo Edit/PNI.

Chapter 20: Page 203, © Gary B. Braasch/All Stock/PNI; 204 (t), © Bill Wittman; 204 (b), © David Young-Wolff/Photo Edit; 206 (t), © Robert Cushman Hayes; 206 (b), © Jim Corwin/Tony Stone Images; 208 (t), © Bob Daemmrich/Stock, Boston/PNI; 208 (c), © Eric Berndt/Photo Network/PNI; 208 (b), © Tony Freeman/Photo Edit/PNI; © 2000 The Crosiers/Gene Plaisted, OSC.

Chapter 21: Page 213, © Index Stock Photography; 214–215 (bkgd), © Corbis/Digital Stock; 216 (t), © David Young-Wolff/Photo Edit/PNI; 216 (b), © Laima Druskis/Stock, Boston/PNI; 217, © David Young-Wolff/Photo/PNI; 218, © Bob Daemmrich/Stock, Boston/PNI; 218 (b), © Chuck Pefley/Stock, Boston/PNI; 220 (t), © Christopher Morris/Black Star/PNI; 220 (c), © Bob Daemmrich/Stock, Boston/PNI; 220 (b), © David Young-Wolff/Photo Edit/PNI.

Chapter 22: Page 223, © Corbis Images; 224, © Lynn Johnson/Aurora/PNI; 225, © Tony Freeman/Photo Edit/PNI; 226 (t), © Corbis/Digital Stock; 226 (c), © Corbis/Digital Stock; 226 (b), © Photo Disc, Inc.; 228 (t), © Alon Reininger/Contact Press Images/PNI; 228 (b), © Stephen Frisch/Stock, Boston/PNI; 230 (bkgd), © NASA/Stock South/PNI; 230 (b), © Wood River Gallery/PNI.

Chapter 23: Page 233, 238, © 2000 The Crosiers/Gene Plaisted, OSC.

Chapter 24: Page 243 (t,l), © 2000 The Crosiers/Gene Plaisted, OSC; 243 (t,r), © Comstock, Inc.; 243 (b), © Mark Richards/Photo Edit/PNI; 245, © Mark Richards/Photo Edit/PNI; 246 (t), © Jean-Claude Lejeune; 246 (b), © James L. Shaffer; 250 (all), © Bill Wittman.

Chapter 25: Page 255, 256–257 (bkgd), © Comstock, Inc.; 258, © Hermitage Museum, St. Petersburg, Russia/SuperStock; 260, © 2000 The Crosiers/Gene Plaisted, OSC; 262, courtesy of Donna Steffen.

Chapter 26: Page 265, © 2000 The Crosiers/Gene Plaisted, OSC; 266 (t,l & t,r), © James L. Shaffer; 266 (b,l), © Barbara J. Feigles/Stock, Boston; 266 (b,r), ©

Uniphoto Picture Agency; 270–271 (bkgd), © Arnulf Husmo/Tony Stone Images; 272 (t), © 1997 Photo Disc, Inc.; 272 (b), © Paul Souders/All Stock/PNI.

Liturgical Seasons: Page 275 (t,l), © Thomas Nebbiangs/Image Collection/National Geographic; 275 (t,r), © 2000 The Crosiers/Gene Plaisted, OSC; 275 (b), © Myrleen Ferguson Cate/Photo Network/PNI; 276–277, © Michael Javorka/Tony Stone Images; 280 (t), © Robert W. Ginn/Photo Edit/PNI; 280 (b), © Robert Cushman Hayes; 282–283, © SuperStock, Inc.; 284 (all), © Bill Wittman; 285, © Photodisk; 286, © Thomas Nebbiangs/Image Collection/National Geography; 288 (bkgd), © James Harrington/Tony Stone Images; 288, © James L. Shaffer; 290 (t & b), James L. Shaffer; 290 (c), © Corbis/Digital Stock; 292 (t), © James L. Shaffer; 292 (b), © Michael Newman/Photo Edit/PNI; 294, © James L. Shaffer; 295, © Myrleen Ferguson/Photo Edit; 298, © 2000 The Crosiers/Gene Plaisted, OSC; 299, © James L. Shaffer; 300, © 2000 The Crosiers/Gene Plaisted, OSC; 301 (t), © James L. Shaffer; 301 (bkgd), © 2000 The Crosiers/Gene Plaisted, OSC; 302, © SuperStock, Inc.; 304, © Bill Wittman; 305, © 2000 The Crosiers/Gene Plaisted, OSC; 306, © Stuart McClyment/Tony Stone Images; 308, © Photo Disc, Inc.; 310 (t), © Bob Daemmrich/Stock, Boston/PNI; 310 (b), 311, © James L. Shaffer; 312, © Michael Townsend/All Stock/PNI; 313, © James L. Shaffer; 314 (t), © David Young-Wolff/Photo Edit; 314 (b), © Bill Wittman; 316, © Fine Art Photographic Library/PNI; 318 (t), © James L. Shaffer; 318 (b), Myrleen Ferguson Cate/Photo Network/PNI; 320, © 2000 The Crosiers/Gene Plaisted, OSC; 322, © Robert Cushman Hayes; 324, © Monastery of Kykkou, Cyprus/Explorer, Paris/SuperStock; 325, © M.K. Denny/Photo Edit; 328, © Bill Wittman.

ART CREDITS:

Chapter 1: Page 11, 15, 17, Dennis Davidson.
Chapter 2: Page 21, Dennis Davidson; 22 (c & b), Bob Niles; 23, Pamela Johnson; 25, 27, Dennis Davidson.
Chapter 3: Page 31, Dennis Davidson; 32, Renee Daily; 33, 37, Dennis Davidson.
Chapter 4: Page 41, 43, 45, Dennis Davidson.
Chapter 5: Page 51, 53, 55, 57, Dennis Davidson.
Chapter 6: Page 62, Jan Palmer; 65, 67, Dennis Davidson.
Chapter 7: Page 71, Bill Alger; 75, 77, Dennis Davidson.
Chapter 8: Page 81, 87, Dennis Davidson.
Chapter 9: Page 92, Don Morrison; 97, Dennis Davidson.
Chapter 10: Page 101, Dennis Davidson; 102, Jan Palmer; 107, Dennis Davidson.
Chapter 11: Page 113, Dennis Davidson; 116 (bkgd), Debi Seiler; 117, 119, Dennis Davidson.
Chapter 12: Page 123, Dennis Davidson; 124, Don Morrison; 125, 127, 129, Dennis Davidson.
Chapter 13: Page 133, 137, Dennis Davidson.
Chapter 14: Page 143, Dennis Davidson; 144, Renee Daily; 145, 147, 149, Dennis Davidson.
Chapter 15: Page 155, 159, Dennis Davidson.
Chapter 16: Page 164, Margaret Sanfilippo; 165, 167, 169, Dennis Davidson.
Chapter 17: Page 173, Dennis Davidson; 177, Dynamic Graphics, Inc.; 179, Dennis Davidson.
Chapter 18: Page 183, 185, Dennis Davidson; 189, Dynamic Graphics, Inc.
Chapter 19: Page 195, 197, Dennis Davidson; 198, © 1996, The Order of St. Benedict, Inc.; 199, Dennis Davidson; 201, 207, Victor Harper.
Chapter 20: Page 205, Victor Harper.
Chapter 21: Page 215, Victor Harper; 217, 219, 221, Dennis Davidson.
Chapter 22: Page 229, Dennis Davidson.
Chapter 23: Page 234, Carol-Anne Wilson; 236, Bob Niles; 240, Jan Palmer.
Chapter 24: Page 248, Renee Daily; 249, Dennis Davidson; 252, Karen Malzeke-McDonald.
Chapter 25: Page 259, Dennis Davidson; 263, Jerry Hopkins.
Chapter 26: Page 267, Dennis Davidson; 268, Don Morrison; 269, Jerry Hopkins.
Liturgical Seasons: Page 278, Karen Malzeke-McDonald; 279, Victor Harper; 280, Cory Davis; 281, 283, 287, Dennis Davidson; 289, Karen Malzeke-McDonald; 291, Jo Arnold; 293, Dynamic Graphics, Inc.; 296, Pamela Johnson; 301, 303, Dynamic Graphics, Inc.; 306, 307, 309, 311, 313, 315, Carol-Anne Wilson; 317, Debi Seiler; 319, Carol-Anne Wilson.